IN THE GHOST COUNTRY

IN THE

A LIFETIME SPENT ON THE EDGE

GHOST COUNTRY

PETER HILLARY

AND JOHN E. ELDER

MAINSTREAM
PUBLISHING

EDINBURGH AND LONDON

First published in Great Britain in 2004 by
MAINSTREAM PUBLISHING COMPANY (EDINBURGH) LTD
7 Albany Street
Edinburgh EH1 3UG

First published in the United States of America in 2004 by
Free Press, A Division of Simon & Schuster, Inc. New York

ISBN 1 84018 835 9

Epigraphs from In Camera taken from In Camera and Other Plays by Jean-Paul Sartre,
translated by Stuart Gilbert (Hamish Hamilton, 1952). Translation copyright © 1946 by Stuart Gilbert.
From The Odyssey of Homer by Richmond Lattimore. Copyright © 1965, 1967, by Richmond
Lattimore. Reprinted by permission of HarperCollins Publishers Inc.

A catalogue record for this book is available from the British Library

Typeset in Futura and Palatino
Printed and bound in Great Britain by
Antony Rowe, Chippenham, Wiltshire

To all those who walked with me in the ghost country

P.E.H.

For my parents, John and Margaret Elder

J.E.E.

PHOTOGRAPHS

Frontispiece   Muir and Philips on the Ross Iceshelf, Antarctica, with spectral halo, 1998. Courtesy of Peter Hillary

Page 2   On the Antarctic Polar Plateau in 1999 with Parhelion. Courtesy of Peter Hillary

Page 82   Matt Comeskey on the Black Pyramid of K2 at about 23,000 feet. Courtesy of Peter Hillary

Page 178   The Hillary Family 1962 en route to America. Courtesy of Hillary Family Collection

Page 298   Hillary and Pearl families at Thyangboche 1966 with Mount Amadablam behind. Courtesy of Hillary Family Collection

Page 339   Mike Rheinberger crossing the "Golden Gate" in the Khumbu Icefall, Everest, 1987. Courtesy of Peter Hillary

CONTENTS

EXISTENTIALISM, a philosophical view that stresses concreteness and individuality in existing things and human experiences. There are two major types of existentialism. One type, called religious existentialism, claims that anguish can lead to a personal discovery of God and a resulting fellow-ship with men. The second type, nonreligious existentialism, is exemplified in an avowedly atheistic form by the French thinker Jean-Paul Sartre. Sartre denies the existence of God, asserting that the world is basically meaningless. He holds that a man truly exists to the extent that he acts and that he alone is responsible for every action he performs. When a man accepts these facts, he becomes capable of positive action.

Merit Students Encyclopedia, 1967

PART ONE

THE OLD ROUTE

GARCIN: **Sorry! I fear I'm not good company amongst the dead.**

ESTELLE: **Please, please don't use that word. It's so . . . so crude. In terribly bad taste, really. It doesn't mean much anyhow. Somehow I feel we've never been so much alive as now. If we've absolutely got to mention this . . . this state of things, I suggest we call ourselves—wait!— absentees. Have you been absent for long?**

Jean-Paul Sartre, *In Camera / No Exit*

CHAPTER ONE

Keep a careful watch for the missing party—they may be anywhere on route. Watch out for tracks leading away from the route. Mark the route taken and leave evidence of passing with flags, cairns etc. and notes left in obvious locations indicating your intentions and time of passage. The lost party might miss you by hours or even minutes, or pass by in poor visibility.

From a government manual for Antarctic operations

Captain Scott was an absentee, officially buried at sea. In the lore he's still hauling, following the calling, and that's how he remains, famously. He's still out there, and that was something Peter Scott always knew for sure. Captain Scott never got to see how his baby son turned out, and he turned out fine, Sir Peter, by all accounts a decent and kindly gent. Captain Robert Scott never knew a conversation with the boy or the man, and his son had to make do with the history books and the legend and what the family told him and what everybody else had to say about him. Later there were terrible things said about "the Captain," as his men had called him, and worse when the son was an old man, twice as old as his father when the Captain lay down in his sleeping bag for the last time.

A year after, a search party found his father in his sleeping bag and later some of them talked to Peter Scott. Some of them visited the family home when he was still small, and he picked up a few new things about his father with the visits and the talks, but he'd read the party's story by the time any of them really talked about it.

The party that found him a year after, they found him with two others only, and not the five that had gone to the South Pole, because two had already died. The first one was buried deep south, on the glacier, and the other one not buried by his fellows, because he'd walked out just a few days south of where everything finally stopped, and the three remaining had no enthusiasm for anything but a quick look around, no great sense of purpose in doing anything but leaving their man wherever he'd taken himself to be buried by the drift that buried everything that lay down, and so just the three found side by side in the tent that had to be dug out of the drift.

The men in the party went in one by one before the tent was collapsed over the dead, and the living said their prayers as the drift pasted the tent and turned it white again. It goes that none of them ever said out loud how Scott and the others looked at the end of it, and at least one man later lost his mind from the burden of seeing it: the color of the freeze dried faces, the matchstick mummified arms, the long unfelt agonies of scurvy and starvation and fear and flesh frozen, and frozen rotting inside and out, and all that had twisted their spines and their features for a long time, and that's how they'd remained.

There was no "they looked so peaceful," there was no bringing them home, no flag wrapped coffin for the Captain. He's still out there. That's why they call him "Scott of the Antarctic," surely. Because he's still out there.

It's less well remembered as folklore that the Captain's rival Roald Amundsen also died in his adventure clothes, that he was still out there, at the opposite end of the world from Scott's remains, under the ice in the Arctic, probably still sitting in the plane that went down at a point vaguely known while searching for a missing explorer who was eventually rescued by other people, disappearing June eighteen, nineteen twenty-eight. He was fifty-six years old. It was a marvelous story that lingered more as a fabled postscript because it was at odds with the core of his legend, his place in things, in part because many people believed Amundsen would find his way home, because he always made it home from the worst places with such predictability that he had ceased to amaze.

He knew it. His place in things was already fixed in their minds. He'd had his time. The polite applause of his later years had clanged in his ears, in tune with the haunted depression that put Amundsen out of sorts with himself and with his fickle countrymen. There were no great journeys left to him, not as he saw it, and none in the public eye. As his story went, there was nothing left, save dying and rolling into the open grave of the history books, where the greater part of his story had already been told. There was the wave of grief when he vanished, the speeches, the talk that he'd be back. But dust drops. For a while Amundsen was known as the White Eagle of Norway, at home, here and there, not said in every household, these days hardly known at all.

This was Amundsen the Norwegian, who got his four men to the South Pole and home again with none of them losing their feet or their minds or even much weight; the first to reach the southern point of the world's turning, a month and two days before Scott and his men made their wretched visit. He was the one. For Amundsen, an absentee complete who knew no great engagement with the regular life, there was no other life.

The house he built in the forest was fitted to look like the inside of a ship so he could dream he was going somewhere else. And so it was with his love life, discovered in middle age and kept as a mysterious adventure, to be taken occasionally as a private pilgrimage into little known country. Apart from a stretch where he talked of marrying a woman who was already married to someone else, the mysterious adventures were taken on the restorative trampoline of affectionate whoring. Perhaps it didn't happen that often because he was always in the deep debt that worried him between expeditions and sometimes worried him when he was out there, probably the only thing from the regular life that hung on him when he was out there.

Roald Amundsen was also known as the Captain to his men: the first man to navigate the fabled Northwest Passage, most likely the first man to see the North Pole (from an airship), the first man to the South Pole, who vanished heroically when there was already too much to remember him by, one of the greats, with no mythic slogan to remember him by.

> Amundsen took dogs to the deepest south, touching there December fifteen, nineteen eleven. Scott and his men walked to the bottom of the world, all tied to the one big sled, finding disappointment and taking second place on January seventeen, nineteen twelve.
>
> Third place wasn't bagged for another forty-six years, until the southern summer of nineteen fifty-eight, taken by a man driving a farm tractor, my father, Ed Hillary, "Sir Edmund Hillary, the conqueror of Mount Everest," as he was most often named in the newspapers.
>
> It was probably at school, when I studied him as part of our national history, when I learned that Dad's trip to the South Pole had been pretty controversial at the time.

❋ ❋ ❋

Ed Hillary was never meant to go to the South Pole. Rather, he was under orders not to go there. He was meant to play a support role only, out of the limelight, no trophy. But from the start he planned for it, stocking his tractors with enough food and fuel to take him all the way, Ed and his four men, the team he always called "the Old Firm." They didn't know they were going for it, the Old Firm. He didn't tell them until they were seven hundred miles out. As he later wrote, "I had my own agenda."

It is one of his great stories.

Ed Hillary's push for the Pole rattled international politics and made headlines, because it played out as a willful duel between Hillary and a British Antarctic veteran of the old school, Dr. Vivian Fuchs. They were part of the same expedition, an epic science project known as the British Trans-Antarctic Expedition of fifty-seven to fifty-eight.

It was the first crossing of the emptiest continent. In fact, it was the expedition's science work drilling into the ice for samples every thirty miles and doing seismic shots that confirmed that Antarctica was indeed a continent. And not an ice covered archipelago.

Fuchs was the overall leader of the trip. Fuchs was the one. Fuchs was going all the way, from the western (or Atlantic) side to the eastern (or Pacific) side, with a team of big Sno-Cats, touching the Pole on his way through, thereby bagging not just the first crossing but also the first overland haul to the Pole in a motor vehicle.

This was the British finally making their mark in Antarctica with something more than corpses. They were still sulking over Scott's defeat at the Pole by the bloody Norwegians.

Well, it wasn't going to happen again, what?

Ed Hillary would be of great use, and he would keep his place, somewhere way off to the side. Leading the antipodean arm of the enterprise, Hillary was given the vital job of laying a trail of fuel depots from the eastern side, with a caravan of Massey Ferguson farm tractors, the kind built for plowing potatoes, modified for the deep sub zero.

By the time the Old Firm had laid all the depots, they were five hundred miles from the Pole, seven hundred miles from the roped down huts they called home on McMurdo Sound. On the day after Christmas nineteen fifty-seven, Ed Hillary issued a press release that went around the world: "Am hellbent for the Pole, God willing and crevasses permitting."

> It caused quite a row, especially in the British press. They felt they were again being robbed of glory in the Antarctic. Dad knew the press would go wild with it, and I doubt it really bothered him. He'd long decided he wouldn't worry about the newspapers. He made his own decisions. He did things his way, and too jolly bad if it got up people's noses. That's my father for you. He uses the word "jolly."

They plowed on for several days, making good progress. Soon after, as the Old Firm were easing their tractors through crevassed country that nearly swallowed them whole on occasion, as they were edging south, Ed Hillary got an urgent message from Dr. Fuchs, who politely affirmed his order against proceeding, argued the point by listing various problems he'd been having with his vehicles, gave Hillary a few new things to keep busy with (clearing a crevasse field, laying another fuel depot just in case), declared his sympathy, said he knew it would be a "great disappointment," and no doubt hoped that would be the end of it.

For Hillary to stay camped on a howling spot of no historical or exploratory importance until Fuchs needed them was all a bit much. From a practical point of view, Hillary didn't like it: staying too long on the one spot, in the leeching cold, asking to be swallowed alive. The Americans hadn't long built their bunker base at the South Pole, with beds and hot food and an airstrip for an easier ride home. That was a better place to be. The Pole. It was . . . there. And he'd planned for it. So the Old Firm pushed on across the howling Polar Plateau toward the Pole.

It ended this way: after laying in more fuel than Fuchs ever needed, Ed Hillary's team stopped for the night within sight of a row of flags near the small U.S. base at the South Pole. It was January three, nineteen fifty-eight, and Peter Mulgrew sent a brief message back to Scott Base on the coast before crawling into his sleeping bag.

"Rhubarb." Then he switched off the set.

The next morning they arrived at the South Pole, on January four, the third to reach the place overland. After posing for photographs and shaking many hands, Hillary and the Old Firm were taken underground, into the American base, to warm up and eat and rest before flying back to base.

Two weeks and some later, Hillary flew back to the Pole to watch Vivian Fuchs pull in, January twenty. After offering his heartiest congratulations, Hillary flew back to Scott Base and rejoined Fuchs's party once they got to Depot 700. Perhaps Fuchs wanted to keep Hillary close, within an arm's length. So it turned: Sir Edmund rode back to McMurdo Sound from Depot 700 in the back of Vivian Fuchs' Sno-Cat, where there was no window, just a dark hole, left back there like a hunting dog.

Whenever the way ahead grew dangerous and uncertain, whenever they hit the long and deep cracks in the ice that could swallow tractors deep—had swallowed them—Ed Hillary was let out to wield his sextant and fix their position, or to walk in front like a hunting dog, to find the good way through and to home where they stood and smiled for the cameras, kept it polite. Soon after, Dr. Fuchs was knighted by his queen, and he made it into the encyclopedias as Sir Vivian.

> So it all ended well. Everybody had their moment. Anyway, I didn't know about the commotion in the press at the time, or for some years later.

❋ ❋ ❋

I had just turned two years old when Dad went down to the ice, and I was talking well as a three year old when I saw him again. I remember missing him. He was already famous

when he drove to the South Pole, already one of the greats by the time I was born, my father, the last of the golden age. I didn't know what any of that meant, and I'm not sure either of us knows what to make of it now, but I believe that even then I was aware that people treated my father as something special. It's one of the things that I can always remember being there: people turning up at the door for an autograph and to have their photographs taken with him, and they always had the same look of awe on their faces that suggested they had just discovered the pyramids at Giza.

They certainly carried on like those tourists at the pyramids who suddenly believe they're archeologists and that they alone will unveil the secrets of the crypt.

   "So, Sir Edmund . . . what was it like at the top of Mount Everest?"

They all wanted to hear him personally tell how it was on the top of the world, and at the bottom of the world and elsewhere if they'd kept up with his travels.

"So, Sir Edmund . . . I heard that you're going in search of the yeti."

It's been said that the Captain wanted the public love, that he would have enjoyed it. My father found it was like wearing a Santa Claus suit all the time. All the time.

With half his soul itching for adventure and the other half lit up by the regular life (the wife and the kids), with his social minglings long cursed with stiff shyness and the burden of good manners (much of the time), with a gift for understatement that sucked the life out of fanciful words like "excitement" and "danger," Ed Hillary wore the mantle of history book hero in the same way soap stars compliantly perform at shopping malls: with the understanding that walking flesh makes a poor substitute for the pictures people carry in their heads, that what people were looking for, when seeking an audience with an elevated soul, was a human unicorn. "So, Sir Edmund . . ."

The "Sir Edmund" business only made the scene feel more fraudulent. As the campfire story goes: Hillary got the news that he was to be knighted while walking downvalley from Everest Base Camp to Kathmandu, having just climbed the mountain on May twenty-nine, nineteen fifty-three.

When a runner brought him the letter addressed to "Sir Edmund," he groaned and joked he'd have to buy a new pair of overalls. He was a beekeeper, from New Zealand, considered then and probably now as the boondocks of the Western world. Everybody called him Ed. He never thought he looked like a knight, because knights then were generally Establishment sorts who smoked cigars and sat on company boards. Now many of them are fading rock stars.

If Ed Hillary looked like a knight of the realm, it was the old fashioned wild variety who traveled in a rough and ready fashion and clobbered anybody who besmirched his honor. For that's how he was.

This was Ed Hillary who walked barefoot to school as a small boy, in the boondocks south of Auckland. He wore shiny shoes later, with a blazer and tie, when he was sent up too early to the prestigious Auckland Grammar School, at eleven years of age, because the local school thought he was a genius.

> **He wasn't a genius. He was bright, but he was shy and too awkward to mix in with his classmates, who were two years older than he was. He struggled. The train ride to school was long, something like two hours. His days started in the dark; they ended in the dark. It was lonely as hell. But he had a lot of time to think and to read books and daydream, so he got lost in those things, which made it a happier time for him.**

This was Ed who started out small and skinny, suddenly shooting up with puberty proper, gangly but filled out with muscles enough and a good reaching arm, clipping the ears of those who had bullied him, and there were train windows broken in the fights with the rowdy and the impudent on the long hauls home in the evenings before settling down for the familiar pleasures of staring out the window and thinking dreamy thoughts.

It stayed with Ed Hillary a long time, the old-fashioned thing of grabbing the people who soiled his honor or mood, his hard and fast sense of right and wrong, grabbing them by the collar and giving them a little righteous what-for, the righteous path dug long before in front of him by his mother, Gertrude, who considered book learning a state of grace unto itself, and Percival, his father, who believed in hard labor and holding to one's principles as something beyond discussion, no matter the cost.

It was his father the hard man who abandoned journalism on principle, with some drama, to keep bees and for whom Ed and his brother, Rex, had worked hard and for no pay as children and then later as men. It was his father who had softened in the evenings when they were small and had taken Ed, Rex, and sister June on his knee to tell them of a little man who lived in a tree stump at the bottom of the garden. The little man wasn't home very much, because he traveled the world and had adventures and did good things, and his name was Jimmy Job, named after Job, the Old Testament plaything of God and the devil who lost everything and kept his chin up regardless.

> Dad did the same with his children (my younger sisters, Sarah and Belinda, and me) when we were small, taking us on his knee and telling us more about Jimmy Job than he ever said about Mount Everest. Whenever we asked him, "Who got up first? You or Tenzing?" he always said, "We got up together."
>
> This was in the marvelous years, after he came home from the South Pole, when it was easier to slide into his awkward embrace.

Most adventurers, many of the greats, in their black and white photographs, in or out of their adventure clothes, don't look particularly heroic. In his canvas parka, the Captain looked like a schoolteacher dressed for a rainy day in the cheap seats at the football. At home, in his waistcoat and with his thinning hair slicked back, Scott looked like a butler. For a long time, to his children and his friends and the newspaper people, Ed Hillary looked the part of the history book hero: very tall and very strong, rough handsome with a long jaw and long cramped teeth, the happy cut lines of a rodeo rider.

He used to whistle cowboy songs. I used to look at him, from the vinyl bench in the back of the car I'd look at him, with his hair cut very short at the sides and the back, and on top he had these curls that fell over his big brow, and I could see he had this strength and confidence that I felt could never be challenged. But he's still out there, my father, in some ways as much a ghost as Roald Amundsen or the Captain, frozen not under the drift or in chilled waters, but in grief.

❄ ❄ ❄

If you are interested in scars I can show you some very interesting ones but I would rather talk about grasshoppers.

Ernest Hemingway, "A Way You'll Never Be"

In the hill countries of India and Nepal, up where there were no tractors, and where the bottom of the world was beyond imaginings save those spawned from fear of the spirits that surely lived there, "the great Sir Hillary" was held as some kind of god and the shaping of folklore a competitive business.

Given that stories about gods and ordinary men were told with a great flexibility and invention, as works in progress, very few pieces of news were accepted as fact. From the start, the story of the great Sir Hillary's drive to the South Pole was passed on as a fairytale. No one ever believed it was true. But it was a great story.

The Sherpa people, claiming Hillary as a thread in their own mythology, especially embraced and embellished the adventure in their fireside raves until there were many versions of it, with monsters and beasts and much suffering, thereby making it true and not true and better than true.

It was among the Sherpa people that Ed Hillary found meaning in his own folkloric hero, Jimmy Job, the stump-dwelling adventurer who did good things in distant places. Soon after the polar trip, Ed Hillary started building schools and hospitals and airfields for the Sherpa people, because they asked him to do it. There was plenty to tell about those days.

From an early project: Ed Hillary and his team had no heavy machinery to flatten the sloping airstrip he and his team had dug out at Lukla, a village at nine thousand feet in the lower Khumbu (now the most popular dropoff point to the Everest region for trekkers and climbers). Instead of bulldozers, he used booze; enlisting a hundred sturdy locals, firing them up with plenty chung (the local home-brewed lubricant), lining them up in one long line, asking them to link arms and dance the stomping dance of fireside habit, for some hours, back and forth across the lumpy field.

Years later, in nineteen seventy-five, Ed Hillary was at another airfield that he had built south of the Everest area, at a village called Paphlu, where a new hospital was also being constructed, when he learned that his wife, Louise, and his daughter Belinda, sixteen years old, the lights of the family, the facilitators of all affection and social ease, had been killed in a plane that had crashed into a paddy field shortly after taking off from Kathmandu's airport. They had been coming to meet him, to spend some time in the hills with him. He flew down to see them lying in rags under smoke, and that was the end of the marvelous times.

> It is undeniably the case that it was the end of Ed Hillary as we'd known him. With the death of my mother and little sister, he just disappeared. They'd lit the way for him. My mother had lit him up inside, and he'd become a much more jovial, confident and probably more outgoing person, at least

in his own circle. It all went out like a light. I couldn't believe it, seeing him emptied out like that, just turned to a husk.

Oh, he still went to the hills. I went with him. Two years on, we went up the Ganges in these jetboats, and when we came into the Punjab, the hills were covered, for miles, with little red and orange dots. They were turbans. Hundreds of thousands of people chanting his name, and bidding that he live forever.

We went up the hills, and he nearly died with the altitude, and I remember sitting outside his tent, just weeping. He couldn't take the altitude anymore. He'd nearly died on three or four trips with the altitude, stumbling and slurring his words, unable to see properly or walk. And that's how he was in the tent, and all I could do was cry. It was too much. We wrapped him up in a sleeping bag and got him down to some sloping ledges where the following morning a helicopter took him out, but the scare didn't shake him out of his shadows.

We later went to the North Pole together, with Neil Armstrong the moon man, in little ski planes. It was a great trip, but he was still out there. He kept busy with the schools and hospitals, the dinners with presidents. That's the Hillary thing: we like to keep busy, and he did. He became an old man, but I never heard him whistle cowboy songs again. He didn't come back.

"What's going to happen, Dad?"

"I dunno."

It was only much later that Ed Hillary took any refuge in being one of the greats—when he was an old man and tired after many years dodging darkness and forsaking his dreams for a sleep where there were no pictures. Presiding in state as the living legend was something done easily enough, even in his fickle weariness with the whole business, and on occasion it was enough to bring the rest of him out for a while.

There was an afternoon when he said, "I'm ancient now," at

eighty-two, and he'd been sitting at the kitchen table signing
a tall pile of photographs, "the picture that went around the
world," of his climbing partner Tenzing Norgay Sherpa standing
on the summit and waving his flags. Tenzing didn't know how
to use a camera and Hillary didn't feel it was a good time for
lessons. There is no photo of Ed Hillary at the top. (There are
no photos of Neil Armstrong on the moon, either. Buzz Aldrin,
the man who thought he'd be the first to step down the ladder
and say some mythic words, left his camera behind with the
craters.)

Ed Hillary put down his pen and quietly said "Right!" when
Peter Hillary knocked on the door with two friends in tow and
reminded him that they'd made a time to talk and have a cup of
tea. He nodded and, half looking at his company, got out of his
chair and went into the sitting room and sat with his back to the
beautiful day on the harbor. This was when the South Pole trip
was just another story that he could pick up in pieces and wave
around in a tired and automatic fashion at first, and then came
long moments when it was like a Christmas light sputtering to
life and the wild man in the old photographs flashed across
the face of the old man sitting in an armchair with a cup of tea in
his lap.

A few steps away from where Ed Hillary was talking, on the
wall of his study, there is a photograph of the Old Firm standing
at the South Pole, Ed to the left of the four other men (Murray
Ellis, Jim Bates, Peter Mulgrew, Derek Wright), all standing in a
loose line at the South Pole in their goggles and heavy polar suits
and boots, and they're all smiling and Ed looks almost naughty
in his happiness, all of them cocky as rock stars, and a little in
love with each other by way of shared experience.

> **They'd all been good mates on that trip. They had their mo-
> ments, but they didn't fall apart as a team. I wish I could say
> the same about my trip south, taken forty years later, in
> ninety-eight. It became a controversial affair too, when it was**

all over, and for a while that's all the trip was about: one man's tantrum, really.

It wasn't the controversy that still gives the creeps to those who participated, because the three of us are still stuck in that traveling nuthouse, when we think of it, and deeper.

I know that it was the loneliest trip of my life. I know that the burning emptiness sucked on my mind and my emotions. Just pulled them out like cotton stuffing. That's the kind of place it is.

I know that the atmosphere in that tent with my companions became stranger and stranger, until it became nasty, alienating. We needed to be mates, like the Old Firm, and look after one another to get through that place in reasonable shape. But there is no happy photo of the three of us on my study wall.

Actually, there are photos of the three of them at the South Pole, and they are smiling with the cross-eyed bliss of people fresh from wreckage, of fishermen pulled from a sinking boat in rough seas, on the verge of tears and violence and collapse.

We went out to complete Captain Scott's journey, to the South Pole and back on foot, eighteen hundred miles, hauling everything we needed behind us, over a hundred days we figured. If we'd done the trip in the Captain's day, there would have been another tent out there with three people lying in it.

Maybe. Maybe not. One of the more disturbing things I thought about: the road to the Pole was a perfect place to commit homicide; one's body would never be found.

It made macabre contemplation, and I was able to flesh it out in my mind as a whodunit in the way I imagined a police inspector would reconstruct the crime. But it was unsettling, this sort of thinking, given the edgy emptiness in our little red tent, the volcanic gases.

By the time I started to feel that I couldn't completely rely on my companions—that I didn't feel particularly safe with them—I was already talking to the dead. More often than not, they were the only thing to see down there, all the dead friends from the hills, the only real company to be had, the dead friends in all their colors.

Fred, on Everest. Tripped and fell. I was there at the time.

Craig. Everest. Tripped and fell. There at the time.

Ken. Ama Dablam. Terrible head wound, most likely dead when we cut the rope.

Jeff. K2. In his sleeping bag. Yes, there too.

Bill. Makalu. Swept off and buried. We had to keep sounding upbeat in case he could hear us talking as we were poking the rubble for him.

Mark. Makalu. Tripped and fell. That's what the tracks said, yes.

Mike. Everest, a few years after one of our own attempts. Fell asleep while sitting down up high. Didn't wake up.

Rob. Everest. We climbed it together, for the first time together, five years before he died near the South Summit. Most famous for calling his pregnant wife from where he lay down. He told her not to worry too much.

Gary. Dead three years after we climbed Everest together with Rob. Dhaulagiri.

Peter. One of the Old Firm. Like an uncle to me. Plane crash, Antarctica.

My mother.

My sister.

The Captain.

Oh, and sometimes the wind made these gusting whimpers off a ski pole or a tent guy rope that made me think of Bruce's mother. I didn't actually see her or walk with her down there on the ice. But they made me think of Bruce's mother, on those occasions when she'd ask, "What happened up there? Was he trying to help the others?"

By the time these things came to mind, the dead friends on

the march, tension in the tent, I'd already started carrying the stove and the bivvy sack, making sure I always had them in my sled. I wasn't going to be left for dead. And that's how things were on our trip, after about two weeks out.

When I talked to Dad about some of these . . . issues, he said, "Well, that's the way it goes sometimes."

CHAPTER TWO

Come on up. Use the red rope.

Alison Hargreaves, K2, 1995

Over the previous year, Eric Philips had talked them all up, the three of them, as the real thing, to the newspapers and the television people, and to the company boards listening to their pitch for clothes, skis, food, a flight to the ice, the million and some.

He'd stand with the air and bearing of one wearing a cape, and tell how they were the men to pull it off. In his spiel he used these words: "We are natural born adventurers."

The people who felt he was putting them on, that he was striking an heroic pose as a piece of entertainment—natural born adventurers? what a character!—were soon persuaded otherwise.

That is, when Philips went on to explain how natural born adventurers were different from the regular lifers, he did so with the unmistakable solemnity, the one-track intensity and the authority of a higher calling that you find in star football players, senators looking for votes, the stack heeled souls who feel most comfortable with the natives on their knees. One way or the other, the assembled went, "wow."

Philips' spiel went this way: as a natural born adventurer he'd "go crazy and pace up and down like a caged animal" if he couldn't get out in the wild places, if he couldn't just leave the family and the regular life and put on the parka and the boots and follow his dream, his calling.

Philips told how he'd gone to Greenland when his wife was pregnant and how lucky he was to have the kind of wife who understood his need to be elsewhere. He said of course he was a selfish man, because he had a daughter now, and she was still small, and he was going to the bottom of the world for three months, and how he had to go there because that's what he was built to do. Likewise, the others, his teammates, Jon Muir and Peter Hillary.

The matter was out of his hands, out of the hands of his companions, because they were marked by the gods. As Philips declared in the spiel, "We have the Ulysses factor. That's what sets us apart."

Ulysses, or Odysseus as the Greeks called him, was the world's first action and adventure hero, the founding father of the big game, the king of Ithaca who won the war against Troy by planting a wooden horse full of his fellows at the Trojans' gates. Have you heard of him?

On the voyage home, he was captured by a Cyclops named Polyphemus, put in storage to be eaten later, Polyphemus having already eaten some of his men. When he used trickery to escape, the god of the sea cursed him and his men to wander lost for ten years to the end of the world. That is, they were sent adventuring, while their wives did a little adventuring of their own back home. **(Still happens in the game. Believe me.)**

While they had a wild and terrible time of it, knowing little peace and much suffering, there were great triumphs, great things seen, greatness felt in their bones. It ended with Odysseus coming home alone, all his men dead or lost. In Homer's epic poem *The Odyssey,* the world's first and best big ripping yarn, nearly three thousand years old, Odysseus tried to trick his way out of going to war in the first place. He never wanted to leave his wife, his kingdom, his nice warm bed. He was frightened of what lay out there. He just wanted to get on with his life.

In a later version of the legend, Ulysses takes on the wandering curse as his reason for being.

> . . . for my purpose holds
> To sail beyond the sunset, and the baths
> Of all the western stars, until I die.

These lines are taken from Lord Tennyson's half marvelous poem he called "Ulysses." The polar explorers from a hundred years ago adopted Tennyson's version as a source of spiritual guidance and inspiration, and as something to read aloud to their fellows as they lay in their sleeping bags: Amundsen, Nansen, Scott, their men.

Best remembered, most loved, and most quoted by the old polar fellows and by the anthologies of classic verse, were the last fifteen lines from "Ulysses," popularly known as "To Sail Beyond the Sunset."

> Come my friends.
> 'Tis not too late to seek a newer world.

From the golden age of motivational speeches, Ulysses' pep talk to his crew should be read aloud in emergency wards and retirement homes, because it's prettier and more stirring than delivering the guts of the message cold: "Sure, things are grim. We're probably finished. But let's keep hanging in there. Just keep going."

One of the men who found the Captain in his sleeping bag, Apsley Cherry-Garrard, in his great book *The Worst Journey in the World,* included To Sail Beyond the Sunset as the epigraph in the chapter that tells what happened to the polar party, according to their dead diaries. It started a trend. If somebody writes about the Captain, they usually throw in a few lines of this poem that has lingered in the big game's mythology like a school prayer vaguely remembered.

As the polar greats had done, Eric Philips declared the last line of Ulysses' speech as his motto and creed.

> To strive, to seek, to find, and not to yield.

For Philips, these words defined what he called "the Ulysses factor" and what he felt it was all about, the business of being out there. And there was nothing he or the others could do about it. Birds had wings, fish had gills, the chaps had the factor, and nature must run its course.

It's not uncommon for adventurers in the big game to carry on in this way, if not always so boldly. Of course they were set apart from the regular people: they did the wild and dangerous things that gave the regular people the creeps when they heard too much about it. The middle was the middle, the edge was the edge, and in between was "why?"

In short, the men told the television people and the company boardrooms about their lives "out there," fueling the mystery of what they were about.

You have to dance the dance to get these things off the ground.

CHAPTER THREE

So you're the guy who's going to write lots of stories about Iridium?
That's great. Don't forget to put our name all over the front page.

John Hayley, Iridium offices, Melbourne, 1998

When they were making their pitch for the million and some, it usually fell to Peter Hillary to talk about the expedition's connection with Captain Scott, because he was a little in love with it, because it was History, it was marvelous being a **minor footnote** to the "greatest polar story ever told," and he looked forward to walking in sympathy with Scott's ghost.

Jon Muir didn't seem to care either way about the connection, although he spoke with a lot of sympathy for the Captain, because his story was so awful, and because he'd really been out there. It was whatever and fine that completing Scott's journey was their expedition's theme, as long as it didn't get in the way of his personal experience of being out there. Eric Philips quietly asked journalists to play down the Scott connection because he felt they'd be making history in their own right. And therein lay a snapshot of the team.

However, thrilled or chilled by the Captain, they all felt at least a little grateful to Scott, because he was helping to float the trip and pay the bills. He was one of their stories. To win the funding required, they needed stories. Without stories, and without means of getting them out, the progress of their trek would have drawn the same level of passing interest accorded to three guys eating nothing but iron filings for a hundred days. No spotlight, no sponsors.

"Completing Scott's journey" did the trick nicely. Hillary even had a letter from the Scott family wishing them well.

Winning both the press and the sponsors was indeed a dance, and a little bit of conjuring. It worked this way: Hillary, the team's deal maker and principal fund raiser, had put on his blazer and tie and shiny shoes, first to meet with newspaper editors and program managers, offering them exclusives to a running story that didn't have legs. Then he'd tell the moneyed moguls how the media was keen.

> That's the way it has always been done. Adventurers and explorers have been promising the world to their patrons for centuries. Perhaps the biggest problem is that many of those promises were never honored. Sponsors and patrons have been burned. Now they want a big return on their investment, and they want it guaranteed, ironclad.

In the end, to make this trip happen, Peter Hillary had to guarantee that the polar trip would be in the news all the way through, and the only way he could do that was by showing the almost-sponsors that the story was already under way, which it was. Still, the sponsors held out for more.

> Our two biggest and most vital supporters each wanted to run the trip as "their" publicity stunt, at which we'd perform, while out on the ice, via satellite telephone. Notably, a daily schedule of newspaper interviews and folksy on-the-spot chats with radio drive time programs everywhere. Things to do between hauling. It was too much. It was a little out of control. It was the only deal going. And I think the Captain would have taken it too.

That's how they got their shot at the Pole: by signing on as a traveling circus of ripping yarns, as a guided return to the golden age, and as a virtual lounge act for people eating canapés.

The Iridium satellite phone company (since folded, later resurrected) was launching itself on the market as the expedition was heading south. Iridium put up a six-figure check, the satellite phones, and free calls home. Their daily media schedule, established by Hillary, was managed by a blue chip public relations firm that was fronting the expedition, but actually worked for the phone company.

In return, the polar team starred in the launch's advertising campaign. Peter Hillary was turned into a lifesize cardboard cutout for in-store promotions, dressed in polar gear and fake beard, satellite phone pressed to his ear, big grin on his face, pretty sunset scene behind him.

Plus, they had to call themselves "Iridium-IceTrek." So they were going out in Scott's name, but the expedition was named after the phone company, in the way that horse races and football stadiums are named after airlines and banks. (The public relations people were insistent that the newspapers carry the trek's full name, calling to complain and make dark noises when the papers didn't comply.)

Our principal supporter, however, was Antarctica New Zealand (ANZ), which runs New Zealand's Antarctic science research program, and which organized our flights down to the ice and ongoing logistical support. ANZ has for some years been flying artists and writers down to Scott Base, to expand its program and public profile beyond science to the humanities. The polar trip was part of ANZ's media and public education programs for nineteen ninety-eight.

There was a potentially awkward sticking point: ANZ operates in a cooperative partnership with the neighboring American operations, at the base called McMurdo Station, Antarctica's largest base. (They share transport planes and airfields, and many of their science programs are intertwined.) However,

the Americans have long been opposed to private expedi-tions, because they're seen as a dangerous drain on resources when they get into trouble. Hence, ANZ felt it a necessary courtesy to ask for the Americans' endorsement of the polar trip as an official ANZ event. And I think everyone was pretty excited when the Americans gave us the nod.

They did so with one condition: if any member of the party had to be pulled from the ice, the other two had to come off too. One out, all out. It was this conditional endorsement that finally put "Event K 390," as the expedition was named in the ANZ paper-work, officially on the books.

But the only reason ANZ gave the expedition a second look at all was the Sir Edmund connection. He was a founding father of New Zealand's southern adventure, his face was on the five dollar bill, he'd built the first Scott Base. The Hillary name was going out there again.

> **The family name was on the line. And I felt a huge responsi-bility for it.**

Among the many guarantees given in writing to ANZ, Iridium, and other expedition stake holders, Hillary signed off on a promise to mention them as much as possible, that there would be no public unpleasantness and that their best interests and public standing would be protected.

> **In other words, we had to be a happy traveling circus of rip-ping yarns. All three of us signed on the bottom line to that effect.**

Among their requirements, ANZ insisted that they carry all their human waste back to base for incineration, that they carry their turds with them, in their sleds, a hundred days' worth of frozen bile bricks wrapped in plastic. ANZ wanted it to be a big part of their story, that they'd left the place spotless.

Hillary argued that the frozen bricks would keep the sleds too heavy, but if the droppings were left on the ice, they would freeze dry and blow away, maybe a saucepanful of dust in total, he fig-ured. There were letters, there were phone calls, but let's just say that Hillary and company took it in the end, the deal: they'd carry all turds, drum up the press at every opportunity, keep it pleasant when talking to the press, and remember to mention the turds. So it turned.

Most evenings, when they got out there, in their little red tent smaller than a double bed, as one man did his turn melting ice for the cooking, with another squatting a foot away singing the hymns of constipation into a plastic bag, the third would take his turn with the phone and the schedule of interviews and sing for their fat soaked suppers.

At first they told the usual stuff, the expected stories of being pinned down by storms that could be heard howling in the background; of being slowed by illness; of days aborted when their hands and feet turned to wood in the sucking cold for the sixth time and no hard banging would bring back the blood or the feeling.

For a touch of true horror, they spoke about the oil and butter soups they were drinking for dinner, about violently emptying their bowels shoulder to shoulder, of their boots falling to pieces, of living in filth and smelling as if they were rotting from the inside. **This is how it was for Scott, what?**

Again and again and again they explained how getting to the Pole from the eastern side, largely following Scott's line, was a journey of three stages.

First: they had to cross the coated tongue of Antarctica, the ragged sheet of ice five hundred miles across, what Scott knew as the Great Ice Barrier, now named the Ross Ice Shelf. At the other end, they'd meet a string of mountains, the TransAntarctic Mountains, two thousand miles long, running east to west **in a tectonic sickle** ten to fifteen thousand feet high.

Second: they'd drag their sleds up and over the mountains, by choosing and following a glacier for about a hundred miles, to nine thousand feet or so, to the splintered edge of the polar ice cap, the Polar Plateau.

Third: another three hundred miles climbing up and across the plateau to the Pole, at altitudes where thinner air further leeched the body and skewed the mind, with deeper sub zero winds that burned the skin like acid, and where there were said to be many impossible visions. Of course, there were six hundred miles to do up on the plateau with the return leg.

Tongue, glacier, plateau; plateau, glacier, tongue.

They told how, once they'd crossed the coated tongue, they were taking the Shackleton Glacier up to the Polar Plateau, a stretch to the east of the Beardmore where Scott had climbed. The Shackleton had never been climbed, therefore it was to be one of their first things. **So we were completing Scott's journey and putting in a new route to boot. All jolly good stuff.**

About two weeks out, they talked of looking around for Scott's body, wondering if they may have actually walked over it.

And they remembered to talk about the dirt they were carrying in their sleds. Shit, crap, turds, poo. The latter was preferred when talking to a radio drive time program somewhere.

Often the journalist at the other end of the phone, having followed the trek throughout and always wondering how to keep it fresh, would sigh and say something like, "I guess it's just white and flat out there again, huh?" So it was.

But Hillary had packed a list of story ideas in his sled, as one might take lumps of sugar to feed the horses at the track. He'd also planned cute stunts, such as calling his daughter's primary (grade) school classroom and inviting the media in through the public relations people. Of course he knew how to play for publicity: he'd grown up in the newspapers, with film crews following the family around and turning their pleasant walks into documentaries.

You may have seen Peter Hillary's bearded withered face on *Good Morning America*, beamed live from the ice at the end of it. He looked ancient at the end of it.

You may have seen him later, still in his orange parka and still thin, but shaved and combed and in the chair with his good cheekbones and his high aristocratic brow and the suit beneath the parka, in the studio, on *The Late Show with David Letterman.*

David Letterman: "Ladies and gentlemen, please welcome Peter Hillary. . . . So you've found a new route to the South Pole, huh?"

Hillary: "Yes, that's right."

Letterman: "What was wrong with the old one?"

CHAPTER FOUR

Or have we eaten on the insane root
That takes the reason prisoner?

William Shakespeare, *Macbeth*

Jon Muir had to be in the mood for television people, but their cameras loved him anyway: he looked and dressed like a caveman fresh from hunting on the plains somewhere, and he lived that way too.

His hair, a long knotted mop, fell in two tangled pigtails that framed his dreamy grin and his eyes that often boggled when he was asked for comment. Around his neck he wore a kangaroo claw, around his barrel torso a roadkill rabbit skin waistcoat. Sometimes a possum skin hat also found on a road somewhere. Feathers behind his ears.

It only made it sexier when he said all the right things with the gruff detachment of a war veteran's ennui, because it lent a sense of jaded intimacy to the exchange. When he wasn't in the mood, he did the haughty gruff stuff without the big eyes.

As Muir told one journalist: "I wasn't built for sitting around on my arse. Getting out on the big journey is so close to what we are, nomadic creatures . . . I mean, our lives are so complex. Advertising people talk about our needs. When you step away from all the other things that people call needs, you find life has a purity and richness that no amount of creature comforts can compete with. Once I'm in the wilderness, I feel more relaxed than in civilization. Even when things are tough."

Muir didn't need much, he said, save for getting out there. And he'd been out there. Muir had pulled off many "daring" and "bold" climbs, on big mountains and nothing-to-grip rock faces, in the European Alps and the Himalayas. He'd been on Mount Everest five times (twice with Hillary), made the summit once, in eighty-eight, got a medal from the Australian government, soon after gave up the mountains for adventuring with kayaks, and then trekking alone through Australian deserts.

Three years after the Pole excursion, Muir crossed the sunburnt country, from the south of Australia to the north, with only a dog for company and a rifle for food and his cart creaking behind him with the only water in the world upon it. The dog died, and Muir ran the last miles, leaving his cart behind, just wanting the odyssey over.

Mrs. Muir—Brigitte—had also climbed Everest. The Muirs caught up between adventures, living simple out on the edge of the red desert, in the shadow of red mountains, in the western region of the Australian state of Victoria. No children, plenty adventures.

Muir had lived in the heat, flies, dust since coming down from a steelworks city called Wollongong (an hour or so south of Sydney), when he was sixteen, having left school to climb the red rock faces so he could one day climb Mount Everest. When he was fifteen, he had put Everest on his list of things to do.

He'd slept in the trees back then, at the foot of the mountains. He kept the taint of the regular life to bare bones since moving

out of the trees. He had liked having no telephone. He never answered the telephone now that he had one.

He wasn't a big people person, Muir. As much as he wasn't
into the modern comforts and concerns of his fellow citizens,
adventurers or not, he often wasn't into their company or their
conversation, either. It seemed that he couldn't be bothered
with the work needed to keep a team happy and sane, although
he could be kind and sort of sweet. But when it got complicated,
he was happier left alone than do the whole reach out and touch
someone thing and otherwise get involved.

> **In many ways Jon's needs are pretty basic. A simple life.
> That's what he likes. He has some challenges and objec-
> tives (adventures) that draw him into the world of other dri-
> ven people, and by necessity into the corporate world to
> achieve his ends. But at the end of the day he thinks corpo-
> rate people, suburban people, most people are too compli-
> cated. He doesn't know what they're on about, and he feels
> that he—unlike the greater body of humanity—"cuts through
> all the crap." That's one of his ways of coping. By saying, "Ah,
> screw it. Can't be bothered."**

Muir's sense of whimsy extended to the organizational and
planning side of expeditions (save for trips he dreamed up himself, and they were usually solo trips). That is, he generally
brought little more to a trip than himself; he was his own contribution, like it or lump it. Muir was the kind of hired gun who you
called because he was usually very good in the field, he was very
strong, he kept to himself, and he was always available. That is,
no responsibilities, free always to go and do as he chose. **There
are very few people in the game who can do that.**

Save for guiding tourists on desert treks, he'd been doing
mainly solo trips for about ten years. "Just me. Me and the
wilderness. That's how I like it."

In nineteen ninety, his medal from Everest still shiny, Muir
wrote to the Australian prime minister, Paul Keating, asking the

government to float a trip to the South Pole. The prime minister's office wrote back: thanks, but no thanks. Muir moved on to other things.

In ninety-three, Peter Hillary partnered up with a friend named Graeme Joy to ski to the Pole. Hillary suggested to Joy that Jon Muir would be a healthy addition to the team, because he was strong and would be a reliable reserve for their team. Joy had resisted the idea, then relented. Muir came onboard, kept on doing his thing until something happened, and kept doing his thing when, after Hillary and Joy danced hard for the corporate people for two hard years, the major sponsors pulled out at the last minute and it went down the drain.

In ninety-seven Eric Philips knocked on Jon Muir's desert door, declared the South Pole his childhood dream, asked that they team up for the big haul south. They didn't really know one another, but Muir was keen to give most things a go if somebody else raised the money. He knew somebody who opened doors. Muir called Hillary.

> I said, "Sure, I'll give it another go."
>
> Soon after I realized that no one in our team had what the field manuals called "deep field" experience. We hadn't traveled (overland) to the ends of the earth, which has its very own cruel quirks and torments conspiring to do one in. We didn't have the knowledge and the habit of the many little things, the particular tricks of the polar trade that make the difference between success or defeat or disaster. I felt it was something we could fix.

Hillary asked Muir and Philips if Graeme Joy could join the team. Joy had been to the North Pole on foot, had studied and practiced Inuit survival and travel techniques, and was an enthusiastic problem solver. Hillary and Joy had led a guided climb of Mount Vinson, the highest mountain in Antarctica. Joy had won Hillary's admiration and gratitude by forsaking his bid for the summit (otherwise assured), by leading an injured climber back down to camp, generously leaving Hillary to bag the top with the rest of the group.

In Hillary's view, the team needed Graeme Joy's experience and generosity of spirit. More than that, Hillary felt Graeme Joy could bring some balance to the chemistry and a pulse to the social makeup of the party. It didn't have much of either. Not only did Joy have the polar goods that would greatly boost their chances of pulling it off, he was an enthusiastic talker, as was Hillary.

Muir and Philips said no way to Graeme Joy; didn't need him, didn't want him.

> **When I'd agreed to join the team, I didn't know Eric Philips beyond a couple of conversations, but I had known Jon Muir for nearly twenty years.**

Muir had been with Hillary in eighty-four when they tried for Everest's "daring" West Ridge route, with four other fellows, without tanks of oxygen, sleeping high in a snow cave and higher still in little tents, but not sleeping at all, and those who weren't feeling poorly started for the top in the very early morning. It was a leeching cold up there as they went for it, the weather bad and darkening, the winds screaming. At eight thousand three hundred meters (over twenty-seven thousand feet) five hundred meters from the top, Hillary decided, **not today, old boy.**

The others started down too.

> **Jon Muir was in front of me. We'd descended to twenty-six thousand feet, about eight thousand meters. I was crab-walking down the slope, moving sideways, with my body turned to the right, when suddenly I felt this wind. I thought it must have been a rock, because something had gone by very fast and quiet.**
>
> **It was Craig Nottle, twenty-three years old, fifth year medical student, light of his family. He'd been coming along behind me, a bit farther up the steep gully. We figured**

he'd probably tangled his crampons and tripped face out. He fell and shot past me like a bullet, nearly took me out too.

The hood of Craig Nottle's climbing suit was up over his head. They'd written their names on their suits, so they'd all know who was who and how they were traveling. But Craig Nottle was looking up as he went by and Hillary and Muir could see the cream on his face and his goggles over his eyes and they just froze at the sight of this falling face, and then Craig Nottle started to bounce.

Boom.

Boom.

Boom.

As Craig Nottle bounced he tried to get purchase on the sloping ice, with spastic reaching arms and sad grasps that held nothing but air. Craig Nottle, the light of his family, tried to stop himself but just kept bouncing and tumbling with the thumping sound of rockfall.

Alone I climbed a thousand feet down the north face to where he lay on stepped ruts of sloping wind blasted snow, calling down to him, hoping he'd somehow survived. I took a photo-graph when I found him like that, and I didn't know why I was taking it.

When Hillary turned to climb up to the route, back up to the others, he saw that his great friend Fred From (ionospheric physicist, light of the family, big heart) had slipped and fallen and was bouncing down the mountain. **I heard him before I saw him.**

Boom.

I just screamed, "Oh, no," and all I can really remember is Fred frozen in midair, in a swimming pose, with a terrible look on his face.

Boom.

I saw the look on his face.

Boom.

> I didn't go down to see how he looked at the end of it. I'm
> pretty sure he went all the way to the Rongbuk Glacier, four
> thousand feet below. And I've always felt him scolding me for
> it and asking me why I didn't come down to him.

So Jon Muir was there for that, but it didn't mean that he and
Hillary were the kind of chums who got misty together. They
called each other "friend," in the way you might refer to anybody
in the gang down at the club. Sharing the trust of the game
didn't require them to be great friends.

> The thing is, you could team up with someone you'd just met
> at the foot of a mountain, as long as they knew their game, as
> long as they had the bona fides. And I don't mean the "wow"
> factor.

Off the mountain, Hillary and Muir had little in common but the
old times, and that they belonged to the same club. I wouldn't
know his politics. I don't know if he bothered having any, if he
cares. If you really grilled me on a whole lot of those aspects
of who Jon Muir was, what he represented, what he held dear,
I'd draw a lot of blanks.

They sort of kept in touch over the years, every two or three
years, made plans, what ho.

Hillary didn't see much of Muir during the eighteen months it
took to pull the expedition together. Basically, Muir sat out in the
desert with his feral cat foot rugs and waited to be called for the
main event.

Two weeks before the team was due to meet up in Christchurch, their launchpad to the ice, Jon Muir called to say he'd
fallen over and hurt his back, and that he didn't think he would
be able to come along. As dismayed as he was and caught under
the clock, Peter Hillary saw in Muir's vague resignation an opportunity to radically alter the team's chemistry.

> So I contacted my old climbing partner, Kim Logan, a power-
> ful man with a powerful heart. Hard worker, with a lot of in-
> tegrity, someone I admire.

Then Muir called again, said he was back in, no worries.

The television people loved the whimsical Jon Muir. He was out there; he was on the edge. When he mentioned he couldn't ski, and that he would teach himself on the march to the Pole, the assembled took it as a sign that he was indeed naturally born to it, that he was the real thing.

CHAPTER FIVE

No field journey may be taken alone. All parties leaving the station will have an appointed leader. The leader is not expected to be autocratic and dictatorial to achieve the aims of the journey, but he is obliged to maintain high standards of safe conduct with a sober appreciation of the risks involved and a clear understanding of the methods used to minimise them. The successful leader will maintain high morale and encourage individual achievement and in return may expect loyalty and happiness in his party and a satisfactory conclusion to the enterprise.

From a government manual for Antarctic operations

All that Peter Hillary knew about Eric Philips, when they entered the magic circle of expeditionary trust together, was this: he had made a neat crossing of southern Greenland, using kayaks, skis, and kites, and he had starred in a documentary of the trip, *Chasing the Midnight Sun,* that had won an Emmy Award.

Philips had also been a private school master, at Timbertop, the outdoors adventure campus of blue blooded Geelong Grammar School, the Australian boarding school where Prince

Charles did time as a boy. (Graeme Joy had also done time at Timbertop, like Philips, teaching the lads to climb and ski and be all they could be.)

Peter Hillary was occasionally invited to play hero for the little Neros by way of telling stories and otherwise inspire their vigorous journeys up the tree trunk of life. **It was on such an occasion that I first met Philips. He seemed all right. A bit pent up, wanting to get out there, and I knew how that could be. Time passed. He was just someone I met.**

Philips later worked as a field officer for the Australian Antarctic program, for the summer season of ninety-six at Mawson Base, west of where the Captain had called home.

In the early pleasant days of their acquaintance, Hillary learned that Philips had grown up in the South Australian city of Adelaide but apparently wasn't fond of the place; was married to a woman called Suzie; was father to a little girl called Mardie, whom he seemed to adore; that he had recently lost his younger brother to death by misadventure; that he had crossed the ice cap on Ellesmere Island, ridden a bicycle over the Andes, wanted to go to the North Pole one day; and that he played guitar and sang in a pleasant if mournful folksy voice suited to the echoes of a church.

> **We heard him sing whenever we got together for an expeditionary dinner. We always had these dinners at a little restaurant where Eric had a regular spot serenading the diners. A romantic place, this dark little trattoria with its low ceiling and the candles on the tables, and always hanging around was that familiar circle of people (in this case, Eric's people) who like to sit on the fringe of adventure talk, and in the middle was Eric with his guitar, holding court.**
>
> **And that was okay. It promised a lighter side to our future tent life together. A few songs, some laughs, all jolly good stuff. I joked a number of times that Maestro Philips would serenade Muir and me after the work was done down on the**

ice. Nice idea, but as time passed, it became clear that we'd need that lighter side, because he was an astoundingly competitive and complex fellow, and that our relationship would be a challenging one.

In the adventuring world, where treks and climbs and feats of derring-do have long been automatically graded by the community into levels of greatness, skiing to the South Pole was "a big trip." Philips was thirty-six years old, a late starter to the big trip. He hadn't been on one before, but he was talented, very driven, very hardworking, very excited about the whole thing, aglow with tremendous self belief, and he had never known "failure."

The Greenland crossing of twenty some days was "a good trip." Philips had done one good trip and several "neat jaunts," always as the leader (either officially or by default), in the spirit of the old time trips when everything went to one man's plan and nobody questioned it more than once. When the newspaper people asked Eric Philips what was the biggest challenge facing the team's stability and emotional well being, he said, "The issue of leadership."

Philips appeared to want to be leader of the polar expedition, knew it could never be, wasn't prepared to have anyone else wear the badge, and insisted that the three of them put it in writing and sign it: an agreement that the expedition had no leader.

What made all this very odd: leadership was never an issue for Hillary or Muir. They saw the expedition as three professionals working in cooperation, with no one playing captain. As a sign of goodwill, they signed.

Still, Philips' open desire to be "the one" continued to find expression. When he took on the core logistical preparations of the trip—the sleds, the boots, the skis—the intensity with which he worked made it clear he wanted no second opinions.

The material planning and provisioning of a polar expedition is a detailed and complex business. A jigsaw puzzle of many parts that add up to the team's life support system, one that has to operate in a relentlessly extreme environment. Think of a space station. They were going into space.

> The sourcing of the equipment is the crux of the job. There are not many people doing south polar trips—perhaps half a dozen a year—and polar standard gear isn't mass produced. It's a specialist area.

To survive and thrive, they needed the right sled, the right stove, the right tent, the right boots that wouldn't shatter and fall apart in the cold, or at least were easy to repair, because all boots fall apart out there. One of the biggest challenges was laying in enough food and fuel to last the distance, while keeping weight to a minimum, with one eye on the details and the other on the big picture.

Philips was a dedicated details man. He worked many late nights on the small details. He wanted to make his mark with this trip and often talked about the expedition being "cutting edge" logistically, and that it was all in the small details. However, it fell to Hillary to find the sponsors to bankroll or supply the desired goods.

> After I secured all our outdoor clothing and down quilted bags, jackets, and pants from an adventure outfitter called Fairydown, Philips insisted on using another brand of parka because it had more zips.

In the end, they sewed Fairydown badges on Philips' preferred parkas, thereby retaining the sponsorship, if not the sponsor's warmest regards. And while Hillary had allowed Philips his way, the episode bothered him.

Meanwhile, there were moments in passing, when they got together socially, that further led Hillary to believe that he and the younger man were not greatly compatible teammates.

One Sunday, a couple of months before the team headed out, Hillary and a friend met up with Philips, in a flat open park that sat behind a Melbourne beach, for a picnic. Philips' wife and daughter were there, two of Hillary's kids, and the friend's wife.

There was a strong wind blowing off the water, and Philips had brought along a couple of the big kites they were taking to Antarctica, to drag them along with their sleds when the wind was right. Philips and Hillary took turns flying the kites on long lines, steering them and allowing themselves to be dragged forward in squatting hops. When the friend took a clueless turn with one of the kites, he kept hold of the steering lines as the gust pulled him over because he didn't want to see the kite fly off into distant traffic. As he felt where his ribs were broken, Philips leaned down and, by way of consolation, said, "Too bad it happened in front of your woman."

A few days before this episode, the men had talked about seeing a marriage counselor, to learn strategies that would help keep things civilized and cordial and otherwise lubricated. In many ways these are true marriages made on these trips, intimate relationships by circumstance, and by the sharing of trust. Polar travel has a sordid history of hatred and resentment laying waste to expeditions. And they didn't want it to happen to their trip.

I remember the day we talked about it.
It was the first day they had dressed up in their new adventure clothes, and then put on fake beards and were painted up with makeup to give them suntans and frosted wrinkles, and stood in front of a pretty sunset scene over an ice sheet somewhere. Sprinkled on the floor and in their hair was snow made from instant potato powder. They were shooting a series of pictures for the phone company's advertising campaign, and they talked about seeing a marriage counselor in between poses.

The problem was, as they stood there with fake snow in their fake beards, resentment was already fermenting, mainly because the newspapers were calling the expedition a "Hillary and company" affair. And because, during the photo shoot, it became clear that the phone company was going to use Hillary as their life size cardboard cutout that would be standing at the counter of outlets everywhere.

That's when I started seeing the old familiar jealousy of the Hillary name lurking in the unhappy soul of my young companion. I just thought, "Aw, not this stuff again."

So I talked to him about it, and told him that he'd have to make the most of it: the two edged sword of having the Hillary name onboard. There's only so many times you can apologize for reality, and I suppose I laid it out like a map of the world.

The Hillary side of the family aren't hostage negotiators. That is to say, my father and I (and to some extent my sister Sarah) don't have a firm or practiced grasp of the nuances of human communication, such that we can navigate the quicksand of edgier emotional interactions to an "I'm okay, you're okay" group hug. When something "is," that's the way it is, and there isn't much point in prettying it up and pretending it's otherwise, and certainly not in a marriage.

I don't know that marriage counselors have much success draining jealousy from an infected relationship. Regardless, seeing a counselor became just another fanciful thing we told the press, because we never got around to making such an appointment.

Meanwhile, the pleasant days of the marriage between Hillary and Philips had slid away, and they were on their way to becoming one of those dreadful couples often seen at restaurants, where the wife nags and bickers and the husband sits in his cave with icy eyeballs. By that sad stage their story was in play, deep. It was August of ninety-eight when they put on those fake beards, just two months out from the trip. The sponsors had just come onboard.

I couldn't postpone and regroup with another team for the ninety-nine to twothousand summer season, because the newspapers would be full of the Olympics, the America's Cup, the APEC meeting in Auckland, and the new millennium. We wouldn't get the media run that the sponsors required. No spotlight, no sponsors.

The summer of ninety-eight, with no scheduled major media events, was a blank slate. It was our only window. In the end I thought, "This is the trip. This is the team. That's the way it is. Let's see if we can pull it off. Let's see what happens."

In shaky marital terms, however, it was akin to saying, "Well, let's have a baby, then." After the polar trip, when reminded of the "in front of your woman" story, and when sent a long list of questions by e-mail, Eric Philips declared he wouldn't have anything to do with this book. However, he provided a long list of family and adventuring friends who could attest to his decency and character. And they did.

His mother, over the phone, named all the Boy Scout virtues to him. He was the light of the family. Mrs. Philips, however, was "surprised" and "unhappy" that her son was carrying a "grudge" because it isn't like him, and she hoped he'd give it up at some point.

After the polar trip, Eric Philips saw a therapist—a research psychologist, actually, with an interest in expeditionary madness. Dr. Peg Levine, Ph.D., was on the list of friends. She said that Philips "came to me at first for a debriefing," and he kept coming because "he wanted my help to understand what happened down there."

So what happened down there, Doc? "To understand what went wrong with this expedition, you have to look for the betrayal. For each of them."

Dr. Levine later worked with Philips on the book. While working on the book—a process Philips described as "cathartic"—they'd become friends, she said.

CHAPTER SIX

And I never did have any doubt, but in my heart always knew how you
would come home, having lost all of your companions.

Homer, *The Odyssey*, the Richmond Lattimore translation

In his shiny shoes, striped tie, and blazer, Peter Hillary looked a
dapper chap, with a vaguely aristocratic bearing. There was
something of that in him, too, and that's how people generally
took him: the starched shirt of good manners and the old school,
removed.

Somehow it wasn't ever fully shaken off when he fronted the
cameras and the school halls and the cruise ship auditoriums to
tell some of his stories with the boyish enthusiasm that also
came to play in the rowdier happy moments with his children.
All the **jolly good stuff** generally warmed up the boardrooms,
the auditoriums, although it tended to leave the more self
conscious attendee a little uncomfortable.

Sometimes, when asked a question, say about one of his
climbs that had ended with dead friends, Hillary adopted the

dissecting gaze of an accident inspector, and the boy's enthusiasm would be no longer there as he talked in brutally bare terms, with no emotion save for a reluctant gravity of chilled certainty, which generally left people cold. Too much barefaced reality.

Often somebody asked, "What's the point?" when the human cost has been so great and the big prizes already bagged. "Hasn't it all been done before?"

The tone of the answer depended on his mood.

If he was feeling sunnyside up, he might embrace the question as if it were an old friend, pukkah up, and say something like:

Indeed, why venture out on such a journey at all? It's something I often ask myself.

Part of the answer is that I'm drawn to the simplicity of the pilgrim's life, and the soaring emotions that go with it. As one Frank Smythe wrote in a little book called *The Mountain Top* given to me by my grandfather Jim Rose, who also climbed mountains: "The charm of mountain-climbing lies not in the climbing, in success, nor in failure, but in the great range of emotions provoked through these physical experiences."

I think this observation was at the core of what lured Jim and my father and me to the mountains, and to adventuring in general.

Another part of the answer lies in the definition of what a challenge is all about. To me a challenge is an undertaking where, at the end of the day, the planned outcome is not assured. There is uncertainty. Hence, the Hillary formula: Challenge = Uncertainty = Excitement.

No challenge worth its salt is going to be easy. I think there is merit in trying things that make you uncomfortable. Tackle the unknown, challenge yourself, and out of the abyss of the unknown rises the specter of your own fear. To swing from the rudder of your own vessel and steer your ship through the weather of life, to chart a journey that you direct. You must do this. Because this is the only chance you will get.

It is being adventurous in the way you see the world and the way you choose to live your life. It is accepting that you must be prepared to risk finding what you would rather not find, and often this is within you. It is being prepared to risk defeat. All this comes at the price of priority: there must be nothing else you would rather do.

Some days, on the other hand, Hillary couldn't bury his annoyance or measure out the jolly good stuff, and he'd give the message cold: it was his life, and if he wanted to spend it in the extreme places where a body dies just by sitting there, where every moment is critical, where every decision is critical to his life continuing, well, that was up to him, and surely it was better than:

Opting for a mollycoddled namby-pamby cotton wool existence in front of a television set.

Either way, to the assembled, it was all good. It was enough that he was "the famous son of Mount Everest conqueror, Sir Edmund Hillary," as it was usually writ in the papers.

When he was in his twenties, the newspapers had a marvelous time with the son of the great Hillary, because he seemed so much the wild young man on fire. Everything he did was measured against Sir Edmund, whose face graces New Zealand's five dollar bill. Part of the fun was naming him as a list of things: "the famous son of etc., adventurer, mountain climber, author, pilot, ski instructor, and daredevil television star."

When he was in his twenties, Peter Hillary felt that people would just look at him, walking down the street with his backpack and his walking boots, and think him amazing. He'd felt like a rock star.

We felt we were. We felt we were the rock stars of our game. I remember I'd just walk around, and you'd think that people would see you and go, "Wow. That's where it's at. They're out there. They're out there so far. They're out there because they're on the edge. The ultimate adventure." And I believe

they are, in a way, ultimate adventures. We operated in moving to the edge and coming back again. And you're totally
blinkered by that. I remember the mountains being what it
was all about. But it was also that blinkered youthful fault:
thinking that it was so important. And of course it's of no importance to anyone unless you choose to make it so.

Hillary was part of the new generation who took on the mountains with a bare bones toolkit. He went up carrying his own
load, with no Sherpas, no fixed ropes, no tent, no oxygen bottles,
no big support team below, just him and his companions breaking trail up the toughest routes, the insane routes, some never
tried, living up high in snow holes and on nothing ledges in a
sleeping bag: a small technical team, alpine style, fast moving,
"daring climbs," that's how he liked it.

But pushing hard lines in alpine style on Himalayan peaks had
its downside if anything went wrong. Out of the four men who
started up the soaring West Pillar of Makalu, fifth highest in the
world, two died, one of them the great Mark Moorhead, a gentle
young man of books and ideas, who moved with great elegance
on the hill, lovely to watch him climb. The other, Bill Denz, one of
the greats, truly, one of the best men **on mixed terrain, on rock
and ice, up high, out at the sharp end of the rope.**

Two out of four, gone; just Hillary and his great friend Fred
From were all that remained of the team in nineteen eighty-
three.

Bill Denz died first, wiped off, buried high.

> And I remember Fred just looked destroyed by grief. Fred
> had been trying to dig him out before Mark and I climbed up
> the ridge from Camp One to see what had gone wrong. We'd
> all been living very high on the mountain, as we pushed the
> route above, living in a crevasse, a long cave of blue ice where
> we cut a long kitchen bench into one of the walls. Mark and I
> had headed down, to take a break from living at altitude and
> build ourselves up with rest and good food. Fred and Bill

**stayed up to push the route, until we returned up the sharply
rising pillar to relieve them of the lead. So we got up to Fred
and we saw Bill's spiky footprints along the ridge far above
and where they disappeared beneath the smooth slice of the
avalanche break.**

A few days later, as the three of them sat in the mess tent at Base
Camp and talked about going home, somebody said they might
as well finish climbing the hill in Bill's memory, and Mark Moorhead said it was awfully strange that he couldn't remember what
Bill looked like. Another few days on, Mark Moorhead tripped
and fell from up high.

Fred From was so distressed he had to walk out from their
camp, leaving Hillary to pack up on his own. When Fred From
got home to Brisbane, he was quarantined in hospital with ty-
phoid, and was very sick with it. As he recovered, he found he
was having second thoughts about going to Everest, as planned
for the following year.

The year passed by.

Peter Hillary and Fred From went to Everest, and Fred bounced
boom.

By then Peter Hillary was the veteran of the big trip and he no
longer felt like a rock star. Along the way, he'd found the big trip
was like raising the dead, like a long night of visionary drinking:
for all the wild joy taken, with or without disaster, it left you in
pieces.

He'd found the big trip was something you got through, and he
no longer wondered if people were looking at him as he walked
down the street. Sometimes they were looking because he was
Peter Hillary and he was in the papers and they would stop him
and ask what adventurous thing he had been doing of late.

Eleven years passed, like diary pages thumbed, with summits
gained, summits lost. His last big trip, in ninety-five in Pakistan
on K2, the second highest mountain in the world, the Savage
Mountain to the community, ended this way:

I just remember coming off our route and into Base Camp, and what remained of the Spanish were coming off their route, staggering in, looking appalling, and everyone just absolutely out of it, and we followed them in. You staggered through their camp, and you knew that half of the Spanish were dead. You staggered through the American camp, and you knew all of them were dead. You arrived at our camp, and you knew that half of them were dead. So, yeah, you got in there and had all these cups of tea and went to bed.

CHAPTER SEVEN

Unhappy men, who went alive to the house of Hades, so dying twice, when all the rest of mankind die only once, come then eat what is there and drink your wine, staying here all the rest of the day, and then tomorrow, when dawn shows you shall sail.

Homer, *The Odyssey*, the Richmond Lattimore translation

It was October thirty-one, nineteen ninety-eight, and their story had already gone around the world, playing out politely in the newspapers and on the radio and television stations back home and abroad. They were happening. Britain loved it. Having long celebrated Scott as their tragic, defiant light of the golden age of exploration, the British press were giving Hillary and the boys a decent and sometimes jealous run, and here he was on Mc-Murdo Sound now, Hut Point Peninsula, the frozen coast.

He woke to the question "Have you been absent for long?" although it came not in words but dreamed faces. How can it be measured?

The number of days Peter Hillary hadn't shaved told part of

the story. They added up to about sixteen years in the field, to the life of sleeping bag dreams and terrors and not sleeping at all.

He was forty-three, turning forty-four in another eight weeks, the day after Christmas, and Christmas to be taken somewhere deep south in a sleeping bag while his children went through the thrill of rising to find what had been left for them by the man in the beard and the North Pole suit and pretending or not pretending to know he was true. Their father would be wearing a beard and his South Pole suit on Christmas Day and his birthday the next day in a sleeping bag, and the day after that he'd be out there and hauling well south he imagined, and they imagined him out there, and that's what they told their friends.

This was their second full day on the ice. He figured they'd be heading out in two or three days. Maybe four. He wasn't sure. The others were close by, still in their beds too.

This was the "new" Scott Base, named after the Captain who had wintered nearby. They were lying in sheets and blankets with fresh underwear, waiting in a long, low green building that looked less ski lodge than artillery bunker as it was swallowed by the surrounding consuming ever-extending emptiness when you beheld it from any great distance. The bunker was dug into the lower flank of a cone shaped nub of black volcanic rock, nearly eight hundred feet high, that stood up like a charcoaled lighthouse on the point of the peninsula.

The giant black finger of the peninsula paled gray and ghostly when seen from the frozen sea, even under an ink sky. It stuck out of the great white everywhere else as a half imagined coast, with its charcoaled lighthouse on the point promising nothing. Observation Hill was most famous as a lookout to disappointment.

The men from Scott's expedition, those who hadn't gone to the Pole, had climbed to the top of Observation Hill to look for their Captain. They later put a cross at the top in his memory, and in memory of those lost with him. They carved the lost

men's names, and they carved the motto To STRIVE, TO SEEK, TO
FIND, AND NOT TO YIELD.

Farther down the sloping foot of Observation Hill, down on
the gravel run-out above the sea ice, in the long shadow of the
cross and the nice words etched upon it, were what remained of
the roped down huts that Hillary's father and the Old Firm had
built in the early days of fifty-seven, the "old" Scott Base.

Hillary imagined the Old Firm living rough through the howling darkness of winter, when there was no sun, but a moon
when the sky was clear and they could see the long walk away to
Mount Erebus, the white volcano, fourteen thousand feet high.

It was under the winter moon that Erebus and everything were
always so beautiful, because moonlight is so beautiful; the ice
plain and the white volcano, the visible terrestrial world a body
of moonlight floating and dancing against the bigger body of
darkness.

The Captain and his men, with no charcoaled lighthouse at
their backs, had enjoyed the floating moonlight in panorama
from their quarters. They had wintered on the other side of
Mount Erebus, up the coast at Cape Evans, in a faded slab hut
that sat in a gentle cove with the white volcano as a distant back-
drop, looking as lonely and lost as a child in a deserted car park.
The Captain and his men had lived rough. Later that morning,
Hillary and party were flying out to see how the Captain had
lived rough.

Meanwhile, the new Scott Base had hot showers, three-
minute showers. It was still early.

It was October thirty-one, nineteen ninety-eight, a Saturday
morning in Antarctica, and back home in Auckland, Peter Hillary had a little boy starting to talk, and two older children who
lived across the sea in Australia, a skinny young girl and a skinny
little boy, and he'd found they all hung from his limbs as a pause
and a brake on the life as an absentee that had long been taken
easily and with no second thought, no pangs save for the sweet-

hearts of his time, and somehow he'd always kept it all separate, because the absent life didn't feel absent at all. It was the best thing, the only thing, and now he was into his second marriage, to Yvonne Oomen, one of the sweetest hearts, who had left him years before. Because he was an absentee.

It was after Makalu in nineteen eighty-three that he met his first wife, Ann Moorhead, Mark's sister, on the visit to pay his respects, and it was after he made the top of Everest in nineteen ninety that she said it was more than enough and he'd better stay home now or else. And still he thought about the other life, like a gambler who talks of reform and yet shivers with the longing, and with the thrill that comes with the longing, and sooner or later follows his bliss regardless.

Peter Hillary stayed home, got bored, started talking about the little family spending a few months or years in New Zealand's Southern Alps. When he started talking about going to K2, the second highest mountain in the world, Ann Moorhead said goodbye, in ninety-three, although it wasn't as civilized or as simple as that.

Nine years later, when Peter Hillary went to the top of Everest again, as he was standing on the top, gasping for breath like a heart attack victim, strung out with the intellectual capacity of a six year old because the big gasps brought in so little oxygen, it so very cold up there, one toe so cold he wondered if it was for the chopper, with his guts raw and sore from months of dysentery and dehydration, with cloud coming in and the need to get down quick—with all this going on, Peter Hillary found the carcass of his first marriage still blowing smoke in his eyes. Back home, Yvonne Oomen had called to tell Hillary's older children, Amelia and George, that he would be calling shortly from the summit via satellite telephone, but she spoke to their mother instead. When Hillary called, pressing each number button with the deliberate lunge of a drunk chasing peas around a plate, he couldn't get through.

He called four times.

    Beep.

    Beep.

    Beep.

    Beep.

    Forgive us this, our daily chess. When I think of middle age, I think of baggage. I am a recycled wedding car that clatters down the road trailing lines of string, tin cans, and cases. "Yes, they all come too." And they do—they come to the ends of the earth with you.

Hillary was in bed, in sheets and blankets, thinking of his children being in their beds, and holding down the feeling that he was about to drop into a hole. The others were close by in their bunks, Philips and Muir. The room was warm and dark. Someone had taped cardboard masks over the glass to provide a sense of the night, to keep the burning emptiness outside regardless. It was around six o'clock when they all suddenly pulled off their blankets, grabbed their towels, and quietly walked down the hallway for the regulation three minute shower, no hearty "heigh ho" to be heard, just a bit of muttering.

Hillary shaved. The others had already let themselves go, by way of declaring the trip already started. Hillary shaved and brushed his teeth and combed his hair, took the towel from his waist, hung it on a peg, and then started putting on his adventure clothes: the thermal long johns, the Gore-Tex overpants, the woolen socks. He put his gloves and big mitts in the pockets of the parka with the big hood trimmed with wolf fur, which hung over his arm as he walked down to the army style cafeteria for his bacon and eggs and beans. In slow motion, with a stirring anthem playing, it could have been hilarious. But the film crew and the television people were at their breakfast too.

Hillary found the others sitting with some people, Jon Muir eating and eating and nodding whenever it was required as Eric Philips held court. Hillary sat down nearby and drank several cups of café au lait from the Scott Base social club's espresso machine. Then they all headed out to the hangar where the sleds were sitting side by side, with the harnesses lying on top, and much of their gear scattered about in a fashion that suggested the place had been burgled, as it always looks when people are going on holiday and find they have left packing their bags dangerously late.

Much of the equipment still needed to be modified before we could start putting together the jigsaw puzzle of the big picture.

But the team couldn't stay long in the hangar because of the demands of the dance.

Today we would fly out to Scott's hut at Cape Evans, and then on to Cape Roberts to make a film about ANZ's scientists and their laboratory on the sea ice (where they were drilling seabed samples that revealed the earth's climatic history).

There were amusing but stirring talks to give to the people living at Scott Base and at the sprawling American base called Mac Town that lay on the other side of Observation Hill. Few of the base people were adventurer sorts. To most of them Antarctica was akin to an oil rig, an isolated and intimidating place where the pay was good but you couldn't just go for a walk around the block to clear your mind. Anybody who wanted to walk beyond the base perimeters had to secure permission first, and thereby have their absence noted. At the various stations on the continent, people have been lost while walking between neighboring buildings in blizzard conditions—lost and frozen solid by the time they were found again.

I was looking forward to visiting Scott's hut: the thrill of seeing where the Captain had eaten his dinner and wrote the first half of his diary.

❄ ❄ ❄

Cold dulls the mind. Plan while you can still think clearly.

The SAS Survival Guide

At eleven o'clock that morning, as per the schedule, Peter Hillary and company flew out by helicopter to Scott's winter quarters at Cape Evans, with the film crew and the television people, to contemplate the Husky skeleton chained to the steps, the reindeer sleeping bags in the bunks, the colorful labels on the tins of food stacked on the shelves, the laboratory with an experiment half done, the penguin lying on the bench, the scene suggesting life still going. On videotape, in the sad light of the swing-a-cat fortress, faces flushed from the cold, the three of them moved along slowly, blowing clouds of steam, whispering, like schoolboys approaching an open coffin in a cathedral.

> **People always say the same thing when they go to Scott's hut: it's like they could return at any moment. And that's exactly what it was like. But I also found it sobering, and very moving.**

Then, as Hillary stayed looking at the old tins of food, the reindeer sleeping bags in their bunks, he felt the familiar fear tug at his elbow and make a dark joke, and all whimsical sentiment evaporated as he realized this beautiful scene made a true picture of what death was all about: everything stops.

And he thought of the sleds lying in the hangar.

> **In the weeks leading up to the trip, the familiar fear had been creeping up on me. I'm not sure why, but I'll spend twelve months organizing a trip and the familiar fear leaves me alone until the last weeks.**
>
> **Fear is a good thing. It keeps you sharp and it keeps you thinking. Fear is part of the experience. Accept it, absorb it, learn from it. Let fear help you take responsibility for your own safety and destiny.**
>
> **Philips was all wound up because he wanted to get back to the sleds and the gear and I was thinking, "Sure, we need**

to do that." But I was thinking there was so much that needed to be fixed, more than could be made right in two or three days.

We were going out there, and we weren't anywhere near ready for it.

The Captain may have been sympathetic, but Roald Amundsen, the Norwegian, wouldn't have thought much of our little band. Likewise, I supposed, Borge Ousland, the new Amundsen. Have you heard of him?

On November fourteen, nineteen ninety-six, Ousland left the western side of Antarctica to get to the eastern side. He set out alone. Alone. Ousland made the South Pole in thirty-two days, refusing a cup of tea as he came through, keeping as best as he could to staying out there alone. "Unsupported," as the community called it. Meaning: no food depots, no packages dropped from planes, no contact with anything but the wild. Using kites much of the way, the supreme allrounder went all the way to the other side. It was his second attempt.

In March twothousand and one, Ousland skied from Russia to Canada, crossing the North Pole, jumping in and swimming across the open leads of water where the ice had parted, dragging the floating sled behind him. He would have snap frozen—pht!—if he hadn't been wearing some miracle suit. Ousland was the new Amundsen. The bloody Norwegians, they had it: the efficiency, good sense, planning, skills.

Hillary and company were running on half a tank of everything, and the familiar fear was whispering in his ear, the long list of holes in their plans and abilities that had queasily threaded his guts as knotted string.

We hadn't done any training together. Not even a camping trip.

The few days they spent together in the snow, in the Australian Alps, with the sleds and skis and kites, were largely spent posing for photographs and news crews.

> We did maybe two hours' actual work in the field between in-
> terviews, and the field was planted with gum trees. I had
> pleaded with them to make it otherwise. I wanted us to make
> a number of skiing and hauling trips in New Zealand's
> Southern Alps, and spend some time in Greenland—but my
> partners always seemed to have other priorities, and Philips
> declared he didn't need to do any training.

By comparison, the two Belgians, Alain Hubert and Dixie Dan-
sercoer, had crossed Greenland twice as part of their training for
a brilliant Antarctic crossing they'd made in the ninety-seven
season. They also went down to Antarctica on a reconnaissance
visit "to accustom ourselves."

> To accustom themselves to the environment, and to each
> other. They're two of the masters of the polar game, the Bel-
> gians, but they recognized the need to bond and work as a
> team, as well as preparing their own bodies and minds. In
> their book about the trip, they said they'd recognized as crucial
> the need to abandon all sense of competition between them.
> Together they pulled it off, and then walked away with the
> warmest regard for one another. Of course, they had the skills.

Hillary and Philips could ski without thinking. Muir could haul
along flat ground all right, but as those two hours in the gum
trees revealed, if the slope dropped, he was apt to slither and fall
over.

Hillary and Muir had many years of experience working in extreme environments.

> There are a lot of little tricks you need to know just to keep
> your fingers warm, for instance. Philips didn't seem to have
> these systems sorted out for himself.

Philips was the only one of the team who was experienced with
the kites. How proficient he was I didn't know. Jon and I were
beginners with the kites.

Kites were the groovy tool of modern polar travel; sails for
where there was no sunset. In the right hands, one could knock
off fifty or a hundred miles in a long day with a kite leading you

on. When the wind was right, a good kiter just sailed along with the sled rocking behind.

Hillary hadn't flown big kites with skis and a sled before, but he'd flown planes and figured the kite as a wing, and taught himself how to fly them in the meadow parkland at the back of his house—how to steer, how to make the figure eights that would keep them sailing in humbler breezes.

But nothing beats experience in the field. Of this sort of travel I didn't have any. That I could ski meant I'd be able to fully concentrate on my flying. How Jon had progressed with the kites, I didn't know.

Because the wind blows mostly from the south in Antarctica, the kites wouldn't be much use on the trip out to the Pole. The fullness of their luxury wouldn't be known until they'd turned for the homeward leg. Without the good winds, the first nine hundred miles, the distance from New York to St. Louis, were to be hauled on foot.

Eric had hauled sleds; Jon had hauled carts. I had done a little sledding in the Arctic and had packed plenty huge loads in the mountains. None of us had hauled the huge gut busting sleds that awaited us.

Hillary had once spent ten months walking the length of the Himalayas, nearly three thousand miles, mostly at high altitude, sleeping under rocks and mostly living off whatever he and his companions found up there, sometimes not finding anything to eat for some days and then it was often barley flour, dry flour, and they'd shove it into their mouths with no saliva to swallow it at first, and then somehow their dehydrated bodies would find the drool.

But I'd never hauled a sled weighing hundreds of pounds for many hundreds of miles. The others said that they liked the idea of it, and they were looking forward to it.

"We're just lunging for the ice. We're itching for the first sting of the harness," Philips said in an interview by phone in the last days before the party's departure.

I wasn't itching for it. I couldn't imagine anyone loving it. It's what you have to do to go the distance.

To prepare for the haul, Hillary had, over many months, gone out each day on long runs up the high green hill that sat in the middle of the parkland at the back of his house, pushing his baby son along in one of those jogging prams with three wheels, and wearing a sledging harness that trailed a rope with an old car tire tied to the end of it. The tire dragged behind as he ran up and down the hills (his son dozing as passing motorists tootled and called out their amusement).

The Belgians did the same thing. Hauled tires. But the Belgians' tires were apparently filled with concrete when they hauled them around, hour after hour. And they were truck tires, by the look of them in the photographs. **The bloody Belgians**.

Down on the ice, Hillary planned to take on the load in the same way he took on the strangling air in the high mountains, by starting out slow and working up to it. He figured it this way: you weren't built to just turn up at the top of the world where the air was thin as charity soup. If you simply rushed up, you died.

I don't believe anyone is built to haul hundreds of pounds for hundreds of miles through leeching cold. But if you worked up to it, you could get there.

Hillary felt the same way about the team. Despite their short-comings, the holes in their talents, there was much good experi-ence and talent between them. They could still make a decent polar adventurer if the three of them rolled into one and became "one equal temper of heroic hearts" (as Ulysses so noisily names it in Tennyson's poem).

Instead, the team was split, in part by the exhausting and un-shakeable realities of the deals they had made to get the trip happening. First, there was the circus and the demands of the dance.

For a week or so, we'd been living together in Christchurch, staying in the home of friends of mine, Dr. Lindsay Strang

and his wife, Genevieve, waiting for our flight south, and trying to make sense of the mess of gear. We completely took
over the house with provisions and parkas and the rest of it
scattered everywhere.

But again, the dance card was full, because ANZ and Iridium
had many meetings and events and interviews lined up, and for
the usual reasons (chief fund-raiser, son of, and this was in New
Zealand) it fell to Hillary to fulfill these obligations on behalf of
all of them. But his companions clearly didn't see his spotlit excursions as expeditionary work.

One evening I returned from the media and sponsor circus, to
shower and change for the next round, and found Eric and
Jon modifying some of their gear. I asked if they could give
me a hand by making a start on some of my gear, as had happened automatically on more than thirty previous expeditions and seasons, where I'd often been obliged to handle a
variety of bureaucratic and diplomatic nightmares. The circus
was just another one to me.

Well, Jon said he'd have a look if he had the time. And I believed he was going to do it. Meanwhile, Philips just silently
looked away. Time passed, and it became very clear that if I
wanted my boots or skis modified too, I would have to do it
myself. I hoped I could attend to some of these things down at
Scott Base, because there wasn't going to be a free moment in
Christchurch, where the circus was at boiling point.

Meanwhile, team spirit and "common advantage," both reliable mainstays of the game as I'd always played it, were being replaced by "every man for himself."

Second, now they were on the ice, Muir and Philips were beginning to openly resent that the expedition was traveling under
Scott Base and Mac Town rules. They felt that in principle and
practice it robbed the trip of its fully "unsupported" status, and
of its independence.

Example: They figured the trip would take about one hundred
days. Regardless, they had to be back at Scott Base by February

seven, when the last of the American search and rescue planes would leave the ice to avoid ruination in the coming winter. **If the Americans or New Zealand decided we wouldn't make the deadline, they'd fly out and find us and bring us back in, no matter how we felt about it.**

Example: If one of them got sick or injured or worn out, such that he couldn't continue, an aircraft would fly out, take all of them back to base, and the odyssey would be over. "One out, all out," was the word from Washington. **Field parties heading out from Scott Base were usually required to have a minimum of four people. They bent this rule to accommodate us.**

And it was becoming a bit awkward while we were staying at Scott Base. There were all these people helping us with our gear and packing—work that really should have been done before we arrived on the ice.

Philips was actually pretty rude to Peter Cleary, the operations manager, a man with more Antarctic experience than any of us, and a pretty decent man too. When it turned out that our HF (high frequency) radio was damaged, Cleary's team put together a neat little unit, better than the original. We were carrying the radio at Cleary's insistence and we were not allowed to leave until the new one was tested. He wasn't convinced that this brand new satellite telephone would give us a guaranteed line back to Scott Base if anything went wrong. Both Philips and Muir were unhappy about the radio situation. Didn't want it. Jon actually said that carrying both the phone and the radio "lowered the quality" of the trip.

I thought, "Jesus. Why did you come?" The life breath of the expedition was its capacity to communicate as we went. But in any event, the reality: it was Cleary's call.

Meanwhile, there was the matter of the sleds. None of the various parts of the jigsaw had been put together, nothing had been tried in the field. The sponsors had come on late, hence the purchasing had also run late. At one point, a promised food sponsorship fell over. Specialist adventure food packs were horrendously expensive, and hadn't been factored into the budget.

> Philips arranged for us to spend a day cooking and freeze drying our oil rich meals with the help of the Royal Melbourne Institute of Technology's cooking laboratory. (Muir had to go to a birthday party.) They did a pretty good job, even though some items contained more moisture than was ideal and hence were a little heavier.

In these small ways, as Philips had worried over the fine details, under the clock, the big picture unnoticed had gone awry. The big picture being: the horror of the sleds.

The Iridium-IceTrek press releases had guessed they'd be towing three hundred pounds each. Now, when talking to the press, they were guessing it was three hundred and some figure unknown.

The sleds, unladen, were more than three times heavier than that used by Borge Ousland and those of his ilk. The sleds were designed by Eric Philips and developed by the Royal Melbourne Institute of Technology. They weighed forty-four pounds without the harness. They were bombproof, but needlessly heavy. Borge Ousland's sled, the one he had dragged across the continent, weighed fifteen pounds.

> The RMIT sled had a lot of potential, but it wasn't really ready to go by the time we had to go. I had wanted us to buy three of the proven lighter varieties, but . . . we didn't.

When the men had walked from their breakfast to the hangar that morning, they had no idea if they could fit everything they needed into them. Because they hadn't seen all their equipment and provisions in the one spot before, not until they arrived on the ice.

> Much of the food and equipment had been sent down ahead before we arrived in Christchurch, where we'd planned to make sense of the mess while waiting for our flight to the ice,

which in turn was postponed for some days because all the planes had been grounded by whiteout conditions down south.

As they were now standing in Scott's hut, with the cameras whirring, with two or three days remaining to pull it together, with the relics of one of the saddest decisions in history lying abandoned under their eyes, at that moment Peter Hillary and company still had no honest clue as to how heavy their sleds would be when they tied themselves on for the march.

And that was the dark joke. We weren't completing Scott's journey. We were repeating it.

CHAPTER EIGHT

Hauling sledges of supplies and other equipment, by using manpower, was a common method in the early days of Antarctic travel. Theoretically, it has economic advantages over other forms of travel, but they are all outweighed by the physical strain it places on human beings. It is difficult enough walking over the many different surfaces inland without the additional strain of hauling a sledge. Nevertheless, man-hauling is still popular for recreational trips.

Allow 45 kilograms per man as a maximum load for a sled. Depending on surface conditions, and party fitness, a man-hauling party can expect to cover 10 to 15 kilometres in one day. Thirty kilometres has been achieved in ideal conditions but in soft snow three kilometres may be the limit. Parties can remain self-sufficient for fifteen to twenty days, and can increase their ground coverage by establishing food depots for use on the return journey.

From a government manual for Antarctic operations

Scott of the Antarctic. What was he thinking? Many heroic thoughts, certainly. His dead diary, found with his body, was one long heroic thought. It later became a best seller, and Scott became as much myth and legend as Ulysses.

The revisionist view is that Scott wasn't thinking at all, and this version of the story has sold a lot of books too, and has long been ahead on points in the debate on Scott's leadership and personality.

The book that smashed the altar was *The Last Place on Earth,* by the heroically named Roland Huntford, who has an interest in dog sledging and was for some years the *Observer* newspaper's Scandinavian correspondent. Page by page, the book worships Scott's rival, the Norwegian, the truly great Roald Amundsen, while painting Captain Scott as a dangerous clown who virtually murdered his men with willful stupidity. Scott's son Peter was still alive when the book was published, an old man; he complained publicly that Huntford's book denigrated his father's name. Huntford later included a passage that noted Sir Peter's unhappiness but insisted he had denigrated no one.

Some of the dirt has been wiped off the Captain's name in recent years by research into various aspects of polar travel, including the basic reality of what happens to humans in extreme cold. Minus thirty degrees. Minus fifty. What does it mean? What does it do?

> The deep field cold soaks through everything, no matter how many socks and thermal suits you're wearing. It leeches out the warmth, freezes all moisture. Boots and bones are shattered, flesh freeze dried. A gentle gust of the deep sub zero burns the skin like acid. The cold eats you alive, quick or slow.
>
> Throw gallons of boiling water six feet into the air, at minus forty, and watch it turn to snow. Snap. Instant snow. Antarctica is called a desert because the deep sub zero keeps the air dry as dry. The dry cold air sucks on the throat and tongue and the lungs, draining out one's bodily moisture. Freeze dried, mummified. Deserts are often called dirty places. Well, the deep south of Antarctica is sterile. Nil life. That's the sort of cold it is.

A human hauling heavy on foot, hour after hour, week after week, in the deep sub zero, struggles to replace the calories lost. Nutritionists reckon a hauling man needs about seven thousand calories a day, but he can probably only digest six and a half thousand calories, and that is once he has worked up to it. The rest goes straight through him.

On a long haul you are slowly running down. Wearing out. Hence, if all the food in the world were laid out in a line across Antarctica, and a man for some reason insisted on hauling a heavy sled all the way across without ever using kites to assist him, and kept up that heavy hauling day after day without respite, he'd most likely starve to death before reaching the other side of the continent.

Eating hearty, the body still withers in the deep sub zero. Eating hearty, filling their plastic bags, Hillary and the boys were withering two weeks out while their bodies struggled to adjust to the fat enriched diet. Scott wasn't eating hearty from day one, two and a half thousand calories short of his needs. His men, likewise.

Two British men, Dr. Mike Stroud and Sir Ranulph Fiennes ("the greatest living explorer in the world," according to the *Guinness Book of Records*) tried crossing Antarctica on foot in ninety-three. They came from the west side, were in bad shape when they passed over the South Pole, crossed the last three hundred of the Polar Plateau, surrendering at the top of the mountains, with the five hundred miles of the coated tongue still below and ahead of them.

They called in the plane because they were starving, walking skin and bone, rotting from the inside, with body chemistry so depleted that their blood samples said they should have been unconscious.

They were certainly out of it, and badly out of sorts with each other. They'd made a number of ice walks together, each one ending the same emotional way: with mutual loathing. Then they'd make up, affirm their vows, and head out again. The

South Pole trip took them to the brink of divorce. Both went on to write books about it.

Leadership was one bitter issue. A betrayal of trust was another. Pace of travel was another again. Plus there was the basic burden of living in misery together.

Mike Stroud is occasionally cited as one of the more honest members of the game, because he has declared over and over that polar travel is an unrelenting horror show.

On an earlier trip, to the Arctic, Stroud and Fiennes carried a gun to scare off polar bears. As the misery ate his bones, and Sir Ranulph got on his nerves, Dr. Stroud started thinking of the gun, and came up with a plan: he'd shoot "the greatest explorer in the world." Put his body under the ice. Walk on for a while. And then get on the radio and hysterically report Fiennes missing. And a plane would arrive soon after to take Stroud home to his wife. It wasn't personal. He just wanted to get out of there.

On the Antarctic crossing, Stroud thought of feigning a hemorrhage by acting out the symptoms, diagnosing himself (well, he was a doctor), and as he was busy clutching his neck, it would be Sir Ranulph calling in the plane.

"A war is like the Antarctic in one respect. There is no getting out of it with honour as long as you can put one foot before the other," wrote Apsley Cherry-Garrard in his great book, *The Worst Journey in the World,* as he was slowly on the slide to losing his mind. Dr. Stroud had read that book.

In nineteen eighty-five Mike Stroud wintered at Cape Evans, in a hut set not far from Scott's hut, with four other men, as part of a British expedition with the daring name "In the Footsteps of Scott." The founder of the trip, the rather handsome and very charming Robert Swan, had read about the Captain at school and decided then he would one day walk to the South Pole in Scott's memory, as a labor of love. *The Worst Journey in the World* was one of the team's holy books. Robert Swan didn't take Dr. Stroud on that walk, but two others, the intense and serious climber Roger Meare and the gently spoken Canadian Gareth Wood. The three of them ended up demented and hating each other. Wood, who suffered the worst of the bullying, later described the expedition as "probably the nastiest experience of my life."

If, while on the haul, Swan and company had begun to think of Scott's journey as a cursed business, they knew it for sure when they reached the South Pole. The American base people there told them that their little red ship, a converted North Sea trawler that they'd bought with public donations, refurbished, and sailed all the way from England, and which was supposed to sail them all the way back again, had just sunk to the bottom of the Ross Sea, crushed by pack ice. The story of the sinking made bigger headlines than making the Pole.

The story of the walk made one very bitter book, written soon after by Swan and Meare, in which they tore into each other but fully put the boot into Wood. Gareth Wood wrote a forgiving and rather generous account ten years later, when his mind and emotions had recovered such that he could see straight.

In ninety-eight, Robert Swan (who in the meantime had walked to the North Pole with Graeme Joy and others) sent Peter Hillary and company a message of "good luck" and an entreaty to, more than anything else, remember to "have fun."

So what happens to you out there, boys? Robert Swan says that Antarctica turns a man into his eight year old self, and it's a mighty neat (if conservative) summation of what the psychologists have been saying about polar madness for the last half century.

❊ ❊ ❊

It's now known that life in the burning brightness (and other closed, isolated, and extreme environments) warps a human's reasoning, and his emotions.

Research into the psychology of polar travel (much of it based on the anecdotes and records of polar trips taken in the latter half of the twentieth century, as well as forays into Inuit anthropology) has found that the isolation, the boredom, the physical withering, the physical pain, the living on top of the same fellows week after week, the mind sapping cruelties of visual deprivation (the blankness of the landscape and human horizon), the jockeying for social position, all of them conspire, in an unseen and corrosive fashion, to turn every little piece of bad feeling or annoyance into deeply held and neurotic resentments that collectively flower as social breakdown.

In short, life in the tent takes on the mood of a prison cell, with the attendant aggression, intimidation, pecking order and turf battles. Men on the haul are often rotten to one another, and they each go to the grave believing it was the other fellow's fault. They rarely have a clue as to the nature and extent of their contribution to the group dysfunction and madness.

More than just losing perspective in the head and heart, psychologists reckon that hauling men actually dissociate, or lose touch with reality, from time to time. Eric Philips' psychologist friend, Dr. Peg Levine, believes all three men probably dissociated at different times. That is, they became borderline psychotic.

Psychotic.

Psychotic.

Psychologists believe it's the visual and sensory deprivation of polar travel (nothing to see but the surrounding whiteness, nothing to hear but a whistling roar and the social and physical isolation in nothingness) that especially plays hell with the mind.

Well, they should know. Psychologists in evil employ have been experimenting with sensory deprivation as torture and brain washing tools for at least fifty years.

Before science could explain what was happening in physiological terms, the evil locked their victims in dark rooms because they knew it would send them mad or break their spirits or sometimes it was just to hear them scream. (They didn't know why it worked, just went with it.)

Decades of experiments, with free and healthy volunteers, in psychology research labs all over the world, have come to the same conclusion: after just two days in a blank environment (be it in a dark and quiet place or in a room painted the one color on every surface), human beings lose various problem solving abilities and long-held skills; some of them will hallucinate and regress. Roald Amundsen discovered and named a mountain range in honor of a friend, only to later realize the mountains had never existed.

The revisionists held that the Captain was Napoleonically pompous and delusional. Maybe he was, out on the ice. And when you consider the sanity of the society that raised him, maybe he was delusional and pompous at home as well. It's worth talking about, because Captain Scott was raised in pompous and delusional times, when good sense had long been abandoned by an Establishment consciousness warped by the excess and glory of empire, where every problem was met by marching at it, where one marched with sheer gall in pursuit of one's glorious dreams. That's how Britain, and everybody else, went to the trenches in the first big war, in nineteen fourteen. And that's how Scott died two years before the war, word of his death coming the year before it broke. When it came, Scott was held as the kind of man everybody wanted and needed to be. The boys mowed down were compared to him. Scott made a great poster boy for heroic disaster born from sheer gall, for the doomed generation. The heroes.

For all of Scott's life, what was called the civilized world had a lust for greatness and for new first things. Inventions, ideas, dance steps. The belle époque and all that early jazz. The world was so marvelous, but not all of it had been touched or claimed or even seen. The "civilized" peoples were unsettled, knowing there were places unmarked with human footsteps. Most vexing was the bottom of the world: it was such a long way away, it seemed impossible to reach and thereby conquer, and nobody knew what it looked like. People had tried for the South Pole and failed, Scott among them, in nineteen one, nearly starved to death on the return leg.

As people started to wonder if the South Pole was beyond the limits of mankind's genius, their wild imaginings took on the fearful coloring of the Middle Ages, as fascination turned to dark wonder and a superstitious dread.

"Maybe the Horned One lives there."

"Or dragons?"

Britain's history was built on slaying dragons, and it was fancied that men were still built that way. The Royal Navy had long been the nation's dragon slayer. It was decided by the Admiralty that Captain Scott was the one: he'd been before, he was strong, he was keen, and he was available.

Military chap, of course he went for king and country. Fatal dreamer, of course he went for the usual personal reasons. The Pole was Scott's golden ring. It was a hot first thing. He wanted to be the first to the South Pole, and he wanted to do it on foot, with his fellows, all tied to the one big sled. That he'd tried before on foot and nearly perished gave him no pause.

It came to be that two expeditions, one British and one Norwegian, found themselves spending the winter of nineteen eleven, hundreds of miles apart, on the Antarctic coast, fretting about the other's fortunes. With little to go on, with no real word save the fact that both parties were going for it and that Scott was unhappy to have a rival, newspapers around the world speculated at length (and with some nationalist grumblings) on what became known as the Race for the Pole.

Roald Amundsen, the Norwegian, did the trip to the Pole on his ear. The time lost to storms and to falling in big holes had been factored into his plans. (**He shot most of his dogs and fed**

their carcasses to the remnants of the pack as tucker, just as he had planned all along.) He made it home, to his hut on the coast, with food and fuel to spare, his men in great shape, everybody feeling top of the world other than the dogs. Hence, it wasn't of the greatest interest to the newspapers or the public who had long expected a tale of desperation, madness, and at least some death mixed with triumph. Sure, Amundsen had his headlines around the world, a period of glory at home, in Norway. After all, he had pulled it off. But, sharing the credit with all his fellows, he'd told the story dry and straight and boring, and it played humbly and briefly to the boondocks on the American speaking circuit of the day and then later in the encyclopedia, just about any encyclopedia.

Stupid and sulking, the British papers grumbled that maybe Amundsen's achievement wasn't such a big deal, because he had used dogs. It brought a little drama to the Pole story until the real thing came along. And it came along, truly. The nightmare of Scott's journey, his fate, was a sensation. Big as the Beatles, baby. There were probably more tears for Scott, more overwrought diary entries.

There are people who can count off the names of Scott's men on their fingers, as one does with the members of a favorite rock group: Bowers, Wilson, Evans and Oates. They were a five piece band, the polar party. However, food and fuel had been factored for four men, and factored poorly. This was the Captain's big mistake in any school of thought. What was Scott thinking?

Captain Scott's party was the size of a football team, with many mascots and cheerleaders of sorts, when it left the expedition's wintering hut at Cape Evans, on McMurdo Sound, on November one, nineteen eleven. They hauled first across the sea ice, then on to the floating coated tongue of Antarctica, the Great Ice Barrier as he knew it, the first five hundred miles. Scott had brought motorized sledges to lay depots across the barrier. They died quick in the cold. He had brought ponies, also for laying depots. They died in the cold, many eaten. There were dogs, and they survived, even thrived, but Scott never quite trusted them, and he fretted they would suffer in the cold. The depots held food and fuel for the return leg, much too little of each.

At the other end of the ice sheet, Scott met the TransAntarctic Mountains, the string of peaks two thousand miles long, running east to west, ten thousand to fifteen thousand feet high. At the top of the mountains, lying high against the sky behind it, was the Polar Plateau. Scott chose the Beardmore Glacier as his sloping highway to the plateau, a hundred miles of steep sloping ice riddled with holes, wide and deep, crevasses hidden by snow bridges of frail standing. Taking a reduced party of eight up the glacier, the polar party not yet selected, Scott said goodbye to the other men and to what remained of the horses. The eight set out for the climb on foot, in boots and skis, hauling monstrous loads, eight hundred, nine hundred pounds, four men to each sledge, two hundred and some pounds each.

It was beyond the top of the glacier, deep into the leg across the plateau, that Scott named his team. It was there, a hundred and some miles from the Pole, with everybody already withering, that he made his sad decision, suddenly making the polar party five, and not the four as always planned. To accommodate the extra man, food and fuel were taken from the homeward sled, leaving the three other remaining men to turn around and haul their horror seven hundred and some miles homeward on further reduced rations, barely making it, skin and bone and half crazy by the time they stumbled through the door of the lonely slab hut on the coast.

The dead diaries say Evans went to pieces after the party (for want of a more cheerless term) reached the Pole on January seventeen, nineteen twelve, a day of no horizon, of no blue sky. You can see it in the black and white photographs. In one of them, Scott, Bowers, Wilson and Evans, standing apart, scattered, all looking in different directions, looking like rock stars posing and sulking in a video clip, with the sky and ground making one flat bright picture show screen. Also in this scene, a tent standing man-high with the Norwegian flag flying from the top, on a thin pole. Inside the tent was a letter from Amundsen, for the king of Norway from Amundsen, and a note asking Scott to please post it. The Norwegian had been there more than a month before him.

Just sad is the group portrait, lined up side by side, everything in their faces, such misery. They were already starving, sick. Some knew their feet—frozen, infected—would have to be chopped off. But they were also deep into the belief that the chopping would never happen. By the time they had turned north, for home, Evans was talking himself to death; a big man, the only enlisted man, what one might call an ordinary man with dreams of the regular life, already withering from starvation, now haul-ing on with dead feet and a dead demented heart, with the hys-teria of knowing he was a ghost in waiting, straining the nerves of his fellows. It got so he was lurching and falling and just lying there with no will to continue. At one point he hit his head in a fall and took to babbling. He died one night, in his sleeping bag, next to his fellows, six hundred miles from where they'd started out, from food and a warm bed. He died deep south, left to the creep of the glacier.

The dead diaries and history books suggest Scott had great af-fection for Evans, and that he was taken along out of sentiment more than sense. They also suggest (claim) that Evans had put all his faith in the Captain, and had hoped that victory at the Pole would mean a comfortable and secure life back home. He was certainly the least experienced of the group, and probably didn't have the mental toughness of his fellows. Hence, fairly or otherwise, Evans has always been regarded as the weak link, the surprise choice, "the fifth man."

The remaining four hauled on, for nearly four hundred miles across the tongue; starving, writing some of it in their diaries,

writing letters of muted bitterness and rebuke, somehow keeping the corks in, somehow keeping the desperate madness unspoken, somehow not ending it with their hands around each
other's throats.

Oates was remembered fondly in the dead diaries, and in the
classrooms still telling his story, for being good with animals and
for killing himself in order to take away some of the strain on the
rations. The revisionists reckon Oates had simply had enough.
Either way, Evans had been dead for weeks. Everybody was dying. Everybody saw it coming, although the dead diaries suggest
Dr. Wilson held on to hope and to his faith that God would help
them out.

The dead diaries say it was Oates' birthday, March seventeen,
when he told the others he was going for a walk and "may be
some time." He turned thirty-two and was never seen again. It
came to him in the privacy of bleached rags, the air was dancing
as bleached rags, white on white. He died in the ghost country. It
was howling at the time.

When the rags and the howling lay down again, Scott, Bowers, and Wilson crawled and hauled on a few days more, making
their last camp on March twenty-one, seventy-nine and some
degrees South. For more than a week they lay in their sleeping
bags with their miserable thoughts, waiting for it. By late March,
eleven miles from food, one hundred and thirty miles from the
hut at Cape Evans, they were dead too.

The Captain and friends had moved on from that spot with
the creep of the sheet, but they were still out there, on the coated
tongue, inside it. One day they would make it back to the coast,
completing their trip, freeze dried, mummified. One day they
will all drop into the sea in their sleeping bags, lodged in an iceberg that will know pretty sunsets and perhaps the flash of cameras from a tourist ship.

As it drifts north, their iceberg will melt, revealing them to the
birds, possibly more tourists. If the latter is so, expect the last

chapter of Scott and his polar team to be written in the tabloids, then in paperback, with pictures. That's how it turned, at the turn of this century, for another cheated British champion, near eighty years dead, found high on Mount Everest in a tweed suit. One of the greats, George Mallory, freeze dried, now a color photograph in a book. So it may turn for the Captain.

What the birds and tourists don't take will fall to the bottom of the sea as bones and canvas. The spot where he lay down with his chaps would always be out there, and for now they were still out there, somewhere, too, Scott and his chaps. It was a great story, with life in it yet.

PART TWO

THE ROPE

> GARCIN: Well, now we've broken the ice do you
> really think I look like a torturer? And by the way
> how does one recognize torturers when one sees
> them? Evidently you've ideas on the subject.
> INEZ: They look frightened.

Jean-Paul Sartre, *In Camera / No Exit*

CHAPTER NINE

Come, my friends
'Tis not too late to seek a newer world.
Push off, and sitting well in order smite
The sounding furrows; for my purpose holds
To sail beyond the sunset, and the baths
Of all the western stars, until I die.
It may be that the gulfs will wash us down;
It may be we shall touch the Happy Isles,
And see the great Achilles, whom we knew.
Tho' much is taken, much abides; and tho'
We are not now that strength which in old days
Moved earth and heaven; that which we are, we are;
One equal temper of heroic hearts,
Made weak by time and fate, but strong in will
To strive, to seek, to find, and not to yield.

Alfred, Lord Tennyson, "Ulysses"

Hillary shaved, brushed his teeth, combed his hair, put on the adventure clothes, walked down the hall with his wolf fur hanging over his arm, lined up for his bacon and beans, sat down with some people who asked the usual questions. This was the last meal that would take any real chewing until it was all over. This was day one, November four, a Wednesday.

At about nine o'clock, with the sleds lined up at the edge of the wide graded ice road that ran flat to the airfield five miles away, Hillary and company walked out of the green bunker, with the television people and the documentary film crew jockeying for position with their fluffy microphones.

It was a beautiful sparkling day. Minus thirty degrees Celsius but no wind. The whole world looked like the Greek flag: two overwhelming colors, white and blue.

The bright blue sky so close and so vast; the face of space.

About sixty people from Scott Base and Mac Town had turned out to see them off, some of them official guests, most of them people who had heard about it as station gossip and just wanted to be there. Hillary and company lined up with their sleds, and the television people came in close, as they always do track-side with jockeys and such. The nation was watching. They strapped on their harnesses, said a few words, accepted a few words of blessing, and then there came a cheer that suggested they'd shot off like greyhounds and then.

For a moment nothing seemed to happen. And then it was like watching three rusty old boiler trains squeaking to life with big grunts of steam, the brake slowly surrendering its fossilized grip on the wheels. So slowly, with big and sometimes terrible grunts of steam, leaning everything they had into their harnesses, digging in the tips of their ski poles, working everything in their arms and shoulders, such that if they'd suddenly lifted into the air, no one would have been surprised.

They started moving, and then Philips was going for it, almost frantically pushing a rhythm into life still so slow when he found it, hitting the lead of what may as well have been an egg and spoon race at a retirement home picnic.

Philips out front.

Muir behind Philips.

Hillary behind Muir; not striding it out, feeling it out in inches at first, trying to find a rhythm that could be called a rhythm.

The media and the film crew were riding back and forth on snowmobiles, passing the men and circling back and turning around for another pass from behind. One chaotic body, moving slowly forward with the energy of a state funeral.

Meanwhile, it was minus thirty degrees. The sixty people and their good wishes went back inside as the men and the circus struggled to make themselves gone.

To Peter Hillary, it felt as if he were pulling out a tree. Each step forward brought a long moment when he was held still in his harness, broken only by his guts squeezing down like a dropped accordion. You can hear it in their film: Hillary's long, high groans. They could have come from a gunshot victim holding his belly together.

Just too heavy.

To the Pole and back: eighteen hundred miles on foot; mostly on skis, really, with skins strapped to the base of the skis to provide the traction. But it was the ropes strung on the bones in the feet to the neck that were pulling the sleds.

They were each pulling the weight of three dead men. **Four hundred and forty bloody pounds.**

In the hangar, at their backs now, was a pile of food packages, ten days of meals, seventy pounds of eating. That pile of food was their "Evans," their fifth man, their last minute change in plans.

On the one hand, as much as Scott's story turns on making that fateful last minute change in plans, nearly everybody in the game had their "Evans," of some persuasion. **The polar geniuses too. The Belgians. Borge Ousland.**

Ed Hillary, with his tractor train, had to dump a load of fuel drums, after traveling some hundreds of feet from the roped down huts, under the gaze of the men left behind in the roped down huts who had argued against him taking the bigger load. The great Amundsen fired two men from the polar trip on the eve of departure.

> **On the other hand, leaving behind ten days of food, from a larder calculated to last a hundred days, was an "Evans" spectacular.**

It happened this way: the previous day, when the sleds were fully and finally loaded and put on the scales, they made four hundred and sixty-five pounds each. Philips insisted the scales were surely broken. He couldn't believe it. He'd worked hard and long, running his mental comb through the fine details. He asked that the sleds be weighed again, and for the scales to be checked. Then Hillary hitched up and took his sled for a sorry spin. **I got to a little hummock, just a suggestion of a mound, and there was no way I was going to get over it. Pulling and pulling and nothing but horror.**

Soon after, the seventy pounds of food were quietly taken off and put into the pile now at their backs.

It wasn't until eight weeks later, just after Christmas, when they were high on the plateau, six hundred miles from where they were snail-dragging now, that the team would find they'd packed a second, equally spectacular, if accidental, "Evans" in their sleds. It made a great story for the newspaper and television people, who at that point started wondering, then predicting, that the trip was in its last days. How excited they would have been to know that "the end" had come to the odyssey during its first two weeks, and had kept limping on as a half abandoned ship, the three of them relentlessly trudging the rut of their ruin.

Meanwhile, this was day one, and the familiar fear had enough to talk about, but Hillary was only half listening as time passed hauling the monster.

> **Mount Erebus and Mount Terror lay off to the left of us as we skied along the road and out toward the ice shelf huge and**

imposing, classic volcanic forms, with a short white plume rising from the summit crater of Erebus. I had a dead friend up there, but I'd think about him later. Once we turned south, Erebus would lie behind us for some weeks to come, and I'd think of him then.

I hoped by then the egg and spoon race would have settled into something else. On reflection, I have no idea why I thought we'd plod along together for the first few days, and work up to the load and to each other, beyond it making good sense. I wasn't going to take part in the race. Certainly the pace wasn't one I could have maintained for any length of time. I'd do what I was doing.

Four hundred and forty pounds. I'd work up to it.

While my mind was going over these things, I found I was feeling pretty emotional. I missed Yvonne and I missed my children. And this place, just amazing. I found it overwhelming, intimidating—the scale of it, and the feel of it. It felt like I wasn't on planet earth anymore, yet here we were, skiing on a wide graded road of permanent sea ice.

They were hauling across an ocean that beached frozen on the peninsula the little way behind him, inching along a road where big trucks and graders trundled back and forth, the drivers in their cabins grooving with their boom boxes and their packets of chewing gum. They all seemed to be women at the wheel.

The road was lined with Day-Glo marker poles, so they could see where they were headed if cloud came over and made the world a great white everywhere. The mail must get through. Polar Americana.

Sometimes they pulled over and jumped down to talk to us and say, "Have a good one, dude," and, "Hey, go for it, man." They were coffee shop encounters, really. The modern world. Hillary found they lent a galling make-believe quality to the day's grinding work. It started to feel like we were starring in an historical parade. And then I remembered: that's exactly what we were doing.

They hauled four shifts, each an hour and a half. The plan was to lengthen the shifts as they settled into the haul. In between the shifts they stopped for a thermos of hot chocolate and an energy bar, or for a lunch of noodle soup and some salami and cheese: always Hillary's favorite (which only meant that the other meals were vile, for he loathed fat and fatty food with the zeal of a catwalk string bean, to the point of shuddering). They made the five miles out to Williams Airfield, **from where ski-equipped Hercules and Twin Otter aircraft flew out to the Pole.**

There was a little village of long domed bunkers set in a row at the side of the runway, where the flyboy residents could see the white volcano framed like Mount Fuji in the tinted windows at the back. The team hauled past the bunkers, for another three hundred yards, and set up their little red tent on the edge of the runway, while the people in the bunkers were sitting down to roast of the day and drip coffee.

At the end of this long hard day we were camping on the doorstep of Ma and Pa America. Like a bunch of little kids sleeping out in a suburban backyard.

It didn't sit at all well with the Ulysses factor, but no one was of the mind to haul on to a more legendary spot. So it was humble pie for dessert that night. There was no sunset. The summer sun sat on a swing; back and forth across the sky, night and day, side to side, never dropping. It burned golden that first night.

In the morning, a snow grooming machine came along and swerved around the tent as it drove back and forth, flattening the verge of runway. The machine brought up a big cloud of crushed glass ice. Hence, it's likely the driver would have been spared the inspiring vision that would have otherwise confronted him/her had the air been a little clearer near the tent.

I woke up to this mighty roar. It was a big machine, and for a moment I wondered if the driver was going to blindly run over us. I sat up and found Eric returning from outside where

he had been shitting on the snow. And by the nose on his do-ings, it wasn't too far away from our small tent—a nylon dome no bigger than a double bed.

Instead of saying, "Did you sleep well?" Hillary embarked on the sort of appalling conversation one generally has in leafy streets with bastard dog owners.

I asked him, "Are you going to pick that up?"

"No," he said, "I'm not going to fucking pick it up."

The stove was soon going. They had their cup of coffee and bowl of porridge floating in melted butter, Hillary and Muir struggling to get it down. It took them five hours to pack and secure all into the sleds.

When they hitched up and headed out, all that remained on the patch of ice where they'd slept was a dark little lighthouse. Eric's farewell to the mortals.

CHAPTER TEN

Complete cloud cover over the snow produces a phenomenon known as 'whiteout.' In the whiteout there is a complete lack of definition and no horizon. The whole visible world, sky and earth, forms a bowl of white surrounding the traveller. Surface irregularities can no longer be detected and a walking man may trip over sastrugi or step unwittingly into a crevasse.

There are degrees of whiteout, controlled by the density of the cloud. In a partial whiteout travel is possible, but it is difficult and tiring because of eyestrain. Providing the cloud is not too low, brightly painted objects and men suitably dressed are visible for normal distances in a whiteout. It is difficult, however, to judge distances because one cannot differentiate between a small object close up and a large object a long distance away.

If you must travel in whiteout conditions (and this should only be necessary in an emergency), then wait until sunset and travel by vehicle lights.

From a government manual for Antarctic operations

Locked in and leaning-to, they put the airfield at their backs and headed east, with a little southerly heading, toward the Ross Ice Shelf. It was cold and windy and the sky was plowed with rows of gauze cotton that went all the way to the horizons: low lying lenticular cloud, dead flat away.

They had their wolf hoods up and their goggles on as they snail-skied the frozen sea that beached frozen the five miles behind them, on the toes of Observation Hill, just below the Old Firm's roped down quarters.

Off the graded road, the sleds pulled back with an unavoidable and often noiseless violence, for they rolled around like fat seals dozing on leashes, twisting and jerking over the wind ruts and shiny scalloping and the little to big pressure ridges, inches to feet high, what the field manuals called sastrugi, that built up in long lines like surplus cement.

Philips out in front again.

Hillary behind Philips.

Muir struggling in his skis on the slippery dip terrain.

They were walking on the ocean, where it met the shelf. Under the sun, the ocean looked as if it had been snap frozen while simmering under a breeze, dimpled and clear and blue enough with the strips of blue above it.

Erebus was to our left, and the frozen sea beached there too. This is how it was in the Ice Age.

Mountains buried in ice, their peaks sticking out like beautiful paupers in the stocks, the sense that one was walking many hundreds of feet above a world long lost to a flood.

White Island and Black Island were on our right, way out on the ice shelf. Not particularly imaginative names, but that is what they looked like. Black Island is largely black, substantially exposed rock. White Island is mainly covered in an ice sheet, low-lying and white, and it almost seems no more than a rumple in the surface of the shelf. But it's notorious for its crevasse fields.

White Island was caught under the creep of the coated tongue that lolled down the mountains to the south and lay flat for the five hundred miles to where the party was meeting it, and some

hundred miles more to the north, where it ran out and broke
away as sapphire blue icebergs into ballpoint blue waters.

**On its way to the sea, the tongue folds into corrugations as it
is drawn around peninsulas and islands.**

Ice is like glass, in that it is a partial solid: it will bend to an
extent before fracturing. When it cracks, the result is not
unlike the fracture patterns on a car's shattered windshield.
Everything still holds together, as one body, but it is riddled
with cracks, many as deep as the glass is thick.

Blow the windshield up to the size of France and the crevasse
fields look like the deep and jagged cracks found on an unhealthy
human tongue that has sucked on too many blue colored cock-
tails.

White Island was a stone permanently cracking the frozen
tongue, birthing crevasse fields, many big holes hundreds of feet
deep, booby trapped with bridges of snow that built up as hori-
zontal icicles. They were traveling east until they cleared White
Island. After some days' work, they'd turn south.

Meanwhile, time passed, pulling out a tree.

Then it started to blow about thirty knots, from the north, and
the air to their waists turned white with spindrift. The air above
their waists had crushed glass diamonds in it, the dreamy spray
of the flurries. They put a halo around the sun.

**Suddenly Eric said, "The wind. The wind. We can sail this."
I said, "No, we can't. It's too strong. We won't handle it."**

**I have no doubt there are people with the skills to fly in
those conditions. For us, as a threesome—we were not one,
we were three—it wasn't an option.**

As Hillary was having his say, Philips was unclipping and digging in his sled for his number three kite.

**I'm thinking, "Jeepers." If he doesn't come a cropper, he's go-
ing to end up sixty miles away. I'll be halfway there. I still
didn't know how Jon's kiting had developed. But without skiing skills, Jon would be left behind at the one mile mark. That
wouldn't be useful. Jon had the tent.**

Philips rigged up, put the kite in the air, sailed beautifully for about two hundred and fifty yards, and then watched dismayed as it was snatched from his hands and spat across the frozen sea to beach somewhere on the flanks of Mount Erebus. He unclipped, started skating after it, soon realized it was gone. Antarctica had sucked down and swallowed the kite like an oyster.

He walked back to his sled, clipped into the harness, locked in and leaned-to.

They hauled on with the wind gusting at their backs, nudging them bodily forward as the sleds jerked and pulled them the other way.

That was day two: about four miles.

> **In the evening, Philips seemed to spend a lot of time worrying over the numbers. Eighteen hundred miles. One hundred days. Eighteen miles a day required, averaged out, of course. The numbers were very clear.**
>
> **We had to work up to it, and as the sleds became lighter and we became more proficient, we would begin to travel greater distances each day. From five to ten miles per day we would eventually haul more than twenty miles and with the kites, perhaps one hundred miles.**

But worrying over the numbers became Philips' habit—for the first fifty days or so, anyway, until they became an irrelevant torment.

❄   ❄   ❄

Day three, five miles: they snail-skied past the base of Erebus, on the wide turn around White Island. They couldn't see White Island. They couldn't see where the cloud met the frozen sea. The wind had kicked up the drift again, in thicker clouds, and they couldn't see much at all. Hauling closer together, they inched through the white on white with the weary frustration of people wearing blindfolds in a party game cursed with no end to it.

Now and then Hillary felt as if he were skiing downhill. There was no horizon to tell him otherwise. The first time it happened, he flinched because he thought the sled would bowl him over, and he half made to get out of its way.

> It certainly caught me by surprise. I'd been thinking about the family and life at home at the time, and half shut Antarctica out. I'd been thinking a lot about them since we'd left Scott Base, picturing in my mind what they might be doing or what we might all be doing if we were together—my wife, our son, my two older children. I was starting to wonder if I had already thought every thought I could think about them.

After the false fright with the sled, Hillary found he couldn't think of the regular life at all for a while, and for the rest of the day he started designing a coffee table in his head, a showcase piece with drawers and display cases. He intended to keep working on it over the next few days, to savor it as a topic of thought, as one savors a hard candy or a piece of gum, to make it last longer, the flavor.

> One of the things that had excited me about this trip was the opportunity to think uninterrupted for hours at a time. I'd planned to wander through my head and visit all the places and the people and the ideas in there.

> Actually, that's not quite right. I didn't want to visit everything in there.

The world was blank, white on white. There was nothing new coming through his eyeballs to think about. Nor through his ears. When they stopped for hot drinks, they'd sit on their sleds with their backs to the drift, and it was so thick they lost their knees. They banged their mitts together and banged their boots together, trying to warm up, saying things like "Damn cold, isn't it?" or "Hope it eases up as the day goes on," and they'd nod and sit with their hoods up like people waiting at a bus stop in the rain.

Then they'd hitch up and haul on again, into the blank.

> That evening, I think we were all beyond tired, and it was all work as usual, just getting the tent up, getting everything inside and sorted, everyone in their own worlds.

> Then we fired up the phone, and I received a message that

my daughter Amelia had been trying to contact me. When I burst into tears, Eric and Jon put their hands out to my sloping shoulders and I thought, "Well, good on you, fellows."

Soon after, we drifted back into ourselves again. Eric to his numbers and making notes, and to whatever else was going on for him.

Jon was reading *The Seven Pillars of Wisdom* by T. E. Lawrence. Which was a great book to talk about. Full of ideas to toss around. But it largely remained one of his private rooms, where he'd retreat and put up his feet.

Jon Muir was the bigger mystery to Hillary, because after nearly twenty years of calling each other "friend," Hillary knew little more about Jon Muir than he knew about Eric Philips, and what he'd picked up had been largely from observation and the circumstantial evidence floated as gossip through their wide circle, or gathered by the way in their occasional cordial reunions.

They got to know various personal things about each other, in the way one reads the "news briefs" column in a newspaper: the bare facts and no more to be found despite reading the same two or three sentences over and over. Jon Muir had never shown any interest in making it otherwise.

Muir is "on" when in the field, otherwise he's just . . . there. It means that when I go to think about him in the "good old days" on the hill, I generally end up thinking more about the other people who were there at the time.

When we went to Everest together in nineteen eighty-four, there were six of us on the team: Muir and myself, Fred From and Craig Nottle in their last days, and two great friends still alive and well, Roddy McKenzie, raised on a large Australian sheep farm, and Kim Logan, son of a Maori chief who later came to K2 (and who I'd called to replace Muir for the South Pole trip when he fell and hurt his back).

We were all put in business class on the flight to Nepal from Australia. The heroes! Come on up! We drank all their champagne and carried on like boisterous but well behaved rock stars. Our rationale, of course, was that the dehydrating effects of the cabin pressure and the alcohol would approximate the altitudes that lay ahead and that this was excellent acclimatization.

On the walk up to Base Camp we bought a yak, which Roddy and Kim slaughtered behind some rocks en route. Roddy was a vegetarian, but he'd grown up on a farm. Kim worked for the national parks service, but it didn't pay much and he'd go into the hills and shoot a whole lot of deer and fill up the family freezer with venison back steaks.

We hung all this yak meat, legs and ribs, out in the dry air of Base Camp at the door of our mess tent, and brewed up beer and carried on like Vikings (who were the rock stars of their day, ten centuries ago).

We ate together and told stories and laughed and laughed to keep the familiar fear away for a while. It's how the story telling business started. To distract everyone around the campfire from the day to day madness of trying to survive a world that was waiting to eat us alive.

Up from the mess tent, we could hear these occasional explosions, like artillery landing close by. It was the icefall collapsing in various places. You always had your own tent at Base Camp, and lying alone, you'd hear these explosions now and again through the night. The sound of blue office block towers falling into a tangled heap. Or the sound of the heap itself detonating under its own weight.

You'd be scared shitless because you were going through there in a couple of hours. I was always grateful for the laughs, because the familiar fear would be saying "Don't do it. Don't do it," and you'd have to hold that down. On the other hand, you'd have to listen to it too. You have to get into a very strange place to go up there.

Sometimes Jon Muir came up and had the few good laughs, but in the early days of the expedition, mostly it was just the five of us in the mess tent those nights. Muir ate in his tent with his wife and his wife's sister. He just ran his own tribe. Then he'd turn up when it was time to head through the icefall.

❊ ❊ ❊

Day four, six miles: The wind blew from the north again, a firm and steady six miles an hour.

The men rigged their number five kites. Hillary and Philips sailed for about three miles, in stop and go bursts. Hillary did his first half mile in about five minutes.

As he wrote in his diary that night, with the jubilation of a teenager who had just discovered the sexual life: **This is the way to go!**

Jon Muir did the six miles on foot. Whenever he put up his kite, he fell over.

> I'd look back half a mile and see Jon getting up. Ten minutes passed by as he sorted himself out, then the kite would go up again and . . .
>
> Bam!
>
> Down he'd go.
>
> That's how it was in the early days for Jon Muir. He'd come staggering in, hauling himself over that half mile, and he'd throw himself on the ground, shattered. It was like he'd gone into the ring with Muhammad Ali and had the living daylights beaten out of him.

It was at this point Muir talked about heading back to Scott Base on his own, without a stove, a tent. "I'm holding you guys up. Take whatever food and gear you want."

He probably figured that, traveling light, he could make the fifteen miles and some back to the airfield in a day. If he was swallowed by the weather he said he'd sleep in his sled. **I just thought, "Think about it, buddy. If the weather stays bad for a few days, your bed the sled will become your coffin."**

> In some ways it could have been the best thing if he'd gone back, because Philips and I would have cut weeks from the hauling if the north wind came up so agreeably again, just

one more day like this one, day four. But it wasn't an option.
One out, all out.

So Jon soldiered on.

Bam!

Bam!

Bam!

❊ ❊ ❊

Day five, November eight, through the boiling misery of a blizzard they turned south to cut across White Island.

**This line of travel wasn't okay with me. It didn't look okay on
the maps we were carrying, either. But our pace of travel was
becoming a source of heavy tension in our little band, so here
we were: cutting across White Island to make up time.**
They couldn't see White Island. They couldn't see more than a
few feet ahead. They were in a storm of buffeting buffeting blindness. **I didn't want to end up in a crevasse field in a storm.**

Time passed with the three of them creeping along, the
egg and spoon race stuck on a tight and difficult turn, creeping
in closer formation; Hillary anxious, dark and then empty of
thought beyond those handed out by the familiar fear; then all
the old animal inside took over. He was wired.

**Absolutely wired with tension, trying to listen for any clues
through the wind, listening for a cracking sound. I was doing
what I'd do on the mountain. Actually, the only time I would
travel through a white storm would be in a desperate flight to
get down from very high on a mountain, in a storm. I'd only
do it because I'd die otherwise.**

**But there was tension, frustration, determination to push
mightily forward. So on we went through the blizzard, each
hauling the weight of three dead men.**
As they shuffled along through the smothering white everywhere, they appeared to one another as blurred smudges on
blotting paper.

And Hillary so wired, caged flies for eyes. And that's what always amazed him when he thought about it later on: he was so wired, so ready to spring clear of a hole that might or might not have been there, when the world suddenly changed color.

It all stayed with him, the fear and the tension, but there was a sudden joy in all of it as Peter Hillary found he could see the dead and the places of the dead. They climbed out in front of him to fill up the boiling emptiness.

At first it felt as if he were going up a hill. **I looked ahead and Philips was way above me, farther up this slope. I looked back and Muir was a long way below me.** Then it became more than a sense of going uphill.

Peter Hillary found himself in a steep grooved ice gully, in what is beautifully named a couloir, with an ice axe in his hand and crampons on his feet, climbing with all his weight on the tips of his toes, where the tips of his crampons were balanced on their points. He could feel it in his legs, always the calves, and in his shoulders too. Instead of the horror of the sled, there was the miraculous agony of hauling vertical at altitude.

He was a fly on the wall and the wall was made of ice.

When he saw up ahead his great friend Jeff Lakes he thought, **"Yes, this is ninety-five."** He was on K2 again.

They'd been up and down this couloir many times, pushing the route. This was one of those days when they were pushing the route. He couldn't figure why he'd remember this day, because it hadn't been a day of any great note. All he could remember was they'd had a good time that day, and he took it as a gift from his mind.

Hillary and Lakes had been friends for maybe two months at most when they shared that good day on the mountain. They were first introduced back in the hotel room in Rawalpindi, with the place looking like it had been ransacked, gear everywhere, barrels of it, and it was **"Pleased to meet you, Jeff Lakes. Welcome aboard."**

Gently spoken, in his early thirties, Jeff Lakes from Calgary was considered one of the "serious hard men" of technical ice climbing. He had a thing for frozen waterfalls, some a thousand feet high, sometimes no friend on a rope, attached by just the points of the spikes on his feet and the axes in his hands.

Lakes had tried for K2 two years before, on an international expedition that had included another member of the nineteen ninety-five team, New Zealander Matt Comesky.

> We just hit it off, Jeff and I. Now there he was up ahead of me as an impossible vision: my friend who loved hanging off vertical ice walls and driving fast cars and talking about the real things. Funny too, in the way he was.
>
> He'd set up his tent in this ridiculous spot at Camp One, twenty thousand feet, six thousand meters. I called it "Jeff's Dangerous Restaurant."
>
> There was this pinnacle of rock that jutted out from the face, on the lower Abruzzi Spur.

(Think of it as the stubby erection on a pyramid-bellied, thunder-thighed steroid user.)

> And there had been this buildup of scree rocks into a little coll of gravel.

(In the nesting cradle where the stub meets the body of the giant.)

> Jeff flattened out the gravel and put his tent over it, on this saddle of rubble, on this jutting pinnacle of rock, with a two thousand foot drop on either side to the Godwin Austen Glacier. The tent door looked straight up the Abruzzi flank where rocks came bounding down from hundreds, thousands of feet above. They generally came pinging and bounding off to the side. Still, it was pretty bloody vulnerable.
>
> Jeff would lie in his sleeping bag with the stove outside the door. I'd go off to get ice and snow to melt for a brew and sit down with my back to whatever was coming down.
>
> Ding.
>
> Dock.

Dang.

The conversations there lasted as long as I could stand the cold, which wasn't very long. Then I'd go back to my own tent, set in what I felt was a more sheltered spot, but a quarter of it hanging over nothing, and I'd clip onto the rope that tied the tent to the mountain, and I'd lie in my sleeping bag clipped to the rope and half sagging with the tent into space.

There was a Dutch expedition up there too at the time. One day we came up there, and a big boulder had come through one of the Dutch tents, off to the side of Jeff's tent, about twenty feet away. I remember this Dutch guy coming up the ropes and pulling himself to the ledge, and looking at the tent and going "Oh, my God," and then just shrugging and going in and making himself at home. The boulder had gone right through all four layers of the twin skin tent. He used a bit of medical tape to patch it up.

They were a funny bunch, the Dutch. They didn't want us coming into their compound at Base Camp. It gets like that with big budget expeditions, political and removed—kind of isolationist.

So in Base Camp, our little band of five would sit in our deck chairs outside our mess tent, set among the boulders, and we'd laugh and gossip about our neighbors, their foibles and quirks, our own foibles and quirks, the usual small town stuff, fart jokes. The laughter of group solidarity. Not sophisticated humor, but that's probably why they call it Base Camp.

It's in Base Camp where everyone finds common ground. It's where you go through the emotional business of tying on to each other with the invisible rope of trust, as a team. It's about getting your head right and feeling right with your fellows.

On K2 (also called Mount Godwin Austen) everybody hunkered in together, in the mess tent or in the deck chairs, and relevant to our situation we made the dark jokes of a kind that doctors and nurses make in emergency wards. To give the horror some distance and get ourselves right with it.

You're going up there.

You're going up there.

It plays on your mind, just knowing where you're going.

Anyway, Jeff and I were just hanging out with the other guys—my old friend Kim Logan from the Everest days, good fellow Matt Comesky, the great Bruce Grant—all mixed in together. It wasn't until we shared a tent together in the fall and die country of Camp Two, at twenty-two thousand feet, that Jeff and I really got to know one another, such that we could talk and talk about our complicated lives. We'd live up there for a few days, while pushing the route above, always starting early to climb in the dark by the light of the lanterns on our helmets. We both loved climbing in the dark.

They'd come down from the route in the afternoons and cook up a vile glug for dinner in the pressure cooker, smelling like dung heaps, the roof of the tent heavy and shiny with their frozen breath, and with a gust of wind a snowstorm would roll over them as they sat in their sleeping bags and looked out over China and talked about the sort of things that people like Oprah Winfrey talk about tearfully on television.

Jeff's parents had split when he was a baby. His father remarried and Jeff grew up in his father's household. It wasn't until he was a teenager that he discovered he had another mother. He started looking for his birth mother. And he found her. He said it meant a whole lot to him to get to know her and connect with her. And it still left that little boy's question: why did she disappear on him like that? And so there we were sitting on a ledge sorting through the heartstrings of a life. It's one of those situations where there's endless explaining, and no real understanding.

Meanwhile, Hillary was two years into a drama that had no end: the volatile aftershocks of marital collapse and divorce.

Since I was carrying a satellite phone, I was able to call my lawyer in Australia and catch up with the latest news on what was happening in the Family Court, where I was engaged in yet another dispute. Shortly after I left for the expedition, my estranged wife tried to sell my house, after emptying it of my possessions. It was deeply disturbing to feel so helpless and remote. But my lawyer told me over a succession of frantic satellite telephone connections that I should let the law deal with the wife and I should deal with the mountain. And that's what I did.

Anyway, it was marvelous: Jeff and I laughing together at the absurdity of dragging this baggage to this little ledge that we'd dug into the fall and die tilt of the slope of hard frozen snow that was glued to the side of the mountain. The snow would eventually ablate back to sheets of ice and bare rock with the wind.

That's where Jeff Lakes and I were headed now, as we fly-walked our way up the couloir. We were going to Camp Two.

Hillary remained in this reverie until he remembered Jeff Lakes wrapped in two sleeping bags, lying in a little slot off to the side of the ledge, just along from where they'd had all their good talks.

They'd all roped up to put him in there, just off to the side of the ledge where there was nothing under the balls of their feet, just thousands of feet, as they'd put him in there. Then they'd fly-walked back to the ledge, to the tent where he'd died in the night, and they'd sat down and howled their eyes out again.

The strange thing was, as Hillary kept inching across White Island through the blindfold storm of day five, thinking about Jeff in the sleeping bags and none of the good times, Jeff Lakes was still up ahead of him in the couloir.

It was at that point that Peter Hillary talked away all thoughts of his friend, and replaced them with the thoughts of an accident inspector.

In dry terms: visual deprivation. Everything was white, and my mind had nothing to read; nothing was coming in, because everything was white. Up and down were difficult to discern, even gravity was shrouded. There were times it felt as if I was walking through empty space and trying to stay upright; swaying from side to side, having to lean heavily on my poles.

I had experienced disorientation of a lesser persuasion as a pilot (when you're looking out at the night sky all the time, you have to avoid looking at the one spot for any length of time) and as a climber (when in whiteout I'd lost the sense of up and down).

But on the shelf it was something else.

With nothing coming in, I believe now everything comes out of you, everything leached out of you like salt is leached from soil by fresh water. That's how I came to think of it over the coming weeks.

I knew what was happening. But they were very powerful experiences.

For the therapists of the world I have called the process "psychological osmosis." The white world is a merciless therapist, one that derobes you and your secrets. Unfinished business just bobs to the surface no matter how well you've anchored it to the riverbed of your mind. It's a cliché that a polar trip is a trip of the mind. It's a cliché because it's true.

My very essence, my history and my heart, were to be projected in front of me.

After Hillary talked himself out of the couloir, and began to put everything in its logical place, he found himself walking on flat bumpy ground. Walking, not skiing. And there were poplar trees on either side of him. The trees were covered in fresh snow. There was snow on the ground under the trees, and none of the buffeting buffeting madness of the storm.

Although Hillary had recovered his sense of up and down, the violent blank had kept its mouth to the hole in his head. It had sucked out something new.

Hillary was walking in a creek bed. There was snow on the

eroded banks and under the trees that sat above them, but there wasn't any snow beneath his feet.

I knew this place. I was coming into a village in the Baltoro Valley in Pakistan. I'd walked through here with twenty-five Baltistani porters, these wild men of the hills, carrying a big load of our gear between them. This was nineteen ninety-five again. We'd come through this village on the long walk into the sloped foot of K2, a week further on.

We'd walked down the creek bed under the shade of the poplar trees.

My mind was mixing things up in a way that was making the old memories brand new, and with a deeper dreaminess than I'd found with the reunion with Jeff in the couloir.

When I went through that village with the Baltistanis, there wasn't any snow on the ground. It was this little dusty village that I recognized because of the poplar trees and the creek bed and then the stone walls of the buildings, not drooping and faded now in the gritty wind and the sun, but a pretty little snow scene that would have made a nice postcard.

Jeff and the others had walked in a week ahead of me, to establish Base Camp.

Hillary had stayed behind to sort out a serious problem with their climbing equipment: the tents for the high camps, the down climbing suits, the ropes and the carabiners, and ice screws and stakes and pitons and all the other bits and pieces that would keep the team pegged to the more exposed sections of the mountain—all of it was marooned at the Karachi airport in a customs warehouse, at a time when a violent and heat-struck unhappiness had taken over the city.

It was a hundred and five degrees (Farenheit) in the shade. There was rioting, people being killed in the street. I'd hoped the customs agents would be able to negotiate their way through the paperwork and secure a speedy release of our equipment, but the taxi drivers didn't want to go across to that side of town, the frantic side of town, so everything just ground to a halt.

So I started calling the various government ministries. Just slowly worked through the system. It was a grind that didn't seem to be getting anywhere; the same conversation over and over with different people, and no joy. At one point I thought of telling customs to send everything back to New Zealand or Australia, when they could get around to it. Meanwhile, I'd fly back home and buy all new gear so the expedition wouldn't collapse. It would have cost thousands of dollars.

And then, after a full week of the dead dog heat and cold calling, Peter Hillary, the son of, was offered a meeting with Prime Minister Benazir Bhutto's financial adviser. I walked in looking very shabby in the heat, and here was this immaculate man who'd obviously gone to Oxford, or something like that. One of those international citizens.

He said, "Peter, what can I do for you?" He was a busy man. He listened to me, didn't say much, picked up the phone, called Karachi, and at eight o'clock that night the gear arrived on my hotel doorstep.

After a long and bumpy truck ride, way out toward the alluvial plains that fall in the long shadow of the Karakoram Range, to where all roads ended, the mountain of gear was divided among the Baltistanis and me, and that's what we were carrying when we came through that village together; these fierce men of the north, with their rolled up caps and hooked noses, very handsome in a tanned Aryan kind of way, leftover warriors of the old Afghan empire, as I understand it.

I remembered we all shared the one spoon, the Baltistanis and me. There was only one spoon to be had until we got to Base Camp.

The sirdar, or foreman, was a squat tough man with an absurdly pretty name: Shiralee. He always made sure I got the spoon first. Shiralee took it next. And so on down the hungry line.

It was on the walk out from K2 that Hillary had come through the village with the remains of the team. They'd come through it at a run. They were running from the mountain. They had felt as if it was looking at them and that it was calling to them as they ran and sometimes staggered with grief and with an oppressive feeling that they, too, could be taken at any time. They were so exhausted that they would later sleep unbroken for days at a time, days at a time, yet they ran.

> At one point the clouds had parted, and all we could see was this perfect triangle, that perfect summit, peeking through this hole in the cloud, making together an all seeing eye, and we ran to get out of its sight.

That he was walking in a similar, if less panicked, communion with the leaching white everywhere didn't occur to Peter Hillary at the time. He wasn't looking for meaning or reason in the village as he walked through it. He didn't think about the customs warehouse at the time, nor about the day they'd come running through to get out of the sight of the mountain. He wasn't thinking about Jeff Lakes anymore. And when he thought of the Baltistanis, it was in passing, in the manner of picking a shiny apple and vaguely putting it away for later on.

Rather, as he inched through the postcard village cocooned in his wolf hood and goggles, unable to hear his gunshot groans in the wind, Peter Hillary abandoned all thinking to lose himself in the wonder of the impossible vision such that the wind's shrieking died for a time on his ears. So, too, the close voice of the familiar fear. Beyond it all, he beheld the vision as if it had nothing to do with him at all, shuffling along with the magical happiness of an overwhelmed grandpa on a day out at Disneyland.

> What a blast.

And then the village collapsed, and there was again only the storming brightness and the blurred smudges upon it and the flooding return to certainty that he was about to jump out of his skin.

> And then I realized my hands were getting very cold. You acclimatize to cold. You adjust to it, but it takes time.

His hands had been "cold" all day, the wind blasting its chill through his mittens and through the inner gloves and the fingers gripping the ski poles, so there wasn't much blood in them anyway. As long as it felt as if each finger was being squeezed from all four sides by two pairs of blunt nosed pliers, Hillary knew his hands were alive.

But they were on the way. He could feel them getting warm, and the relief of the warmth ran through his body like a taste of something he wanted to get drunk upon.

> **That's the problem when your hands and feet start to go numb—it's so easy to just let it happen. They were falling asleep.**
>
> **When I stopped to bang my hands together, they woke up screaming, the pliers squeezing tighter such that your eyes kind of roll to the back of your head. And that was okay.**

Time passed, inching and banging and wired again with no joy in it. They were cutting across White Island, three blurred smudges. **It was a freak show. For the second time I got up and said it was crazy walking blind into who knows what kind of country.**

> **We stood there and talked about it, having to yell at each other to be heard. My hands were turning to wood again. We were all cold, getting colder as we, ah, debated the issue.**
>
> **So we stopped early, at two miles and some.**

Putting the tent up in the hard gusting winds and the cold was like trying to wash a big rabid dog that had already eaten their hands.

And then crawling inside its belly.

CHAPTER ELEVEN

I wish that such an Odysseus would come now among the suitors. They all would find death was quick, and marriage a painful matter.

Homer, *The Odyssey,* **the Richmond Lattimore translation**

The routine was the same every night. They set their sleds in an arrow shape, into the wind, around the windward end of the tent, to protect it from the breeze or blast.

Before unrolling the tent, no matter the weather, they always anchored it first, by putting in an ice screw or tying a corner loop to one of the skis or to one of the sleds, so it wouldn't be suddenly swallowed and spat beyond salvation.

Once the tent was up, they staked it down securely with stakes, ice axe, skis.

Two of the men stayed out to shovel snow on the flaps, so the tent would freeze to whatever patch of Antarctica they were calling home that night, while the cook for the day threw his gear into the tent and started setting up the stove, pots and food in the "main vestibule"; which had room enough for a man squatting low, so it served as the toilet as well as the kitchen.

The cook always slept in the middle of the tent, with his head near the cooking area.

The other two slept either side of him, with their heads down toward the small vestibule; just big enough to crawl through, and set as an arrow against the wind, behind the arrow of the sleds.

Once the tent was sealed to the ground, the two outsiders dug out a ring of snow blocks a foot high, and built a pile of snow inside it, all at the cook's door, so he could reach out and grab a chunk for the pot as he sat in his sleeping bag, facing into the vestibule, bent over a stove the size of lingerie gift box, getting the first hot drinks on the way.

The rest of the gear had to be inside the sleds or tied to the sleds, so it wouldn't get drifted over in the night.

And the sled covers had to be sealed or we'd end up with sixty pounds of spindrift in them. When everything was accounted for and locked down, the outside crew crawled into the tent.
If it was blowing hard, they'd throw their sleeping bags and mats—and their personal kits, toolkits, the satellite phone kit and whatever else was needed for the night—through the cook's door and over the cook's head because the windward door was locked down.

And suddenly there would be three people up to their waists in bags of gear and everybody covered in frost and frozen drool and nostril juice, jackets full of frosted ice, the wolf fur all iced up, everything iced up and on the tent floor no bigger than a double bed.

On top of each other, we'd get our mats down, the insulated foam mats, and the Therm-a-Rests. We always kept the Therm-a-Rests inflated, from day one, and never inflated them again, because to do so would soon fill them up with ice. Breath, moisture, ice.
They'd lay their sleeping bags down and ready before getting out of their iced up clothes, hanging them on mesh netting in a

hanging area. The stove helped a little to dry them, to a cold damp.

By the time we were ready to take out the GPS (Global Positioning System) and note the position report, and got the satellite phone going and the diary out, generally it would be time for the first of the drinks, two or three hot electrolyte drinks depending on how the stores were going and how hard the day had been.

And then the cook got on with the main meal (say, pasta Alfredo or creamy chicken and rice, whatever it was, always floating in a soup of extra virgin olive oil and anhydrous butterfat). Finally, he made up the lunch bags for the following day and filled up three two-liter thermoses with boiling water. Much reaching out for many chunks of ice.

It was a major job on top of the four hundred and forty pounds; some pounds off as the meals were consumed, some pounds back on as we filled the plastic bags.

Generally the cook would be going relentlessly until ten or eleven o'clock at night.

And there were always repairs to do to the gear, cook or not.

Even with the twenty-four hour daylight we slept like logs.

It came in the night as it did in the day, the sun's light, in colors according to the weather: the burning magnesium that came to them through the storms that only shrouded them lightly; the shiny silver gray screen of flat cloud cover; the marvelous warming—warming!—rays of a golden sun in an open sky that kept them almost toasty at midnight. Because there was no night. They never got to see the terrestrial world dancing as a body of moonlight against the bigger body of darkness. There was no darkness from above.

Which was handy too. Because you didn't need your light to find your pee bottle in the inconvenient hours.

At five o'clock in the morning, the watch alarm sounded and the cook would sit up and get the stove going, start reaching out for the first chunks of ice. (Someone else would take his turn at the stove at day's end.)

> One cup of coffee each. One large bowl of porridge, butter drenched. We hadn't prepared our insides for this diet (as was the practice of the greats of polar travel) and for some time we suffered the cramps and indigestion, the runs and the greater indignity of losing a portion of what we had hauled behind us with such gut-busting effort.

In the early days, when various bits of hair from various bits of the body turned up in the dinners, they'd pick it out with at-home sensibilities. Later there was hair everywhere. It seemed the tent was filling up with it. By then, when they found strings of it floating in their fat soaked suppers, they'd drink the strings down with an almost welcoming affection, such was their easy happiness when something different and new put a benign bump in the repetitive rhythms of domestic details and duties and only the weather to talk about and "pass the salt" and not even the strings of hair worth talking about, for the novelty passed quickly into the jaded monotony of their marital life, such was its flattening power.

❄   ❄   ❄

Peter Hillary was cook for day five, November eight. He took turns with his icicle hands, keeping one near the stove and the other reaching for the chunks of ice.

He hated cooking, in part because he had no talent for it. On his regular sojourns across the Tasman Sea to Melbourne, to spend time with his children, Hillary invariably knocked together his masterpiece, one of the truly clueless dishes of all time: soggy pasta swimming in a soup of canned salmon, green olives and canned tomatoes. **(Canned goods because an empty fridge is a clean fridge.)** It went down the throat like chunky salt water until the palate adjusted to the various ingredients, and then it had the disturbing addictive quality of potato

chips. As soon as his daughter Amelia could look over the top of
the cooker, she asked to take over the duties for everybody's
sake.

The polar meals were much worse, of course, but that was the
case no matter who cooked them.

> It wasn't brain surgery. Just throw in the meals packets and
> the extra oil and keep stirring until it melted into a lumpy
> syrup of grease. There was always half an inch of pure oil and
> butter floating on the top.

And on that storming afternoon, inside the red belly of the rabid
dog, Hillary was glad to have a warming distraction from the
buffeting buffeting, and from the others and the unhappy frustration with the two miles and some, especially that he'd been
the unfortunate who called for the plug to be pulled that day. It
was but the latest layer in the tension that had been growing like
an onion in the community garden of mood since they spent
that first night by the airfield runway.

> How and when were we going to find our happiness? Where
> were we to look for it?

It was clear the tent wasn't a happy place. As Hillary's automatic
hands reached out for the ice, fiddled with the stove, set out the
mugs, he looked over the day out there and quickly decided it
hadn't been a happy place either. This opinion was supported by
small waves of the day's plagues as he thought about them: the
anxiety, the fear, the wired side, the frustration with the loss of
control, the vexation that democracy was impinging on his core
belief of self reliance and would no doubt continue to do so.

And when he decided to "look for the good," as it is writ in the
self help books he generally despised, Hillary was disturbed to
remember that the day's one ray of light had come from a place
he generally regarded with dread.

> That the Hillary side of the family tends to see the world in
> black and white terms extends to the concept of happiness.
> "You're either happy or you're not. Which are you?" When it

gets more complicated than that, I admit I get a little out of my
depth.

For a while he sat confused in the undeniably strange mix of
happiness and dread; and at first the happiness seemed to be
winning, such was the joy he found in remembering the impossible vision of the postcard Baltistani village, and how marvelous
it had been to see Jeff Lakes in the couloir again.

Neither had stayed with him for long out there, some minutes.

**But they were such intense experiences. More startling than
the storm. And that's what it was all about for me.**

When talking to the school halls, the convention centers and
cruise ship auditoriums, **"such intense experiences"** was all
Hillary could comfortably offer by way of explaining **"what it
was all about for me."** Because if he'd laid it out straight, the assembled, trying to give it a point of reference, would simply as-
sume he was a Pentecostal evangelist and become fretful.

Because Peter Hillary would have to stand up in his blazer and
tie and say something like:

**The sick madness of living with fear screaming in my ears,
and acting against its pleas, is in its finest moments a visionary state unto itself and, in collaboration with external pressures, the conduit to an even greater rapture.**

The rapture wasn't the heart of the game, but the heart of the
heart: the most elusive and mysterious of all the jewels hidden
in its chambers.

And that's what Peter Hillary was looking for when going out
there, those finest moments, the rapture that overwhelmed the
agonies such that there was no confusion or ambivalence or
doubt. **"You're happy or you're not. Which are you?"** The rapture wiped out the question.

This version of the thrill, however, was new to him: walking
with ghosts in living color.

He knew people who lived with ghosts every day of their lives.
How they thrived, he didn't know.

They either seem in desolation or dedicated to bringing loved ones back to life in their minds. I've seen the desolation, and I've dabbled with bringing the dead back to life. Then it got to the point where there were too many of them. The burden was that I'd often been there at the time, or knew well how it would have been for them, and after a while you're this "survivor" watching all these final scenes play over and over again.

I felt that K2 was still too fresh to bring out of the vault. Just too heavy.

That's why I'd been surprised to see Jeff Lakes again, in all those memories, because I thought I'd locked them well away in the vault, to let them age.

The more Hillary thought about how surprising it all was, the more the dread pulled on his better mood as an undertow, out of habit or not he didn't know. Regardless, he kept working the stove and surrendered to sadness.

Well, you know, Jeff. Jesus wept, they say. It always seemed so cruel to me because Jeff had fought so hard to save himself.

We didn't know the full horror of his odyssey until he collapsed in our arms as a zombie, and even then we didn't know how little was left in him. He was already dead and we didn't know it. We had him propped up against us in his sleeping bag. He took automatic swallows of the drinks we were pouring into him, and we were thinking we'd saved him, and we told him everything was going to be all right. This was at Camp Two, where we'd become friends.

We never heard his story, how close he'd got to the top or otherwise. We knew there were six other people up there, who'd been ahead of him, and that they were all dead. One of our fellows, Bruce Grant, was dead. Jeff didn't talk about any of that.

He couldn't talk when he got to us. He couldn't say a word.

The last face to face conversation of any coherency that Jeff

Lakes ever had, with anybody, certainly with anybody still
alive, was with me.

Hillary and Lakes spent the first half of that day together, the day
of the last conversation. They were going to the summit and
they'd started out for it together, ahead of the others, leaving
their camp at eleven p.m., heading up in the dark.

They were above the summit shoulder, at twenty-six thousand, heading up, their legs like dead men, each step an agony
that caused them to suck desperately for the air that wasn't
there. Four desperate breaths of too little and then another dead
man's leg to swing up and against the ice.

It was very cold. Brutally cold because their blood had turned
to sludge with the effects of the altitude. They weren't carrying
supplemental oxygen, and they were above the magical eight
thousand meters, high in the death zone.

They climbed up the ridge of the shoulder toward the base of
the Bottleneck, a steep ice gully that led up to the summit ridge,
jutting out over the eleven thousand foot South Face. There was
the top, just over a thousand feet above the throat of the Bottleneck, K2.

And then we both felt it, the cold that said, "I'm going to kill
you." It was forty below zero, and at altitude you have little inside to ward it off. Our blood had turned to engine oil. We
were dehydrated. We were unable to move with the sort of
vigor that warms a body. "I'm going to kill you."

We headed down to the Spanish high camp to warm up,
and we met the others in passing, as they were coming up. My
teammate Bruce Grant was way out in front of the others,
moving like a robot. I gave him the rope.

Bruce was a famous superman in New Zealand. Later a local current affairs show did an "investigative report" into
what happened to Bruce Grant, because it didn't seem possible that anything could happen to him, that anything was beyond his astounding physical powers.

But K2 is K2, and when I gave him the rope he wasn't saying much, and he didn't look great, but he wanted to get to the top and that's where he was at.

As Alison Hargreaves went by she said, "I'm going on." Nothing more. Eyes straight ahead.

Alison was a British climber who had just become famous for climbing Everest without oxygen and without clipping onto any of the ropes. For weeks she'd wanted to get to the top of K2 and go home to her children.

And then well below her came the already ghostly Rob Slater. Head down, resolute. "Summit or die," he had said before leaving the States. "Either way I win." He had been looking exhausted for days now.

I had the intellectual capacity of a slow six year old. And when Alison said "I'm going on," I remember she wore the face of a child whose heart was defiantly set on one thing, and that little else existed in her world at that time. Bruce was the same, couldn't say much. He wasn't a talker at the best of times.

But who can say how they were? I was retarded at the time. Oh, handicapped, challenged and the rest of it. "Retarded" works because that's how you feel. But I knew enough to say they were walking simple too.

When I later told one reporter that I felt Alison and the others had been "blinkered from what was developing around them and that the group chemistry seemed all wrong," it hurt people, families. In at least three countries. Then the reporter suggested, "Did they have summit fever?" Well yes, I suppose in a way they did. And so I confirmed the media prognosis. But to know summit fever or even to have a notion of what it might be, you would have to go there yourself.

This report was picked up by newspapers everywhere. It went around the world like a bad smell. Love and truth. When they stink, they stink.

And still this hurting family, Bruce Grant's family, wanted me to tell them what happened up there, to their boy, their amazing boy. All that I could tell them with any certainty were the same things I'd already tried to tell that reporter, the bare facts of the event as I knew them, and my appraisal of what went wrong for them.

So I couldn't tell them much at all. I sat with them and looked at all the old photographs of Bruce.

The last time I talked to Bruce was when I gave him the rope. We didn't talk long. It was cold. I was very cold.

Bruce headed on up. I followed Jeff down to the Spanish camp, a few hundred feet down the shoulder.

They crawled into one of the tents, climbed into the sleeping bags there, warmed up with a brew, resting without recovery, violently shaking off the lethal grip of the cold only, their brains slowly shutting down regardless. After about two hours in repose, they headed up the shoulder again, dead men for legs, dead everything because that's how it is up there, with the altitude, the cold. They were dying.

That's what this "living on the edge" business was all about with extreme altitude adventuring. It wasn't the edge of the ledge, or the beckoning edge of insanity or simplehood; it was about functioning, in critical circumstances, while hovering on the edge of death, every cell of the body torn between giving up, clinging on.

As we moved up, we could see the others. They were inching their way, slow, hauling themselves up the Bottleneck and onto the exposed traverse to the summit ridge. Hard going, clearly.

I was some way ahead of Jeff, the ground getting steeper as we climbed. This was the highest he'd ever been before, nearly twenty-seven thousand feet.

When I got to the Bottleneck, I cut a ledge in the snow and sat down in it to take a drink from my thermos and wait for him. As I watched him come up the sloping ground, I noticed there were clouds swirling over the summit. Snowflakes kept landing on my mittens. I suddenly felt it was all wrong.

Jeff came up, cut a ledge and sat down, and we talked about it. I told him it looked bad to me, and that I was heading down, not to our high camp, which was just below the Spanish camp, but all the way down to our happier spot at Camp Two, a drop of about five thousand feet.

I was getting wired with the whole thing. I was wired anyway. If a man was suddenly transported from the death zone, high on a mountain, to the front window of your house, you would believe that a homicidal maniac was looking in at you.

That's how I would have looked, with or without these huge clouds coming in or feeling that it was all wrong. I'm not sure what my face conveyed as I talked to Jeff. We had grown used to seeing each other freaked out. And we had half a brain between us.

You're a walking nerve ending and not much more up there. The reality in detail and my perceptions at the time, to what degree they matched up, who can say? All I could hear in my head was "Get down now."

Jeff Lakes decided to go on for a while. He said he probably wouldn't keep going for too much longer, that he'd probably turn around sooner than later, but he also said he couldn't bear the disappointment if the others got up and he missed out. That he would never forgive himself for turning back if they got up. And that was our last conversation.

What was Jeff Lakes thinking?

As we sat there, we heard a woman's voice calling from up above. It was Alison. "Come on up. Use the red rope."

So Jeff went on up, used the red rope. What were they all thinking?

"Come on up. Use the red rope."

I remember hearing voices at the top of Everest in nineteen

ninety. I had used bottled oxygen to get up, and it ran out as I started down from the summit. All the way down I heard voices. When I was coming down the last of the ice gullies to Camp Four on the South Col, I saw what I thought was a yellow tent. Then I realized it was a knee, sticking out of the ice like a little crumpled tent. I knew that knee, not beyond hello and good luck and take care up there, but he seemed a nice fellow. He was a Yugoslav fellow who had been on the mountain the previous year, eighty-nine.

It ended for him, and for another man, a Sherpa, in the last of the ice gullies. They were descending, having successfully reached the summit. They must have been on a rope. One of them probably tripped and fell and pulled the other one off, and they bounced some hundreds of feet—who could say how many, who could say with certainty what really happened? I knew the knee belonged to him. I was hearing voices when I saw it.

Now, on the ice shelf, I was seeing Jeff Lakes.

I wondered what was going to be dragged out of me next, and if I was up to seeing it.

❉   ❉   ❉

Hillary stirred a pot of gruel that could have lubricated a car, putting aside the quandaries of rapture to stare into the stove's chuffing blue flame.

A confusion of mood returned, however, when he drifted into the couloir again and followed Jeff Lakes up to Camp Two for one of their good conversations, and found there was no dread up there. As he settled into this surprisingly easy happiness, as he appraised its potential for the weeks to come, it occurred to him why he was having such a good time with the dead Jeff Lakes: he was lonely.

We all feel lonely every day, in passing or in bouts, and there is a loneliness just in being alive, one's path and all that. And

Antarctica was "the loneliest place on the planet," as writ in all the coffee table books. But I hadn't been "a lonely person" since my adolescence at school, a place that one school friend described as "the gourmet sausage factory" where we were trained to be "tomorrow's leaders." And then there was the desperate loneliness, the horrible emptiness of the years after my mother and sister were killed.

Life in the tent was like being part of a machine. It was all work. Work conversations. Work tensions. Office politics. Sailors in a submarine. Shh. We did our job, we kept to ourselves, and indeed I felt myself becoming "a lonely person" again.

The phone calls home were more a cruel tease than a comfort, as was always the case no matter what part of the world one called from. And in the first weeks out, Hillary found the lack of privacy and abundance of tension allowed for no relaxed intimacy with his wife, heart to heart, and the longer it went on like that, he wondered if he'd ever be able to whisper sweet nothings again. **(Well, as close to sweet nothings as I can get.)**

The media calls were interesting sometimes, when he didn't simply have to perform, but could instead talk at length, in two-way engagement, without the burden of emotional attachment.

The journalists talking with the tent could hear the buffeting buffeting, the clanking of plates and mugs, but rarely a voice in the background. No happy chatter or the long vowels of considered discussion. No evidence that the fellow talking from the tent was in the company of others, that there was anybody else there. When, say, Muir talked about them all "smelling really bad," there was no raucous chorus as one might get from an unwashed football team or even a bunch of astronauts. Before long, it started to feel as if the team was wearing the frozen happy face of a marriage keeping up appearances. It never felt as if it was a good time to talk.

When Ed Hillary was driving his tractor across Antarctica, he was able to call the family home once a week, via a radio signal that was patched through to the telephone system. The calls were prone to cut out at any time, with no opportunity to learn why one of the children was suddenly howling until the next scheduled call. Ed Hillary later wrote how easy it was to imagine himself with his wife and children, in the warm air of the living room and the sun coming in off the harbor, and how suddenly it all vanished, with a slap in the face as the big white place crashed all over him again.

Ed said the Old Firm often felt lonely, but they were never really alone. And they'd done what they could to keep it at bay by generally adopting the campfire attitude of community when gathered around the stove. But it came easy to the Old Firm; not because they liked each other, although they apparently did well enough, but because they were personalities open to conversation.

Hillary and company were relying on a dozen or so exotic variations of bus stop conversation, and occasional bouts of by-the-way locker room banter. **It was kind of perfunctory communication. "Would you pass your mug."** Only rarely did they have a rave together. When they did it was more like a forum. It was never about getting to know one another.

For Peter Hillary, "as good as it gets" in this awkward and sorry environment amounted to sharing an occasional moment of small comedy with Jon Muir. Only once did they ever laugh, fully laugh, with the booming abandonment of the old days on the mountain. It wouldn't come to them for weeks, until they'd crossed the five hundred of the coated tongue: it broke open like the old times and then went on for a long time, as the hysterical, shrieking happiness of the insane.

Philips didn't catch the bug with that one. That he just sat there and looked at them only added to the hilarity.

And was it God or the devil who designed the perversely impotent yet poetic piece of small comedy that came at the end of day five's two miles and some?

When I first crawled into the tent, I realized I had forgotten to bring in my food bag for the evening meal. I called to Jon who was still outside, and asked him to get it from my sled. He lifted out what he thought was drinking chocolate but was really my poo bag. It brought up a half smiling shrug between us and that's all. "Oh yeah, right. The romance of polar travel! Ha ha ha. Well . . . better get on with it."

Anyway, he was done in. Lost. We were all a bit lost. The mood was the mood.

Muir was probably getting sick at that stage too, with a flu from Scott Base. Two days on, he'd be laid out with it. So he was probably at that stage when all one felt was a heavy fatigue, but that early symptom went unrecognized in Muir's case, because he assumed his exhaustion was born solely from his labors, and the heaviness of the ordeal.

If Robert Swan's assessment of what Antarctica does to a mind was accurate, then it made a prediction too: that the men would turn into their eight year old selves. For Hillary, if he were to truly fall into the patterns of his playground days, as "a lonely person," he'd find himself staging and suffering an emotional siege. The polar and isolation research psychologists were predicting an emotional siege among the three of them as a matter of course, to some extent; dysfunctional unit or not.

Was it happening?

Well, of course. Eric and I seemed to be continually at odds. Jon just wanted to go home, and couldn't do so without pulling the plug on the whole trip, and so it wasn't a happy situation for him. And the way of life itself was a siege. Three men against the elements. Locked in together. Locked in their heads. That's the misery, that's the challenge. What do you do about it?

I mean, there we were in the tent, the belly of the rabid dog, three men sharing a double bed, the wind howling, the world outside a monster, and as I'm handing out the bowls of gruel

to my companions, the only conversation going on is between
me and Jeff Lakes.

I didn't feel connected to these guys, and we were out here
on a rope together. Yes, they had shown a little compassion
when I learned my daughter had been trying to call, but compassion between strangers gets old quick. And we were
strangers to one another.

What do you do about it?

Hillary knew enough to make his own prediction: if they didn't
somehow "connect" and find "the good" in each other, all
they'd remember in the end were the little human hatreds that
come easier than compassion among strangers, and they
wouldn't be little hatreds anymore. Hillary felt they needed to
do something to make the tent their Base Camp instead of their
bus stop in the rain.

**Limbo land, really. Purgatory: the place to wait while Antarc-
tica decided to give us heaven or hell with the weather.**

The only antidote, as he saw it, was to conjure up the old campfire mood by drawing the other men out; get them talking about
themselves and their lives, away from the game and the thrill of
being adventurers. He'd been trying to do so since their first
night, at the airfield.

**I tried to make it happen as we ate our dinners. But it wasn't
happening. They responded with the polite or indulging
murmurs one generally gives mad strangers on the street.**

On the evening of day five, a Sunday evening, with the mood being the mood and no end in sight to it, with the shuddering return of his old loneliness, with business the only topic of
communal interest, Peter Hillary dropped all subtlety and, as a
matter of business, suggested they establish a Base Camp social
club, by way of a regular conversational happy hour, for the sake
of the expedition's mental health.

They hadn't seen the marriage counselor, or done anything
else that might have taken them to common ground, to a way of

talking with each other and a sense of "team." So why not a social club?

> It was pretty contrived, I admit. I just suggested we make a
> regular time to get together and, yeah, make it like a social
> club, make it part of the routine: we'd talk a bit about our-
> selves, our hopes and dreams, how we viewed the world, how
> we viewed the world when we were children, anything, I
> don't know. I wanted to institutionalize it in some way be-
> cause I knew it wasn't going to happen automatically.

It was always going to be the best time or the worst time to bring
up the idea, given the two miles and some. And when Eric
Philips and Jon Muir murmured their lack of interest, Hillary
looked for the good, found temporary comfort in denial:

> The mood's the mood. Tough day. No problem. Another time
> perhaps.

By the time the meal was done, and everyone had finished their
chores and repairs, it was still early, and it was as if they rose
from their personal tables, in their personal dining rooms, and
headed off to their separate rooms for the rest of the afternoon;
without speaking or acting in any way that suggested there was
anyone else present, let alone jammed up against their rump.

It intrigued Hillary, that he never knew where the others went
in their heads. He wondered if his reclusive companions were
seeing dead friends out there too, and what a campfire they
could have made with them.

He and Jon Muir shared some of the same ghosts; if and how
they walked through the halls of Muir's head, he couldn't imagine. Then he thought about Eric Philips suffering the death of his
younger brother.

> It happened quite soon after we teamed up, and he'd talked
> openly about it at the time, in that aftershock that leaves peo-
> ple mute or needing to get it off their chest. It was just terribly
> sad, because the family hadn't seen the boy for some time,
> and it was Eric who found him cold and just hugged him.

That it was hurting him or riding him during the odyssey became clear some weeks later. Over the first days out, the curtains were drawn. And I suppose it wouldn't have made a
very happy hour if we'd really got into it. Not then anyway.

This life, eh?

What a day.

✻ ✻ ✻

Hillary built up a campfire in his mind and played ghosts with
his children, a favorite game. On summer evenings, after dark,
he took them to a big green park wooded with old spreading
trees and standing lamps planted sparsely along the walkways
so the rolling lawns were a spooky gray, and where the trees
stood away from the lamps their shadows made caves. They'd all
run over the lawns and lurk in the caves and spring out with
their white sheets held over their heads, floating and trailing and
snapping in the air with their shrieking laughter.

It was always good for forty minutes, an hour, as an outing.
And not so long as a reverie, on its own, but Hillary purposefully
stepped from that scene to another and to another, consciously
looking for connections, seeing if he was capable of building
long trains of entertainment from his "happy" catalogue.

**I was frightened of getting bored, and becoming a too easy
touch for bad memories.**

And lonely too. Bored and lonely: the easy as hell recipe for a
slow cooked insanity.

**Bored and Lonely: the parents of delinquent and disruptive
children everywhere.**

Perhaps Tennyson could make it prettier: "Come, my friends . . ."

**I'd already tried that one. And it didn't look like my friends
were coming to the party. What do you do about it?**

**In my private room on the evening of day five, I decided I
needed to develop strategies that would make me capable of
a protracted and profound self containment, such that I could**

survive as if there were nobody else out there with me, for the
nearly one hundred days, while in the company of others, and
remaining on agreeable terms with them.

Which was akin to finding himself in a maximum security prison,
something else the psychologists had predicted. Worse, it was
volunteering for solitary confinement. The hole.

It was a bizarre challenge, to say the least. But if I couldn't get
the social club off the ground and there was no real company
to be had with these fellows, that was the weird place I had to
take myself to. To cope, I had to be capable of generating my
own company. Hence, my attempts to generate a string of
reveries at will. It was a mental exercise. I always do mental
exercises on big trips. You're always looking for new and better ways to cope with the stress and the long stretches between drinks. This was just another one, I figured.

From the shrieking ghost game with his children he stepped off
to watch his father and his father's old climbing friends riding
around the living room and the perilous fringe of a swimming
pool on bicycles, under the hilarious blessings of whisky and the
wonder of easy fun.

From there it was easy to step off and see his father doing an
impersonation of John Wayne knocking a wayward cowboy on
his ear, "I wouldn't do that if I was you," with the poplar wood
fire behind him, and his old friends and the family looking up at
him from the blankets on the ground and the stars out and the
smoke of the poplar wood sweet to the nose, but that was a
scene he'd thought about so many times that it inspired an affectionate passing glance before he stopped the train to wonder
how many times he could look through the old family album
without it becoming just another door to madness.

He started over with the memory of the legendary Dr. M coming to the door with his bearded face full of optimism, a bottle of
oxygen under one arm, a loaf of bread under the other, wanting
the Hillarys, Ed or Peter, to go climbing with him.

He was this local doctor, a fabulous eccentric who wanted to be the master of the seas, the mountains, and the sky. He had just returned from the Auckland to Suva yacht race, where he had been a navigator on one of the competing yachts. They had become lost; the yacht demasted and had to be towed back to New Zealand. Now he was looking for a climbing partner. How the oxygen bottle fitted into this, I never understood.

When Dr. M got a temporary position in a little rural town in the central district of the North Island, the story goes, he decided to take all the local women off birth control because they were all overweight. Then he sent them out jogging. They all ended up pregnant, and with strained muscles. It caused a bit of a row.

Dr. M was married for a time to a glamorous newsreader. She had all these beautiful groovy clothes and Dr. M started wondering if she loved her clothes more than she loved him. He had to know. So, the story goes, he got his surgical scissors and cut all her favorite dresses into precise two inch strips, and then sat and waited to see if his wife's dedication to their marriage went beyond the destruction of her precious clothes. It did not.

Dr. M was a great story to be told over a glass of wine. Isn't that how it is for everybody? No matter how marvelous the past, we need new things to happen.

That was the paradox: the new things always remind us of the old things, or cast us among them. In the end, when the campfire died to ash, Hillary reluctantly but inevitably thought again about where he'd been cast that day, among the impossible visions..**Time travel by hallucination.**

Reluctance gave way to gratitude when he saw it as another mental game, to be enjoyed for its own sake. **I did find it intriguing. How it all worked. Why particular memories?**

Did Antarctica come and scoop them up from the top of the

pile, or was the vault in Hillary's head just full to bursting? **Or were there a variety of factors that had to be in place to make it all happen in a particular way? I wanted to know why I'd been thrown back to K2. Twice in the one day. On the mountain and in that postcard village.**

Hillary went step by step through the chain of events that had led up to his meeting with Jeff Lakes in the couloir, looking for the connections with the unmoved but involved attitude of someone doing a crossword puzzle. That's what was so great about being an accident inspector. It made Hillary a Teflon outsider to his own situation, himself. The uncomfortable part was coming back in. As was the case that night, after he'd found a logical solution (to the question of memory selection by the hands of the great white everywhere) that half satisfied, and his blood had thawed and once again started pumping through his veins.

It was almost too obvious. Pure clichéd therapy stuff.

As I previously explained: the only reason I would willfully travel through a white storm into crevasse country would be to escape an otherwise certain death up high.

In fact, that was the situation on K2 for me, a desperate blind run for my life where I reversed backward down the steep face, kicking snow behind and below me so I had some guide as to where to place my feet.

If it tumbled and stopped somewhere below me, I put my foot on that spot where the shadow of the clump of snow was cast. In the white on white world of the storm it was difficult to see the snowball. If it seemed to disappear, then I assumed the ground fell away there and I'd deviate across the face and kick the snow in a new direction. At one point, when I did my little mule kick to send off another snowball to scout the way into the white oblivion, the entire slope broke loose for several yards in every direction. Perched upon a rambling carpet of rapidly descending snow, I shot down the face. It was steep country. I wasn't on a rope. And the last words of many absentees flashed somewhere behind my eyes: "Oh, fuck."

I clawed at the face, opened up my body like a skydiver trying to catch an upward breeze, and flew across a crevasse, a crack that sat across the slope, with the lower lip well below with the drop in the slope. Happily the scouring of my crampon front points and the tearing picks of my axes reined in my slide and let the carpet of cascading snow rush from around me and descend into the white void beneath my heels.

The trained animal inside took over. I eased my ice axe into the slope, easing it in so it wouldn't be torn out of my hands. When I stopped, I just stood there against the face, heaving air into my lungs and wanting to howl, to cry for help, for company. But hugging the snow wall wasn't going to get me down. I pushed myself out from the face and started kicking snow into the whiteness below me again.

That was the storm born from the clouds I'd seen building up while having a swig from my thermos at the Bottleneck with Jeff Lakes. I met it later that afternoon, as I tried to run ahead of it, only to find it was coming up the mountain, a thousand freight trains screaming upward. People later said, what a strange storm it was, climbing up the mountain like that. It went all the way to the top.

The punchline for the television chat shows would go something like, "And I guess hauling through the buffeting, buffeting whiteness brought it all back. It kinda felt the same. Can I cry now?"

❄   ❄   ❄

It was a few days after his walk through the impossible postcard village with the Baltistanis that Peter Hillary remembered a bothersome conversation he'd had in ninety-five in Islamabad, in that week when he'd stayed behind to rescue the K2 team's gear from the custom sheds.

On the third or fourth day of the saga, as Hillary sat at a desk in the expedition agent's office, going through the paperwork and feeling it a waste of time, he realized that the expedition's liaison officer was staring at him as if he'd just seen something troubling.

Climbing expeditions to Pakistan—and Nepal, India, and China—must be accompanied by a military officer, basically to ensure that the climbers stick to the mountains that they've paid for at so many thousands of dollars per permit, depending on the hill's popularity; and to watch that nobody wanders off to collude with spies from the CIA or hostile neighbors; **or so they say.**

> In other words, they don't really do anything, by and large, but turn up and get paid. And we have to pay them, and kit them out. It's a perk of military service. We ended up with this young army officer, Sohail. He wanted a thousand dollar sleeping bag, of the sort we'd be using at high camps. He wanted all this gear he didn't need, so he presumably could sell it off later. Frankly, I couldn't blame him if he did.
>
> Anyway, I was sitting at this desk and realized Sohail was just looking at me. He'd been quietly sitting across from me for some time. I raised my eyes and asked, "What is it?"
>
> He asked, "Is it too late?"
>
> He was just looking at me.
>
> And I said, "It's not too late. I mean, just because we've had a few delays . . . It's the perfect season."
>
> He said, "No. Your age."

CHAPTER TWELVE

But when the young Dawn showed again with her rosy fingers . . .
Homer, *The Odyssey*, the Richmond Lattimore translation

Day six, November nine, they crossed seventy eight degrees South, and although everyone seemed a little cheered by the eight some miles, their best to date, the two miles and some of the previous day continued to silently stir the pot of unease.

It was a beautiful sparkling day. Clear and calm, no buffeting buffeting. The tent warm on the sunny side, its walls a still red glow where the nylon was stretched against the rays of the sun.

We put our heads out and found we'd camped in an area free of crevasses. And the way ahead looked reasonably clear too. No trouble in sight. So much for my fears.
Hillary said something sheepish by way of lubricating whatever awkward emotions were quietly running wild in the hearts of his companions, yet he remained unapologetic about calling the halt in the storm. He'd do it again, if he felt they weren't in control of the situation.

We skied south, with sunshine reflecting brightly off the snow and ice, under the face of space. I was finding my rhythm, where I slowly punched my way through the day, sore and tired, pulling out a tree.

Two or three miles on, we ran into a field of large bridged crevasses. We skied over them without any trouble, but it took us the rest of the day to get through them. And then.

❄ ❄ ❄

Day seven, two miles and some through a boiling blizzard, the shortest day's hauling yet.

And yes, it was me again. My hands.
Hillary and company had woken to find themselves once more in the belly of the rabid dog. It took the three of them to wrestle it to the ground, roll it up.

Strong winds, drifting snow, a fog of spindrift, intensely cold conditions, no sky, no horizon, white on white on violent white.

I kept losing my sense of up and down, but no dead friend came to see me. Maybe it was too cold for them. It was too cold for me. By midday my hands were freezing, completely turned to wood, the color of bone. I couldn't warm them no matter how hard I banged them together. Jon Muir came through in champion fashion, by getting me to put my hands on his tummy to warm them. He'd put on a lot of weight. Which was a good thing, stocking the larder against the withering. He'd really put it on and that tummy felt pretty good to my cold white hands. It was amazing, because it didn't seem to bother him.

Hillary had put on a stone (fourteen pounds) but it had barely smeared a layer of fat over a body that had remained naturally and then willfully free of such a thing, always, boy to man. He still didn't have what you'd call buttocks. Big hands and feet; skinny arms, legs and body. A human gibbon. Great for climbing, not a great help in the cold. Well, Hillary?

Anyway, Jon's tummy thawed out my left hand fairly quickly, but after fifteen minutes my right hand was still wooden, so we put up the tent in the maelstrom and stopped early again. And then we found we couldn't call home. When we tried to charge the phone batteries, the charger setup seemed to keep shorting out. We didn't know what was wrong.

Strangely, while we all said, in our own way, that we could take or leave the phones if we'd had a choice in the matter, after a week with the luxury of calling home we're all unhappy that we've been cut off.

"We must fix the phones!"

Eric and I set up the HF radio and the antenna and called Scott Base to discuss the situation with the technicians there. They said they'd investigate. The good old radio, eh? Not that I said such a thing at the time.

The problem with the phone gave them something to talk about for a while, with an anxious edge to it. What if they had to be resupplied with a new charger system and batteries? It meant a helicopter would fly out from Scott Base, and their coveted "unsupported" status would be soiled, if not fully compromised.

The reality is, no trip is fully "unsupported" when everybody knows you are out there, and there are planes and helicopters to search you out and bring you home when things go wrong. They can fail to find you. They can get there too late. But it's a luxury the Captain and Amundsen never had. In modern times the most you can aspire to is traveling in "great style."

Borge Ousland had new gear flown in to him, early on his North Pole trip. He was still the one. Odysseus took some years out from his great wanderings to make endless love to the enchantress Calypso. He was certainly the one.

I felt we could live with this . . . shame. We needed the phones. They were as essential as the tent, because they were

paying the bills. Plus, we were also anxious about what a visit from the modern world would do to our sense of being "out there."

The latest curse to their odyssey had changed from a practical problem to an existential crisis. Actors talk about the burden and necessity of "staying in character." Imaginative love play thrives on staying in character. If the mood is lost, the entire enterprise is immediately bankrupt, until the required store of focus and enthusiasm can be mustered again. Hillary and company were living both scenarios. The media actors keeping it upbeat; the swinging lovers of adventure.

Meanwhile, as the phone ceased to be a topic of conversation, and became instead that evening's patch of quicksand to quietude, the phantom arms of illness were laying Jon Muir down and out and dead in his bed. Again he assumed he was merely surrendering to bone weariness. The talk died with Jon Muir, with the phones, with the two miles and some.

When Hillary raised the social club idea, he watched it hang in the air as a rhetorical question until he figured the mood was the mood was the mood, and the party lay through the afternoon in their three quiet rooms, removed from all storms but those of their own private making, as the belly of the rabid dog continued its spastic violence into the night.

By the time the dog died, to an unreal silence aglow with a graveyard sun, Jon Muir was shivering and then sweating and shivering again, in full conversation with the Scott Base flu.

※　※　※

Day eight, November eleven, a Wednesday, seven miles under a blue sky with some cloud in it, thin trails of sugar grains spilled over blue glass, and Jon Muir miserably ill.

He was suffering, but he just soldiered on, mile after mile with the fevers and the shakes, dragging his four hundred and forty pounds.

The sleds were particularly boisterous that day: surfing crazily over the shiny wind ruts, pitching like holed ships as they crested the serrated waves of sastrugi, pulling pulling on the traces, knocking the men out of their strides.

> Exhausting, hurting work. How Jon Muir coped, I do not know. It would have been hard enough just to stand in his condition. There wasn't much we could do for him. The horror of the sleds was such that we couldn't lighten his load. It wasn't even talked about for the sake of politeness.
>
> I couldn't have pulled anything extra. By then, in the mornings, I was bleeding into my plastic bag, because the strain of the sled was tearing me a new one.
>
> If I'd taken on a bigger load, I would have got to a bump in the ice, and found myself as stalled as I'd been on that hummock on the eve of our departure—and found that I'd finally given birth to my insides.

They snail-skied toward Minna Bluff, a whalebone of black rock that poked high out of the ice to the south of them, meek more than magnificent. Mount Erebus and Mount Terror were prominent to the north at their backs. And still in sight, as a little black bump now, was Observation Hill. All they had to do was look over their shoulder at the little black bump and imagine, at its foot, the little beds in the little bunker where people took hot showers and ate bacon and beans at table, with talking too.

> Even as a bump it made you feel as if it was only a few hours' happy skiing away.

Satan came to Jesus in the desert when he was suffering and offered him all the marvels of the world, which had to include a hot bath, pleasant things to drink, and explicit respite from his tortured but visionary wanderings. All Christ had to do was abandon the righteous path.

Observation Hill was Hillary's Satan. It said to him, "It's very very nice here. You could be here in no time. Because you're not very far away, are you?"

The Captain and his men would have suffered similarly, because Mount Erebus looked over their homestead, and it stayed on the horizon for a longer time than the little black bump.

Did they find the whiteouts a blessing in this respect? I always did.

❄   ❄   ❄

Hillary was cook again that night. Muir was laid out, shivering, sweating. Philips worked the phone, the batteries dying now. Muir's illness was talked about on a radio show somewhere; made a few extra lines in the newspaper reports.

After a day with Observation Hill poking him in the back, Hillary's automatic hands were in play again, reaching for the ice, filling the mugs, stirring the gruel as the half removed clatter of bowls took him to various elsewheres, his eyes playing with the little blue flame, his ears tuned to the cheery sound of the burner. The stove made a place beyond the wilderness, beautiful or otherwise.

I've always felt that way about a stove. If you get caught out in bad weather on a hill, the best thing you can do is dig out a snow hole, climb into your sleeping bag, and get the stove going. Soon you have a brew in your hands and life starts to feel pretty damn good.

The meal was taken with occasional business or banter exchanges, fits and starts and momentary murmurs, all of which he automatically fielded and returned and didn't notice that they'd stopped coming and everyone was in their rooms again. Philips may have been repairing something or making his notes, his head down the other end of the tent with the mucoused Muir. Hillary was blind to them, such was the stove's enchantment.

There were still the three thermoses to be filled. His reaching arms did their automatic swing as the cheery chuffing of the little blue flame made a choir with the soft roaring sound of water on the boil. It was a familiar song, welcoming him to the kitchen table in the old family home, where his father was sitting with a cup of tea in his hands.

A cup of tea around the kitchen table in our family was more often than not about drinking tea, not light conversational chatter. And so it was on this occasion, an afternoon in eighty-five, except after the second cup Dad said, "Would you like to go to the North Pole?"

My jaw dropped as he laid out the plan.

Dad had just been named New Zealand high commissioner, or ambassador, to India and was due to fly over and set up house in New Delhi. I was shortly off to Nepal, to lead a trekking group; paying the bills, enjoying the hills.

Just a few weeks after that cup of tea in the kitchen, our chores on the subcontinent completed, we found ourselves in Delhi for a few days before flying out to Canada. It was the premonsoon, and conditions were typically dry and desperately hot. Every day there were reports of deaths from heatstroke and dehydration, and the mercury seemed to live around the forty-four to forty-six degrees Celsius mark. A hundred and ten Fahrenheit and then some. It was cooler on the plane, and cooler again on the ground in Edmonton, where we met the rest of the team—notably, Neil Armstrong the astronaut. Quiet, serious, dead to the attentions of anonymous admirers, but he didn't mind the few good laughs.

There were also a number of people from the Canadian climbing community coming north. I already knew one of them, Pat Morrow, who had climbed Everest in eighty-two, when I was in Base Camp and going for neighboring Lhotse. I knew of the prominent polar traveler Martin Williams, while I had never heard of the quiet and pleasant Stephen Fossett, whose company I enjoyed over the two weeks of the trip. Later Steve would attempt Everest and the Seven Summits, although he wisely turned around at Camp One on Everest, and soon afterward changed his focus to balloons and the circumnavigation of the globe, for which he's now famous.

Most hilarious was a marvelous character called Mike Dunn. During our travels, Mike told me that he'd had a troubled childhood.

"What happened?" I asked.

"I ran away from home a lot."

"How old were you?"

"Oh, about thirteen," Mike replied.

"Where did you run to?"

"Mexico."

It was the runaway Mike Dunn who came up with the idea of landing at the North Pole in Twin Otter planes fitted with skis.

In Edmonton, however, we all boarded a Boeing 737 that flew north over the freezing tundra of early spring, first to Yellowknife in the Northwest Territories, and then over the ice encrusted islands of the Northwest Passage to Resolute Bay, where we landed on an ice slick runway.

We disembarked into the minus thirties. I remember the shock of the cold as we left the aircraft and walked across the ice to the small terminal building. After the artificial comforts of the plane, the cold hit us like a wall, and all my time in high frozen places was temporarily forgotten.

We spent a couple of days at Resolute Bay, and visited the neighboring Inuit village with its simple houses and heated water pipe lines and rows of trucks and snowmobiles. There were Huskies tethered to a rope and simple wooden sleds and one large white polar bear skin staked out by the wall of a house to dry in the frigid air. It was minus thirty-five on each of these two days, and there was a light breeze blowing, which made the cold even more brutal. Amazingly, the Inuit children wandered about the village in blue jeans and ski jackets, while we marched about awkwardly like Michelin men in our voluminous insulated clothing.

In the evenings, the younger members of the group gathered at one of the aircraft hangars at the airstrip, to shout our tales of derring-do at one another. We had to shout because the scene was owned by a motley group of locals who stood around in the lounge of one of the offices, drinking, with very loud music playing. In the corner, a television set screened a succession of depraved blue movies, and the music drowned out the "ooh ah" soundtrack.

At one point I was talking with a young Royal Canadian Mounted Police officer, and I noticed his eyes wandering to porn corner. Then he'd wince and raise his eyebrows as he looked back at the shouted conversations.

On the second evening, an executive jet flew in, and the Australian captain told us a few wild stories of his own. He said that his client had come to the icy wastes with his son, to shoot polar bears with bows and arrows, after tracking them down from small airplanes.

A few months earlier he had flown a man across the Atlantic in his 707 to Marseille, where they had picked up two missiles and then flown east with what he described as "carte blanche" clearance into Iraq, where the missiles were removed. The captain maintained that the missiles were fired upon Iran a short time later.

"And what did you do then?" we asked.

"We flew back across the Mediterranean to Sicily. (The man) wanted to party. He told me to take the plane over to France and get him some girls. So I did. He's the boss."

A day later we flew north again, to Ellesmere Island, in the Arctic Circle, landing on a frozen oval of ice called Lake Hazen. We were to wait at the lake for the right conditions, for the last legs north to the Pole. Banks of low cloud drifted in,

filled with ice mist. It was minus thirty, minus forty. We retreated to an insulated Quonset hut, where we drank endless
cups of tea and listened to everybody's stories: my father and
Everest and his other adventures, Neil Armstrong and his
mission to the moon.

I'd really wanted to ask Neil about his lunar experiences,
but I'd seen my father suffer the endless question "What was
it like on top of Mount Everest?" and knew well enough to
leave the moon man be. I think everyone was a little conscious of this . . . sensitivity, in respect to Neil and to my father.

But the mountain hut atmosphere brought out the stories,
as we all hoped. Neil talked about his life as a test pilot and
his interest in aircraft. He had read a lot about the Arctic and
was very knowledgeable about early Arctic exploration, particularly the early attempts at exploring the high latitudes
from balloons. And finally, he told us how they had guided
the landing vehicle down to the surface of the moon, constantly changing their approach path as they descended toward the lunar surface.

"I had a pencil and a piece of paper up against the window
to help me calculate the angle of approach," he said.

It was just what I wanted to hear. They really did steer that
thing and land it on the moon. Living breathing beings did
the job, not a pre-programmed computer.

By the second day, with the cloud still drifting in, people
were getting a little restless, even bored, and Mike Dunn announced we should go fishing. It was around thirty-five to
forty below outside, and I couldn't imagine the fish were
jumping.

One of the pilots who was taking us north brought out a
chain saw, the other a strong reel of fishing line. Out we
trailed after them, in search of fish. In less than a minute
a thick sewer lid of ice was cut from the surface of the lake.

The cold water steamed with the differential of water and air temperatures, and into this seeming cauldron we lowered the line.

Within a short time we had nibbles on the line. I don't remember that they even put bait on the hook, so the fish (Arctic char) must have been very hungry or not particularly discerning. One by one we hooked them, reeled them in. As they emerged from the water, they only got three kicks on the end of the hook before they were "schnap" frozen. We ended up with a pile of them; some right hooked, some left hooked, some S-shaped and a few straight ones too. The Arctic char tasted delicious whatever their orientation.

After nearly three days waiting on the banks of Lake Hazen, our two captains announced that conditions were suitable for the polar leg, and we scrambled into the aircraft, bundled in all our warm clothes and breathing clouds that frosted up the windows, plated them with ice. As the planes taxied and scraped over the lake, we rubbed the windows and peered out, and when the engines roared loudly we watched and felt that strange and hypnotic phase of flight where the three dimensions are experienced at their greatest: as you pull away from the ground.

Soon we were climbing through the thousands on the altimeter as we droned north over the icy hills, to the northern tip of land at Alert, and on out over the frozen sea. The delineation of land and sea seemed indistinct, but the concentric lines of pressure ridges and crumpled plates of ice told of the war of oceanic currents below. We flew in tandem at ten thousand feet for hours. I stared down in amazement at the plates of sea ice and occasional leads of open sea that cut across the fields of white.

At eighty-six degrees North we glided down toward the sea ice. Through the rimed window I spotted a cluster of tents upon the ice. I felt a moment of confusion, and even wondered if we had turned back without my realizing, and then I saw we were coming in toward a short squat plate of sea ice fringed by tall pressure ridges. The captain engaged the reverse pitch, which growled loudly, and we slapped down upon the plain of ice. Turning the plane sharply, we drove across toward the cluster of tents. There was a group of men standing out there encased in their polar suits, standing motionless and watching our approach. They looked lonely and rather cold in their ice encrusted suits. As we climbed out of the two little planes, they weren't saying much either. But they were friendly.

Soon we were refueling the aircraft from fifty-five gallon drums and walking around the camp.

"What do you guys do here?" I asked.

"We're a research camp. Studying the ice and atmosphere and listening for whales," said a bearded man who seemed to be in charge.

Then into my ear one of the flight crew whispered. "They're listening for submarines. It's classified."

The bearded base leader continued. "See, over there . . ." He pointed to a number of ice drills set up near the tents. "We lower sensors, hydrophones, down into the sea."

"Amazing," I said. "Do you have to be careful about leads ripping through your camp?"

"That happened not too long ago," he said. "The ice sheet split through the camp, and we had to move quickly to prevent the tents and equipment from falling into open water. Say, it's a little cold out here. Do you want to come indoors?"

Their insulated tents were equipped with floors and gas heaters . . . and computers, video screens, books, family photographs—all the comforts and mainstays of home life. There were six of them camped there, as I recall, and they came from all over the United States.

We talked about the cold and the isolation. "It's tough," one of them told me. "I'm from Southern California!"

Their stove made a cheery chuffing sound too.

❅ ❅ ❅

Day nine was a good day, a new best at eight miles and some, halfway to their required daily average, but Jon Muir still very pale and out of it with his sickness, no sign of it easing, still soldiering on.

There was a **cool southerly** blowing a dry scald in their faces, and they pulled up their neck warmers to sit over their mouths, their cheeks, over the lobes of their ears. Then they put on the plastic masks that covered their faces from chin to hairline, looking half samurai, half astronaut. Their goggles like windows in the masks.

Minna Bluff was drawing closer as they worked their way up the distant coast of White Island, but a large field of small crevasses and picket fence sastrugi kept robbing them of their straight line of travel.

While many of the crevasses had strong snow bridges, there were almost as many better avoided. And in stretches the jagged shards of sastrugi weaved around and in between the cracks in the ground, and beyond, making mazes of knee high impossibility for the sleds.

Their route wandered drunkenly from trouble spot to trouble spot until they made clear country again.

> For the most part we navigated using shadows that moved around us at fifteen degrees per hour. At midday, our shadow was directly in front of us. When it lay to our left, we knew that it was six o'clock and time to stop for the day.
>
> We also used compasses, but the great magnetic variation at the bottom of the world meant that the compass needle— dragged one hundred and fifty degrees East on the dial—appeared to be pointing more to the north than the south. Our headings were commonly around thirty degrees magnetic for most of the journey. At the end of each day we would check our GPS units to get an accurate fix on where we were and how far we had traveled.
>
> While we occasionally veered off to one side or the other,

on the whole our headings each day proved pretty accurate. The natural navigation of steering on our shadows or steering relative to the oncoming wind or cutting across the lines of sastrugi at a particular angle proved very reliable.

In many ways this was all part of becoming acclimatized to our environment. The Aborigines of desert Australia were masters at reading their harsh trackless landscape. The Polynesians were masters of their watery domain as they traveled and colonized the length and breadth of the Pacific.

In a similar spirit and with similar tools, trusting the wind and the shadows and the shapes, the gadgetry left in the sleds, the party sought a similar confident communion with the white plains. To find their place upon it as well as through it.

If the visionary states and the rapture had the color of godhead, walking in communion and under the guidance of the physical landscape was for Peter Hillary akin to submitting to devotion in a church. It was the closest thing he ever got to any sincere faith or belief.

I believe we come from dust and we go to dust, and our lives are what happens in between. I don't believe in God or a spiritual dimension or that there is anything else but wind and chemistry. Our memories and emotions are equations, to me. The mystery is in those equations, and how they flower into physical feeling from dust. It's a cold church but a very beautiful one.

❉   ❉   ❉

Day ten, Friday the thirteenth, another beautiful sparkling day, another record haul of nine miles. But when they set up their tent at the end of it, they were less than sixty miles from Scott Base, and it didn't take the helicopter very long to reach them.

They'd known it was coming.

After lunch we were buzzed by a low flying Hercules aircraft, during my lead as navigator. It was looking for us. There was no wind at all, so we heard the plane's hum come from the

north and suddenly—RIOWWWW!—it was over our heads.
It was something so new and different and magnificent to behold that it almost brought tears to my eyes, this big four engine bird circling about us and waving its wings at us, and you
could see a little man in the cockpit and then he was gone as
the plane turned to the north, to land at our first campsite, the
airfield.

As it disappeared, some of our "staying in character" went
with it, for sure.

The helicopter arrived at about a quarter to eight that night.
Peter Cleary and two technicians, Mike Mahon and Anthony
Powell, were onboard, with new battery charging gear for the
phones and presents of beer and apples.

We heroically said "no, thanks" to the beer and apples, for
the sake of integrity.

Hillary thought they probably should have said "yes, thanks"
and had a blowout. Start over with a party, say to hell with the
last ten days, tie one on, and if it ended in tears and a brawl, then
it was best to get it over with. They needed the beer to bring it
on, and they needed the beer to numb them if it went to hell.

And when he said "no, thanks" too, to the beer under his
eyes, it was with a private, dignified and horrified grief.

We got quickly to business, checking the new charger system,
talked a couple of things over, pleasant but all kind of
brusque. And then off they flew in that gorgeous mechanical
dragonfly, our guests leaving us to our solitude on the ice
shelf.

But not for long. We had our phones again.

"Think I'll call the wife," said Jon. He was still pretty sick.

Observation Hill was a pimple at their backs now. They wouldn't
see it again until their return to it.

And finally, Peter Hillary's social club and Base Camp bonding
ambitions were laid to rest too. He'd brought it up in the lull that
followed the helicopter's departure, by way of putting on a party

without beer. New tensions were accruing daily, so there wasn't going to be any "good" time to bring up happy hour as anything but a possible cure for what was ailing them. This was the time. The night of the helicopter. There was no better time to start over. Why, it was almost mythic.

And then, through the filter of his companions' compassion, Hillary finally got it: they weren't interested, because they . . . weren't interested. To the Pole and back, that's where it was all at, by way of discourse.

That was their equation, and they hadn't kept it a mystery.

❊   ❊   ❊

Day eleven, eight miles: the world was flat, not round. Flat like a sheet of typing paper. No wind early on. Not a hint of it. Everything lay still but the men and their sleds, and they would have appeared to be walking on nothing if anyone had been out there to see them pass by from a distance.

Over their heads a canopy of cloud, spreading low in all directions to the horizon and never meeting it. Under their feet the coated tongue, lying in all directions to the sky and never meeting it. Reflecting off one another, the cloud and the ice were the same color, the same texture—to the eye and the mind they were the same thing. The world was a lighted picture show screen and they were unwashed specks upon it. Still inching along, the scrape of the sleds calling the name of their bodily cargo.

"Sht."

"Sht."

The disquiet inspired by the helicopter's visit the previous evening had lingered on over breakfast and beyond as a communal flatness that matched the world of the day. That they had come and gone so quickly, their hot showered pleasant smelling visitors, only added to the party's sense of marooned dislocation. Muir was in the last of his illness, slowly coming to, but washed out. Philips was talking of pushing harder, going faster, go go go. Hillary was bleeding into the bag again, his shoulders aching constantly now, his belly button wrapping around his spine with each grunt of steam.

>And always, daily, you had to fight off the profound feeling that we weren't getting anywhere, toward anything or any-place—the feeling of being on a treadmill with no end to it.

>Hence, I thought less about the South Pole and would we ever get there, and more about the fact that in another thirty minutes or whatever I'd be enjoying some hot chocolate. I broke each day down that way, into parts, as I would on a long and hard trek through the hills.

But every day was a new world in Antarctica. And some days were impossible to break down into parts, because they were of a seamless construction and persuasion. The still blank immensity of day eleven put the beautiful sparkling yesterday beyond imagining. Hillary's comforter thoughts of the next hot drink were likewise put out of reach. As it was for the eye, it was for the mind: there was nothing to fix on, no sense of scale or perspective, no evidence that there was any other world.

>It was pretty spooky, really, the way it muddied the mind, and this overwhelming feeling that yes, we were in the middle of an everlasting nowhere. The others seemed a long way away, much more than they really were. At one point they melded into one creature, the two halves of a ladybird walking up a white wall.

Maybe Hillary was just going cross eyed with the empty enormity, for there was no easy way to think beyond it.

>And it brought my spirits down.

Now and then through the day, a soft breeze came from behind.

>Eric tried using kites several times as these little tempting puffs of northerly wind came along to frustrate us, petering out as quickly as they came.

That evening Eric Philips started building a large snowblock cairn, to mark their first depot for food, fuel and waste to be left here for retrieval on the return journey. There were to be eight depots in all, placed every hundred miles, with about fifteen pounds taken off each sled at each depot. The food and fuel were buried in the cairns. The turds were put in a red bag and stuck on top of the cairn as a beacon. (Amundsen often used a dead dog to marker his depots.)

Hillary was inside, at the stove again. For a while he brooded uselessly about it, reflecting with bad humor as he thought of Muir promising to do extra shifts at the stove by way of making up for his lack of contribution to the expedition's planning. That the Hillary side of the family saw the world in black and white extended to the notion of "fairness," to honoring one's promises, and to doing one's share. These considerations gave his brooding a fatal righteous tone that stopped the heart, and then he thought of Muir still sick with the flu, and he cringed at where his mind had been taking him.

It was later the cooking matter became a spoken campaign. In the end, Hillary did more cooking than Muir because Muir later got ill again, farther on, when he started exploding, his bowels blowing shrapnel without warning, on occasion taking out everyone and everything in the tent. During that time he was excused from stirring the gruel for everybody's sake.

> **Anyway. It had been a darkly dreamy day outside in the blank and it took a while for the chuffing sound of the burner to sound cheery to me. And then I began enjoying the warmth of the little blue flame rather than just finding relief for my fingers.**

When Hillary built up his campfire that night, he found himself in company with Jon Muir, by way of remembering another time when Muir had been ill. It was one of Peter Hillary's great ripping yarns: the time Jon Muir threw up and saved both their lives.

This was in eighty-seven, when they'd returned to Everest for another bold attempt on another bold route, the South Pillar, one of the steepest on the mountain—a straight "elegant" line nearly all the way to the top.

There were four of them: Muir, Hillary, Hillary's old friend Kim Logan, also back for a second attempt after eighty-four, and another chum, Mike Rheinberger of Melbourne, making his first try.

> One of the things that gave eighty-seven its dark comedy was poor old Mike Rheinberger's hemorrhoids. Mike had them bad, about as bad as you can get them, I believe. Huge, apparently. Mike shared a tent with Kim Logan, up at Camp Two, and we could hear Mike having all this gruesome trouble because these varicose veins were just hanging out of there. One night we heard him making these strange grunts, as if he were trying to pull on tight socks, and then he said, "Kim. Kim. Can you get the torch, mate, and push them back in for me."
>
> Kim's reply: "Nuh! Jesus! Oh, Jesus. Get 'em away."
>
> So Mike started asking everybody.
>
> There was this Austrian eye surgeon on the hill. I think we were peasant farmers in his eyes. However, this didn't discourage Mike Rheinberger from knocking on the surgeon's tent door and asking if the good doctor could put his magic hands to work and heal him. Mike probably thought that making the request in German, with a display of the finest German manners, would make all the difference.
>
> And it did. Instead of saying, "No," the surgeon politely said, "Nein," explaining that his fingers were fine surgical instruments for use around the head only.
>
> Jon Muir was also in hilarious form that year. He could be pretty outrageous in his younger days, Jon Muir. Mostly physical humor. For a while he was the Harpo Marx of mountaineering.
>
> Although I'd seen Muir around the climbing scene in New Zealand in the late seventies and early eighties, we didn't ac-

tually meet until nineteen eighty-two, on an Air India flight out of New Delhi, where I also first met Mark Moorhead, Craig Nottle and my good friend Roddy MacKenzie. They'd just done an excellent climb on Changabang, nearly seven thousand meters. I'd been on Lhotse with Fred From.

Anyway, Muir made an impression because he kept asking for the leftover meals from the trolley. When he finished with one, he asked for another, and he made this great slobbering spectacle as he polished them off, licking the trays clean, just camped it up. He kept asking for the meals until there weren't any left.

At Everest Base Camp, in eighty-seven, Jon Muir was even more ebullient.

There was a glamorous expedition camped nearby, driven by a glamorous American woman named Karen Fellerhoff. Her boyfriend was a well to do Swiss fellow, heir to the Toblerone fortune. So Karen was accustomed to the good life, and she brought a party atmosphere to Base Camp by planting pink flamingos in the moraine rubble around the American tents, and generously opening up a crate of French Champagne as the need arose. Veuve Clicquot—La Grande Dame, s'il vous plaît.

Karen Fellerhoff loved the expedition scene. She was urbane and articulate and elegant, with long blond hair, very good at getting into boardrooms and raising funds and other expeditionary necessities . . . like crates of Veuve Clicquot.

I was always pleased to be invited over, when they'd pull out another bottle, and what a sadness each time as a third of the precious cargo came gushing in the low atmospheric pressure at seventeen thousand six hundred feet. Then they'd pour the remainder into old furry plastic mugs that had had soup in them half an hour before. Barbarism, really.

Jon Muir took great pleasure in wandering over and freaking out their more conservative sensibilities. He'd smear bright red and purple lipstick all over his face. (He was using lipstick instead of sunblock because it was thicker, I think.) He'd paint his entire face until it was a gaudy plate of red and purple.

Then he'd put on a broad brimmed hat and a red sash and wander over in this, um, mincing fashion. He'd walk up to whoever was most visibly squirming, put his arm around the shoulder of the discomfited soul, and drawl in his ear for some time. He's a hairy fellow, Muir. It was quite a show. The antics helped pass the time. No one had climbed the mountain the previous year, because of bad weather and deep unstable snow up high. The nineteen eighty-seven season passed the same way.

We walked in on the first legal day of the season, and Muir and I were still there at the end of it, after everybody else had gone home. We walked out on the last legal day after living above seventeen thousand feet for two and a half months.

What happened to Kim Logan and Mike Rheinberger in the meantime was one of the strangest things I've ever seen. What made it even stranger was that Kim and Mike's odyssey was presaged by a conversation we'd had in the mess tent before heading up.

It was an old conversation. It was a conversation I've had many times over the years. It was all about the deals you make or don't make to get to the top. In the case of the eighty-seven mess tent talk: how many fingers were we prepared to lose to frostbite in exchange for the summit of Everest? I remember Kim saying, "Oh, I suppose if I lost a little finger . . ."

I could understand it. Sure, if I could be assured of it: alpine style, without oxygen, South Pillar, get up and get down, and yes, lose most of the little finger on my left hand, I'd go for it and I'd feel eight feet tall.

But, really, it's not like that. It's not a deal made. If you're prepared to make a deal, it's likely to get out of control. If you're prepared to lose one or two fingers, then you're going to lose both your hands. If you lose your hands, you're going to lose your life. It's the boring old "thin end of the wedge."

I always go out with the attitude that you're not going to lose a fingernail. The reality is, I've had injuries, I've nearly been killed and the rest of it, but you can't go out prepared to sacrifice pieces of your body for the prize. It's all about knowing when to push, and when to back off.

Soon after having the finger conversation, there was a break in the weather, and Hillary and company went up through the icefall, and up the sloping glaciated highway of the Western Cwm to Camp Two, at twenty-one thousand feet. The weather was unpredictable. When a brief window opened, Logan and Rheinberger wanted to go for it, try for the top. Hillary and Muir argued that the conditions didn't seem quite right.

It's always a gamble. You never really know. So Kim and Mike went up. They climbed for a long day, and then climbed on for a second day and then got stuck in a storm at about twenty-six thousand five hundred feet, in the death zone. They didn't have any supplemental oxygen. We weren't using bottled gas.

I later learned that Kim had wanted to turn around and reverse down after the first day's climb up the pillar, but Mike wanted to keep going. I don't think Mike was comfortable with the steep and technical terrain, but he wouldn't back off, probably because he didn't want to reverse down the exposed face they had just climbed. Kim wanted to back off, but Mike wanted to keep going, so Kim kept going with him. Soloing up and then the storm came in.

It was so cold up there that their breath froze in thick plates onto the walls of the tent, and the wind was so wild it whipped up dense blizzards, full storms inside the tent, again and again. It happens sure, these storms inside the tent. But it was so bad for Mike and Kim that they could hardly breathe.

> They were drowning in it, in this storm of ice particles inside
> their tent.

Hillary hadn't seen them for two days, couldn't spot them
through the storm or through the cloud that hung around after
the storm. He started to think they were dead. He did the numbers, and the numbers said they were probably dead.

> Initially I thought perhaps they'd gone for the top. But condi-
> tions changed and they had to get down, so they couldn't be
> at the top, so where were they? And I remember thinking,
> "This is it." They were up in the death zone. I believed, by my
> calculations, up around eight thousand meters. No bottled
> gas. Gone two days, we're into a third day. Caught in a storm.
> It was shrieking up there. We could hear it from Camp Two:
> the squadron of falling jet planes. You had to wonder if their
> tent was being shredded up there. It was very cold at Camp
> Two, so it would have been brutal up top.
>
> I was out of my mind, and I was furious with them too. Stu-
> pid bastards and the other things you say when you're out of
> your mind with worry.
>
> It had been hard coming back to Everest. From Camp Two I
> could look up and see the site of our old snow cave, where
> Fred From and Craig Nottle spent their second to last night,
> three years before, in eighty-four. And here it was all happen-
> ing again. Two more mates. I was physically sick with waiting
> to know what had happened to them.

On the third day there was a slight break in the weather, through
a window in the cloud and there they were, Kim Logan and
Mike Rheinberger, coming down the ropes on the Lhotse Face,
rappelling over the Yellow Band and down the broad central ice
gully, and Hillary could see that Kim Logan was out of his mind,
frantic.

> We saw him unclip from the rope, and he kept on coming
> down the gully, solo, no rope, and Jon and I were thinking,
> "What the hell is he doing?" Fall and die.

When we got to them out in the Western Cwm, I was shocked at how they looked. They were such a mess. They were chronically dehydrated, and they said they had frostbitten fingers and toes. They were on the edge, and I wasn't hugely confident that we could bring them back. I mean, if they'd both fallen down dead, I wouldn't have been that surprised. Unbelievable, how they looked.

Kim was in his mid thirties; Mike was in his forties. But they looked as if they'd aged another thirty or forty years. More. I've never seen anything like it in my life. They looked like prune people. Ancient people.

Mike looked like he was a hundred years old. I remember thinking, "Jesus, he is done for."

Back at Camp Two, Jon Muir took Mike Rheinberger into one tent; Hillary took Kim Logan into the other. He took off Logan's boots and socks and mittens and gloves, to check out his fingers and toes. They were all black sausages.

Could we save them, I had no idea. Once they turn to black frozen sausages, it's marginal. Chop, chop, chop, chop. Chop.

I started pouring electrolytes into him, probably a gallon of liquid, more. I gave him a vasodilator drug to help get the circulation going again. Jon was doing the same thing with Mike. We both worked on our person, getting him out of his damp gear, putting him into fresh dry things, and getting him into his sleeping bag.

As I was tucking Kim in, he said to me, "Pete, it's gonna be all right. We'll be able to go up again tomorrow."

It floored me. I just quietly said, "No. No. We're gonna go down."

The biggest concern was that once Kim's feet and hands started to defrost, he was going to be in terrible pain. Bad bad. We had to get him down fast, before he started to defrost, while he still couldn't feel anything.

We had a devil of a time getting them down. Mike's frostbite wasn't as bad—a couple of toes, a finger. But he was still out of it, from being up there too long. There wasn't much we could do for Kim but walk at his side, and help him stay on his feet. A big man, he was suffering, but he was amazingly stoic. It would have felt as if they had already been chopped off.

By the time we got to Base Camp, Kim had forgotten about going for the top, and he focused on saving his digits. We went to work defrosting them, by bathing them in a warm potassium permanganate solution, in less than sterile conditions, but we did our best. Kim still can't fully straighten the fingers on his left hand: they're slightly atrophied. But he didn't lose any of them, fingers or toes. He got away with it.

Kim had to get to a doctor and to the thick air of lower altitude, but he couldn't walk downvalley, so we put him on a yak, and he rode out with some champion Sherpas to care for him. It took some months before his black sausages looked like fingers and toes again.

Mike hung around for a while, talking of going up again. It disappointed me that he couldn't see reality. Sometimes you have to say enough is enough.

After a while Mike saw how it was, that he had nothing left inside, and that he'd certainly lose his frostbitten parts if he didn't move to warmer climes. And eventually Mike followed Kim Logan downvalley, limping all the way with his bad toes.

❋ ❋ ❋

Mike Rheinberger came back to Everest the following year, the year after that and again, and again, every year for eight years, he came back and tried for the top. His quest ended in ninety-five.

He summited very late, at seven p.m., with the light all but gone and his oxygen tank all but exhausted. With seasoned Himalayan climber Mark Whetu, he descended a short distance down the North Ridge. They were both struggling, washed out, near zombies.

On a narrow ledge high on the northern side of Everest, Mike Rheinberger sat down. He planned to spend the night and descend in the light of the next day. Mark Whetu sat down beside him, telling himself not to fall asleep, banging his boots together, his hands together. Mike leaned across to Mark Whetu, put his arms around him, and they both fell into oblivion.

Some time later, Whetu woke up horrified to find himself still sitting near the top of Everest. His feet were frozen. He found people trying to call him on the radio.

Whetu then woke Rheinberger, found him making slurred sounds, found that he was flopping about and couldn't coordinate his movements. He got him propped up, urged him on. They began an agonizingly slow descent until Mike Rheinberger couldn't stay on his feet. Once he sat down again, he couldn't be roused.

Meanwhile Base Camp got through to Whetu over the radio. Mark Whetu told them about Mike Rheinberger, still alive but sinking, with a cerebral edema brought on by the altitude. Rheinberger's head was filling up with fluid, squeezing to nothing his mind, his ability to stand or otherwise move, all of him. Base Camp immediately urged Mark Whetu to leave Mike Rheinberger and get down as fast as his frozen feet and wooden hands would allow; they told him to save himself.

He couldn't do it at first. He couldn't leave him, and then he had to leave him, and he left Rheinberger sitting there with who knows what going through his mind. Before heading up, Rheinberger had looked into a video camera and declared the climb "a do or die effort."

One of the fellows blown from the top of K2 said a similar thing, smiling beautifully at the time. "Summit or die. Either way I win." That was in ninety-five too.

※　※　※

Half their team was gone, the team of eighty-seven, but Peter Hillary and Jon Muir stayed on. The bad weather stayed too.

Back up at Camp Two, they noticed a three millibar drop of pressure on the barometer. A thirty or forty millibar drop at sea level is a warning that a hurricane is about to come through and trash all the resorts. At twenty-one thousand feet, a three millibar drop gives the same warning. The shift in the air to violence was in play as they started down.

American climber David Breashears (of IMAX fame) and some of his team stayed up, and when the storm hit, Breashears was rolled in his tent one hundred yards or so down the Western Cwm before he managed to get out, lucky not to be killed. The storm had torn the tent from its anchors.

The bad weather followed Muir and Hillary down to Base Camp, sat on top of them for a few days. Then it lulled and they went back up the icefall again. At Camp Two, they found their tents destroyed, their sleeping bags filled with ice.

> So we painstakingly rebuilt our home away from home and waited for the elusive window in the weather, the good moment.
>
> It never came; people started leaving. I remember when the Austrian team left and Hanns Schell, the leader, walked by our tent in the Western Cwm. He was on his way down because he had decided enough was enough and as he came by he said to us, short and sharp, "Gut-bye . . . Unt gut luck."

By the end of October, they were the only souls left on Mount Everest. They were spent. If the window had suddenly opened, they wouldn't have been fit to take advantage of it. They were wearing out their welcome at altitude. On the way down from Camp Two, for the last time, they were nearly killed in the icefall.

Muir wasn't feeling well. And at one point he stopped to vomit in the central icefall and Hillary stopped there for a minute as Muir cleaned himself up. They moved on, with Muir leading, maybe thirty feet ahead.

They were coming through what is known as the atom bomb area, as named by Ed Hillary on the first foray through the ice-

fall, in fifty-one, on a reconnaissance expedition with the great
Eric Shipton. (It has been called the Traverse and in recent years
the "eggshell area.")

> The atom bomb traverse area is an unstable and tangled part
> of the icefall, where the ice piles up like a logjam, and period-
> ically collapses without warning—blue office blocks of ice,
> five stories, seven stories high, leaning towers, human mouse-
> traps.
>
> This was where people had been killed in two accidents in
> eighty-two, three Sherpas and a Canadian dead. I was in Base
> Camp, going for Lhotse, and the Canadian fellow, a very per-
> sonable fellow, had come to our mess tent and shared the
> good laughs and campfire stories the night before he died.

As Hillary and Muir came through the tangle, following the fixed
ropes, where they were standing suddenly started tipping,
everything around them tipping. Just like in the movies. With no
clue where to go, they unclipped from the ropes and started to
run and move around, to keep their feet.

> It was like a huge earthquake. Everything was collapsing and
> moving. I'd started running back up the hill. Suddenly it just
> stopped, and Muir and I looked at each other silently for
> about thirty seconds and sort of shook ourselves. Shrugged.
> Carried on.
>
> The area in front of Jon, a platform of tangled office blocks,
> had just dropped away. Everything that had been there be-
> fore was gone; all that remained were shards of clean sharp
> green ice, old glacial ice, shards of it, razor sharp, the size of
> small cars and refrigerators.
>
> And that's where we would have been if Jon Muir hadn't
> vomited—minced in that collapse, impaled. I've carried the
> remains of people out of this place, out of such a mess. I knew
> what we'd missed.
>
> Jon and I had been up and down the icefall and through the
> atom bomb area about twenty times, acclimatizing and haul-

ing gear to the high camps, because we weren't using high altitude porters. Sooner or later something had to give.

*   *   *

Day twelve, ten miles under a sky that blew sunny to overcast, the blue glass above periodically scrubbed by fleeting fat rags of cloud, until all the rags were herded and the sky became overcast again. The wind came up at their backs, from the north, steady and firm but not speedy. They hauled the first ninety minutes as the wind found its measure. After the hot drinks, they put up their number seven kites and let the wind do the work.

It was fantastic. Figure eighting, the elegant curved orange canopies dragged us along on our telemark skis, with our sleds attached behind, at between five to ten miles an hour.

It was salvation from slavery, sailing across the wretched sastrugi with a concentrated ease, over the coarse sandlike snow patches that made me pant when man hauling, and on toward the southern horizon. There was a horizon. All I needed was a wayward bird to fly in my wake and I might well have burst into song. But not for long.

Sadly, Jon's skiing and kiting skills were not good, and we spent much of the day standing, waiting, freezing as the northerly gently streamed south. While we didn't travel a great distance, it was a respectable day with lots of learning about flying kites with sleds in tow.

We stopped at half past six, or eighteen-thirty on the expeditionary twenty-four hour clock, and made camp on a patch of flat white snow that was indistinguishable from what lay all around and out to the horizons.

Eric had showed a great deal of patience with Jon, and I must say it impressed me. It had been particularly frustrating, because if we had really applied ourselves with the kites, we would have covered about sixty miles. Ten days in one with much less effort and much more fun.

We crossed our fingers the northerly would stay with us. But at eleven p.m. it slowed and turned to a southerly.

I was disappointed that Muir hadn't got the basics together before the trip. He didn't look too happy either. Four days of illness. Wanting to head back to Scott Base, because he was slowing us down on the days we could have most gained ground. It was hard on him. He was having a hell of a trip.

* * *

I remember too, from eighty-seven on Everest, Muir was quite troubled and sad in himself. It became more apparent as we stayed on for that last week of the season, when we were the only two people on Everest and nothing was really happening. We were up at twenty-one thousand feet and just sat there for a while.

It was a spooky time, alone in the Western Cwm, at twenty-one thousand feet. That's one thing I remember. We were so alone. Camp Two had this feeling of a deserted camp, a big junk heap of abandoned tents and gear.

It was brutally cold too. We were only getting four or five hours of sunshine because it was getting toward winter and the sun didn't peep over the Nuptse Ridge for long. We were talking about going up to the South Col if the weather was fair, but we weren't up to doing anything, really. We were run down, nothing left.

We recognized some of our gear from the eighty-four expedition, which had been blown away and down to the cwm, and that was terribly haunting. Fred, Craig, what had the wind done to them over those three years past, where were they? Much of the week was spent remembering them.

Most of the time, Jon Muir and I just lay in our sleeping bags, in separate tents, and occasionally got together to eat. Anyway, he was quite troubled and sad in himself at that time. He thinks about things for a very long time before speaking of them. And it was about the only time he ever really talked to me, heart to heart. "The wife's gone walkabout," he said rather obliquely one day.

We made it down, both of us unscathed, Muir and I. Time passed, years, then the South Pole trip. Bit of a shame, really.

CHAPTER THIRTEEN

A few months back I had an odd experience. I had entertained a young Greenpeace couple who had been working in Antarctica. On the last day the young man asked was I Bill Denz's mother? The following week I had a very vivid dream that I was watching the interior of a hut in Antarctica and Bill's voice came clearly as if in the same room. "Hullo, Mum, how nice to see you again." I gasped and said, "Bill, what on earth are you doing there?" "Oh, I am now looking after the boys in Antarctica," he said. It gave me a nice warm feeling inside.

From a letter to Peter Hillary, written by Cecily Denz,
Bill's mother, five years after he died on Makalu

Day thirteen, a Monday, eleven miles, and the world was a flat sheet of typing paper again, and again everything lay still but the men and their sleds. The northerly that had blown to a southerly late in the night, had blown itself out as they'd slept.

No wind. No sky. They wouldn't see a sky for the next three days, no sun for three days, nothing but variations of the great white everywhere, where there was nothing to fix on, for the eye or the mind.

Antarctica, their beautiful torturer, following the tradition of the best tormentors, had taken the first dozen days to slap them around and soften them up, get their hopes up with some good weather, only to slap them around again with a new set of plagues. For the next three days the blank came to play with their heads, like an evil psychologist.

Hillary was already shifting into his siege, still with half a hopeful eye that the social weather might change, but standing sentry nonetheless against the boredom, the loneliness. When he locked in and leaned-to, conscious of the blank immensity and its thought robbing powers, aware that his mind would be muddied if he didn't lock himself away somewhere, Hillary fixated on furniture and home decoration by way of keeping the day at bay. It held him for two shifts, through the bus stop lunch.

Weary of stained floors and carpets, he brought his wife into the scene, and had the sort of long conversation he might have otherwise had with her from a hotel room somewhere. He was away a lot; the lecture scene, leading trekking parties, paying the bills, telling his wife he missed her. As they had their conversation in his mind, after a time it started to feel as if he were talking to a picture postcard.

When he found himself moving uphill, and unable to talk it away, he took it as a teasing prod from the blank, as a personal message that there was no resisting it. And there was no resisting it. The sled took on the extra weight of being hauled uphill, even when he closed his eyes and tried to put himself on a piece of familiar flat ground, for there was none to be found.

From time to time the world changed direction, and he found he was heading downhill; he could feel it in his shoulders, the slight respite. It was better going downhill until he found himself turning forty-five degrees to the right and then following a track between two stone walls where there was a smell of lighted cigarettes and wet dust and then a hot breeze in his face, and then just the flat sheet of typing paper and the breeze remaining, a burning whisper from the south that stayed throughout the afternoon.

The breeze was something to think about, and then worry about because they needed a good wind from the north. He spent the rest of the day wanting a good north wind, wanting one to come up steady and firm and everlasting, and wanting Jon Muir to get it together with the kites and the skis so they could all sail and sail across the coated tongue, because he wasn't able to hold it off, the feeling that they weren't getting anywhere.

They hauled an extra twenty or thirty minutes that day, made their best distance.

Hillary called Yvonne. They talked about decorating the house, how they missed each other, how busy he'd be when he got home, traveling, working. Pretty much everything he'd already talked about with her in the imagined sitting room with the stained floor and Nepalese carpets.

The wind picked up in the evening, buffeting the tent. He sat and had a hot chocolate and tried to have new conversations with his wife, his kids, friends. Everyone at home was becoming a picture postcard. The regular life was becoming another album of stilled memory. It amazed him more than it bothered him. It would have made a great philosophical discussion over a glass of wine somewhere.

❉   ❉   ❉

Day fourteen, eight miles. They woke to find themselves in the belly of the rabid dog again. Outside the tent, they found the cloud ceiling from the previous day had fallen to the ground. As Hillary noted in his diary:

> **A windy, cloudy, lost-in-space day. Where the three of us trudged south on our skis as if moving upon a layer of cloud within clouds and surrounded by them. Our white world is without boundaries and orientation. The world goes on indefinitely.**

Today all our breaks were spent sitting on a mat on the snow beside one of the sleds with our bivvy sack pulled over us. As the sack cracked and whipped in the savage winds, we huddled together and drank from our mugs and ate from our food bags until time was up and we returned to the wind and spindrift and the eternity of man-hauling.

Each of us cocooned in our jackets and tucked away behind our goggles and masks in our own isolated worlds of thought. They are the only thing that sustains you out on the ice shelf when there is no horizon, no visual context upon which to focus and make your goal.

The problem was finding the thoughts to sustain him, beyond an appeal to boredom to stay well away. And again he found himself walking uphill through a boiling brightness, no matter how the accident inspector tried to explain it away.

They were sly little visions that day, rising up and falling away, filling up the picture show screen and leaving it blank again until something new was projected there for a moment. It was like attending a lazy slide show in a smoky room.

Most things he recognized; some things he didn't.

He saw an overhanging boulder that made a cave the size of a downed cow, and there was a fire smoldering in there, and for a moment he had the sense of lying by the fire in a sleeping bag, with two other people in their bags beside him, their heads tucked inside from the cold, for the light beyond the cave was a dark blue of early morning. He knew the place but couldn't name it. Somewhere in the Himalayas, but where and with whom he couldn't say, because he'd slept that way in many places, with a good number of people, and it wasn't up on the screen for long.

That it gave him something to ponder, he took as a gift from his mind, until he was distracted by something new, a vast field of barley through which he once strode with a thick head of hair and a beard the color of the field, the grained grass coming halfway up his chest, the whole world gold but for a blue sky and only for the moment it took him to recognize the place and then it dissolved into the clouds within clouds that surrounded him.

In another moment he had the view from a corner table in a café called Tiamo in the Italian quarter of Melbourne, where there were heavy wood paneled walls with smoke stained posters pasted and middle aged Italian women in cook hats and floral dresses and aprons silently toiling over the stoves across the counter at the back, and too many young people wearing black and the froth on top of the coffee colored caramel, and cigarette smoke making streaked clouds in the slivers of light that came through a high window, and everywhere else dim and populated with chatter, and always those old men in their felt hats and waistcoats and faded suits who seemed to live at the table across the aisle with a platter of smoked meats and cheeses.

The café then lit up bright and faded bright as the clouds filled up with a train station in India, on a very hot day where a man wandered up and down the platform with a platter slung from his neck bearing bread and mysterious fillings and the man calling, "Samweege. Samweeeege," until he was lost to a cloud of steam from the old train's boilers.

Soon after, Hillary saw the great Fred From walking up a steepening slope in a balaclava that put an oval frame around his face.

He saw baby photographs of his children, strange faces from over the years, some dogs running wild and they gave him a start because he'd been attacked once by dogs while cycling the back roads near a Victorian country town during the early days of exile from his children.

He only saw the dogs as four legged smudges.

Philips and Muir were blurred smudges on blotting paper.

In the afternoon he saw a line of blurred smudges to the west of where he was hauling, ponies and men in balaclavas, and he figured it was the Captain and his caravan.

And there were blurred smudges that Hillary didn't recognize. Shapes of people who lay down before he could ponder their identity, if he'd been so moved.

Now and then a fragment of conversation would come into his head, and for a moment he would pick up that conversation before it was lost to him or before it fell away to a single line for contemplation that couldn't be avoided. There was one line that kept coming up, and Hillary considered it a dark joke:

"We know you guys are out there. We're here for you."
Now and then the wind would punch him in the face. It was streaming from the south against his face and chest, but sometimes it gusted and shoved him around. Still, he stayed wherever he was, with the vision of the moment, or the violent blank in between. It was an exhausting day inside and out, body and soul. And it didn't end when he crawled inside the belly of the rabid dog that night.

As Hillary noted in his diary:

> **Today my compass housing broke and needed repair, my mitten leashes needed improvement, the skins on my skis needed adjustment, a cord needed to be attached to my mug's lid so I don't lose it, I have a small blister on one toe, this journal needs writing, there are coordinates recorded, and I am cook for the night. Six liters of boiling water to be created from snow and poured into our three thermoses, dinner, four drinks each, and preparations for breakfast at six a.m.**

The cheery chuffing sound couldn't work its magic on his weariness, couldn't take him somewhere pleasant. Half his mind was out there with the slide show, the other half distracted by his chores and the call to lie down and pass out. From his postscript to the day:

> **Tired. We are all. And so to sleep. For far too few hours. In a tent warm and cozy that sits like a tiny red cell upon a white plain of cold and wind and sterility. Nil life.**

❊   ❊   ❊

When the dead friends lay down again, they took all color and conversation with them. They drained the world, leaving again the burning emptiness to behold, the great white everywhere.

His grandfather taught him how to bury and raise the dead. As a small boy he had found it a sad and marvelous thing to do. Later Peter Hillary found that he had to bury the dead over and over, and that any joy taken from raising them often left him as one was left after a night of visionary drinking: swearing you'll never do it again. He had spent many years holding them back, all the dead friends.

Well, isn't that how it is for everybody?
Down on the blank there was no holding them back now. Two weeks out in the deep sub zero, there was nothing to see but the dead friends, the greats. Mostly they'd quietly come and go, making the world a picture show.

As Hillary hauled south, the coated tongue was creeping beneath his feet, creeping to the north where it poked into the sea. It lay flat in all directions to the sky and never meeting it, **white into white.**

He couldn't see the sun on its swing through the blank.

There was no sun.

Hillary had seen one, three days before: yellow and orange and gold. He had seen a sky too—blue glass scrubbed with rays. He'd almost forgotten there could be lovely days like that one.

There were frozen waves on the sheet, but he couldn't see them either, white on white. The ragged sheet lay flat in all directions to the sky and never meeting it. White and bright, the sky and the sheet made one lighted movie screen for the dead friends in all their colors.

On day fifteen, eight miles and some, a Wednesday, seventy-nine degrees and a bit South, the cloud that had surrounded the previous day had turned to snow, and when the dead came up, his grandfather was among them. He called his grandfather Jim. Jim Rose climbed mountains too. He used to live next door.

Jim would lead us around the garden, pointing out the cicada cases high on the bark of the peach trees, the wetas lurking beneath the thick bark of the totara trunk, toadstools pushing through the cold grass beneath the fig tree and watching the beautiful bellbird song of the native tui, with its white ruffle of feathers beneath his bill. Learning how to know when a feijoa is ripe to eat and how best to climb back down through the branches of the great deodar at the bottom of the garden.

Hillary was exploring the old garden in short pants, smelling the damp earth and the flowers and climbing back down through the branches, under a blue sky and a yellow sun.

It was great.

He had found his grandfather by trying and failing to conjure up the big sloping garden in his own backyard, where his wife sang heartily to their little boy while hanging out the laundry. None of it would come to life. Picturing it was beyond him. His grandfather's garden came up in its colors instead.

He was amazed, is amazed now, how all thoughts of the living and the regular life wore out on days like these, how they went to nothing in the burning emptiness, as mints dissolve on the tongue. The wife, the kids, the plans, the dreams, the automatic garage doors. His wife made spaghetti bolognese with carrots to sweeten the sauce. Her name was Yvonne. Their small son was walking now. Hillary's older son had skinny legs and lived in another country. Both were little boys. His father was in the encyclopedia, just about any encyclopedia. His father answered to Ed. As Hillary reached for such thoughts, they were sucked from his skull by the blank. Three days, white on white.

This was the ghost country.

Come, my friends.

He was open to them.

Mostly they'd quietly come and go, and Hillary would drift in the afterglow, of the greats, keeping the hum of old times in his chest until it surrendered all companionship to the grind. So the

Wednesday morning passed, hauling through bleached rags, engaging with whoever came to his side. It went on through the afternoon until a sudden shout of longing sent them back to their graves.

All Hillary heard was a choking sound, the shout's collapse. It sputtered out. The snails in his nose turned to glass in the deep sub zero.

> **Ever since I can remember, there were a number of elements to my life that had always been there and I assumed always would be.**

He'd been with his grandfather, the man he always called Jim, in the old garden, learning to name the wonders. Then he'd been on the wide black beach, out on the west coast, at the place they called Anawhata, where the family had made their retreat and lived in bare feet, for eighty years, and where his grandfather taught him how to bury and raise the dead.

> **He showed me how to clean the carcass of dead birds I found on the beach after there had been great storms at sea. The salt layered feathers looked sad and dry and the stench was terrible. We buried them in bags in the garden, and after a couple of months I retrieved the bones and threaded them together to be standing skeletons. There was a wandering albatross, a sooty shearwater and a spotted shag, and I set them up on a shelf above my desk in my room.**

He could see the skeletons on the shelf above his desk in his boyhood room, but he couldn't see them on the shelf in his study back home, in the regular life with the wife, the kids, the garage doors. There was a lovely photograph of his mother in the study, on the bookshelf, down from the dead birds. Her name was Louise. She was smiling and engaging the camera dead on with her brown eyes big and twinkling. He couldn't picture it. He couldn't conjure the lovely photograph, but he found his mother on the black beach with Jim. Jim was her father. They were down on the black beach and that was fine.

Hillary never believed in magic. But he understood when people he'd taken to Anawhata called it a magical place. Ancient, and thereby brand new, in that this was how the world looked when it was young and steaming.

The road to Anawhata ran west of Auckland, up and along an ancient volcanic range, through tangled and dank forest, and the road was a dirt road long before the forest opened to rolling hill country, lumpy green velvet with black and white cows upon it. From the edge of the green velvet, the track dropped as a slippery slide, dropped near five hundred feet to an eroded valley of primitive plants, a leftover from the dinosaur days. The black beach sat another three hundred feet down, at the foot of a steeply sloping green wall, banded with rock, that fell from the edge of the valley.

Wet and crumbling above the beach, misted in the mornings and nights, the sloping wall had rain forest all over it, binding it; ferns and vines and elegant reeds with furry spear tips, trees hundreds of years old.

The green wall curved to the north and south, making two jungled headlands shaped like the knobbly knees of a giant old boxer. Indeed the green wall and the knobbly knees boxed the little black beach with the sea. It always felt as if the rolling sea were above his head when he looked out at it, and especially so when he had just climbed down to it.

Hillary climbed down to it in short pants and grammar school hair and walked with Jim and Louise to the southern end of the beach, to show them the shiny black mussels, **green lipped,** on the rocks, the three of them laughing together because it was a big sea breaking and it always felt it might suddenly swallow him.

Along the way Jim said a hearty goodbye and went back to his grave. Hillary and Louise took one of the muddy skinny tracks up the slope at the back of the beach, through the ferns and the trees bearded with moss and lichen, everything green and wet and the air flavored with the chocolate and tobacco of rotting leaves, the track dropping sharp off the right hand side on the climb to the little house of planks and glass (**and corrugated aluminum**) that sat above the beach, on the southern headland, just back from the drop to the rocks where the shiny black mussels were glued.

It was always warm in the late afternoon, with the windows floor-to-ceiling and the sun coming off the sea and with the light streaming red with the red curtains and then with the evening turning and the sun meeting the sea. They brewed their tea. They lit their twenty candles, made the fire, happily followed the rituals of the simpler life, talking and talking, mother and son. It came as they were talking together, the single shout of longing. She was gone with the shot of it. The moment of frailty ringing in his ears soon dead too.

The air was dancing as bleached rags, white on white. It being a Wednesday afternoon had no real meaning for him. One of his boots was falling apart; the sole was peeling away from the toe, where it slotted into the ski. The toe of the sole was flapping about like a slackjawed fool, would keep flapping for another week or so.

With his ears clear, the world drained, all longing turned toward the promise of a hot drink, until that too was lost and there was only the scraping of the skis, the horror of the sled that was truly tearing him a new one, daily. He found it hilarious to think of it now: that he was towing his own blood streaked dirt, stored in the sled with the food, the stove.

Part of the contract, what? Leave the place spotless.
Spotless it was, in all directions, yes, save for the smudge up ahead. The great white not everywhere. Almost everywhere, almost spotless. Hillary was a smudge upon it, of course. An unwashed speck. Five hundred yards ahead, the others making just the one smudge, their tracks lost to the drift, his unwashed companions.

What marvelous marchers they were, the others. Up ahead, to the eye, they were climbing steadily toward the sky, yet not getting any closer to it. It was as if the white plain was moving endlessly over a rise on the no horizon toward them, as if they were walking against the world's turning.

> **Trick of the eye, old bean. The mind makes it up. Comes with living too long in the blank.**

They were marching marching all right, and if Hillary had said to hell with the tearing, gave everything to catch up with them, they would only pull away faster.

> **We are not now that strength which in old days moved earth and heaven.**

There was no company to be had up ahead.

> **We are not now that strength.**

When he contemplated the climbing smudge, he did so with a blankness that matched the air.

❀   ❀   ❀

In the account that he later wrote, with the help of his psychologist friend, Dr. Peg Levine, Eric Philips noted that the group split apart after two weeks out. Dr. Levine later told a journalist that to understand what went wrong with the expedition, one had to look for the betrayal. "For each of them," she said.

For Hillary, it came two weeks and one day out, as he was lying in his sleeping bag, some hours after his afternoon walk on the black beach with his mother.

Muir had cooked that night, so his head was down the other end of the little red tent smaller than a double bed. Hillary and Philips were camped with Muir's sleeping-bagged feet between them.

It wasn't dark, because there was no sunset, but the mood was of the night. Lying there, thinking about the day out there and trying to think of the living and the regular life, Hillary heard Eric Philips on the phone, speaking in low muffled tones, telling his wife, Suzie, how Hillary and Muir were proving hopeless and useless and disappointing.

Muir kept falling over, slowing them down. Hillary was slow and causing them to abort days because he didn't like traveling among crevasses in whiteout.

So lost was he in his review of the team that Philips didn't stop to think if anyone was listening. Muir was apparently out like a light. Hillary lay on his side with his eyes open and not blinking, like a hospital patient in shock that his life support system has been switched off without anybody asking how he felt about it.

Just before lying down and hearing these unfortunate things, Hillary had written up his diary. He mentioned his mother, and he mentioned the Captain. He then mused on what is probably the most quoted line from Scott's diary:

> "Great God this is an awful place."
>
> It's not too difficult to agree. Another day of snow, cloud and lost horizons. Our daily life on this Ross Ice Shelf is a monochrome of misery. There is nothing to see. Nothing happens. Your sustenance is all from the thoughts in your head.

PART THREE

THE HILLARY STEP

> GARCIN: Couldn't you have held your tongues? Now
> it's over, he's stopped talking, and what he's think-
> ing about me has gone back into his head. Well,
> we've got to see it through somehow. . . . Naked as
> we were born. So much the better; I want to know
> whom I have to deal with.
>
> INEZ: You know already. There's nothing more to
> learn.
>
> GARCIN: You're wrong. So long as each of us hasn't
> made a clean breast of it—why they've damned
> him or her—we know nothing. Nothing that counts.
>
> Jean-Paul Sartre, In Camera No Exit

CHAPTER FOURTEEN

Twelve o'clock,
Along the reaches of the street
Held in a lunar synthesis,
Whispering lunar incantations
Dissolve the floors of memory
And all its clear relations
Its divisions and precisions,
Every street lamp that I pass
Beats like a fatalistic drum,
And through the spaces of the dark
Midnight shakes the memory
As a madman shakes a dead geranium

T. S. Eliot, "Rhapsody on a Windy Night"

After the demented skeletons of Dr. Mike Stroud and Sir Ranulph Fiennes were flown off the ice in February ninety-three, they told different stories as to why they'd abandoned their walk across Antarctica, five hundred miles short of the coast, as if they'd had some sensible say in doing otherwise. Each said he would have kept hauling if it hadn't been for the appalling condition of the other: Fiennes claimed he'd called the halt because Stroud would have otherwise died from hypothermia; Stroud said they'd run up the white flag because Fiennes was at risk from fatal blood poisoning, from the rotting of one of his feet, his toes "black bags of pus." They both wrote books about the trip, in which they made further conflicting claims of burdensome behavior against the other. Each portrayed his companion as one more horrible obstacle to overcome, like the cold, the wind, the bodily decay. At the end, they weren't able to declare with grace that "we were done in" or "we couldn't continue," because at the end there was no "we." It was fated to play out this sad way once each had felt betrayed by the other out there. Hence, at the heart of it, they told the same story: it was the other guy. That was the darkness of their odyssey. "He was the one."

People divorced; in bitterness the things they say, the way they remember the why and the how. Even when talking about love and life and the big picture of what they'd aspired to, and what they felt it was all about, their stories may only match up when they describe the motivation and the damage of betrayal. Because the motivation is always the same: a "frustration," be it from a position of principle or confusion, be it from selfish, primal or whimsical quirks of reason and desire. Likewise, the damage is always the same: a message that lodges in the heart, the psyche, that stains the mood of the most virile egotist. The message being: you are no good.

In the Stroud-Fiennes affair, it played this way: Sir Ranulph declared himself "leader" of the team of two, regardless of how Mike Stroud felt about it or argued against it. Fiennes, the older man, mostly led from behind, for he was the slower man on that trip, and he didn't like it, seeing his companion way out in front, and he didn't like Stroud forever pushing him to pick up speed.

He refused to do so, asserting that his "polar plod" would better see him through the journey. As Stroud's pleas of frustration turned to nagging and then nastiness, Fiennes anchored his position with scorn and righteousness, cloaking any and all injury. Therein lay Sir Ranulph's tools of vengeance, notably when Mike Stroud's bowels became a running riot, for days to weeks, laying him out, slowing them down.

One evening, and this was about eight weeks out, Fiennes ripped into his companion, declaring it best that he call in the plane and have Stroud flown out, because Stroud was a burden, Stroud was slowing him down; he'd proceed without Stroud. When the steam ran out, the world's greatest explorer saw devastation in the face of his companion, realized he'd gone too far, realized some of the damage he'd done, and he begged Mike Stroud to forgive him. He tried to talk things up between them, tried to act as if they were mates again. "You're a brick," he told Stroud. British men call each other "bricks" when assuring each other of their solid worth as human beings. "You're a brick, Mike."

Later that night Stroud answered the jolly compliment in his diary: "Ran is a real prick." Stroud couldn't let it go. Not out there in the polar pressure cooker, where every little thing itches hotly, where "trust" is meant to be sacred, currency solid as a brick, yet so vulnerable to every little thing. As any self help guru will attest, once the trust evaporates, so does the love, good will, capacity to forgive. From that point on, every little thing is flavored with the darker doubts, self doubt. All apologies: worthless.

For it is this that keeps the gurus in business: where a consuming enchantment with "beauty" can be purged from the universe by nothing more than an indifferent blink of the beholder's eye, breaking from the "beastly," from the dirty magic of the "beastly," is never so clean or complete. Having laid its scent and spore in the beholder's heart, having been there and been there before, it is the beast that enjoys the more lasting purchase. When freshly fed, it flowers there like a fungal complaint stirred from dormancy.

❊   ❊   ❊

More than the lyrics, it was the music of his companion's moaning that moved Peter Hillary, playing in his ears a familiar song from unpleasantville. He could feel it digesting where the evening meal was wriggling; a greasy eel with electric twinges. He held it down, listening and not listening, thinking his thoughts, wandering the darker halls and nothing to be done about it, with only the spastic tent giving voice to the way it was.

I was just so tired.

Little time passed before Hillary felt he was falling backward through water, and that was all right. Under the smother of exhaustion the wriggling spark stilled to a warm and pleasant coal. He couldn't hold it off, didn't want to hold it off, yet he clutched at his thoughts, his Antarctic thoughts, as if to take them into oblivion, as a child might hug a teddy bear with the hope that it will be there in his dreams. He didn't feel a thing as mercy palmed his thoughts, put them away for the morning, leaving him to the beautiful nothingness and then the dreams, and to the dreams the howl of the night returned. The stove, the tent, the rattle of the tent. They were in the belly of a rabid dog. The stove wasn't chuffing but in roaring chorus with the freight train winds outside. The whole world was screaming. They weren't actually saying anything. They didn't need to say anything. It was all on their faces as they sat over the stove and brewed up the next hot drink, pondering what would happen the following day. But there was some confusion about who he was with, and where they were camped, where they were going.

Most of my polar dreams vanished as I opened my eyes to the drumming nylon of the tent. But sometimes in that state of half sleep, my dreams were as vivid and consuming as the im-

possible visions populating my days on the haul. When I think of them now, the dreams were a fractured and scrambled continuance of those visions; that my mind was on some frantic mission to show me everything I had ever known, to make sense of it all, or to prod me into making sense of it all.

There are people who spend a good part of their lives looking for meaning in their dreams. They must scare themselves silly. The "snake" means . . . The "bridge" means . . . I wonder what the "tent" means? I've always loved living in a tent. Actually, I can't remember not having slept in a tent. So it should be no surprise that I do feel at home in a tent. I like its compactness and the function of the shelter and the practical objects you have in a tent. Everything is there for good purpose.

His sisters, his little sisters, seemed to be there much of the time, in the tent, their faces illuminated by a paleness of shadow that was cast by what he didn't know. They were sitting with their sleeping bags drawn up to their chins. The tent was green, with heavy walls, the doors closed against the wind and grit in the wind. Somehow he knew there was grit in the wind, and it bothered him. He pondered if it was snowing as he lived through the dream. He looked for signs of time and place and prevailing conditions.

It was dark outside the tent. It was a night with no sun in it. He enjoyed that dreamed darkness. He found it welcoming. A pressure lamp was mysteriously placed against the tent wall, in the corner, but the darkness had soaked into the tent from the outside world; a fog that sapped the lamp's magnesium glare, holding it down to a glow no mightier and no less enchanting than moonglow through cloud. It was a warmer light, a more generous light that paleness of shadow on his sisters' faces, so gentled in their features that he squinted in his dream to see them clearly in the brief teasing clarities of dream land. Sometimes he had an urge to look over his shoulder, to see what was lighting their faces, but was always somehow distracted from doing so. He resented the distraction; he felt stifled by it. Likewise, when he tried to question his sisters about what was going on, he was always somehow distracted from their reply, somehow estranged from them yet feeling they remained close by. That vexed him too. And it chilled him a little when he realized his sisters weren't touched or even aware of the anxiety that Hillary felt ruling his time with them.

> **The tent, the dream tent, was a way station in my dreams, where I returned from other dreamed places, and where I always seemed to be no matter where else the dreams took me. Sometimes my sisters came with me.**

In that subconjured world of dissolving moments, the pressure lamp came for a time a red lava sun when Hillary realized his eyes were open, and had been open for some time. They were very cold when he blinked, sharpening the feeling of being awake, and yet equally sharp the running pictures in his dreams, and he lay there for a time blinking the cold from his eyes, conscious that he was living two, three lives at the same time.

There was the blurred ball of the sun through the wall of the red tent. There was the pressure lamp too in the corner of his eye and his sisters huddling, and his conscious mind juggling memories from a long time ago with memories of the days and the evening just past, and everything sharp. Then the sharp feeling of needing to pee with the dream moving on to the back seat of a car with his sisters there and the red lava sun hanging out the back window, misted through the dust brought up by the car and with his eyes open he thought about the car and the dust and the road that rutted rough all the way out to the Matuki Valley, where the family often went camping in their summer holidays, for he felt that was the road they were on. He knew it was the road because it always smelled of sump oil, where it had been splashed onto the track by the homesteaders upon the stretches of dirt that ran past their houses, to keep the dust down and prevent it drifting into their houses and sheds. He could smell it in his dream, with his eyes open. Living between two places, it smelled bad in both of them, and everything sharp. Hillary reached for the pee bottle, had his communion, emptied it out, settled deep into his bag, closed his eyes; all the while caught in the string of memories that ran parallel to the dream, until the dream fully took hold again.

❄ ❄ ❄

Come in, laddie, and warm yerself by this roarin' . . . candle.

The Goon Show

The dream ride in the back of the dream car didn't last very long, through the time I was half awake and gone soon after that, I suppose. There wasn't much to it. I remember there being a little black dog in the back of the car, wriggling and jumping around, my sisters and I trying to grab the dog or fend him off. We used to have a little black dog with a white chest, at the family home in Auckland. The only little dog we ever had that was black all over, from nose to tail, was in Nepal. And yes, we called him Blackie. It would have made sense if Blackie had been in the green tent rather than the dream car. Blackie belonged in the way station tent of the dreams.

Through the time I was half awake, using the pee bottle, half asleep, riding in the back of the dream car, in that extraordinary in between state of being, I was making all these connections between the places in the dreams and the places I'd known. I remembered the green tent after a time, the whole story. I remembered it the way you remember something like "Little Red Riding Hood." You know and remember the whole story in an instant. When you are thrown into the middle of that story, you know without thinking exactly where things are at. What's gone, what's to come, the chaos of dreams notwithstanding.

It was clear to me that we were up around thirteen thousand feet, and that it was nineteen sixty-six. If so, we were feeling pretty poorly then. Lindy would have been seven then, Sarah was ten, and I was eleven turning twelve. They were my little sisters in the dream. Wherever we were, it was cold. I never saw outside the green tent. Everything was happening inside the tent. But it felt to me that this was sixty-six, that we were camped above the village of Kunde, in the Khumbu region. The family was walking to Everest. In the waking life I remember it. How much I have taken from the family photo album, and from hearing about it, and how much of the story I know as a true recollection, I cannot say. But I remember it well.

We'd trekked in to help Dad with the finishing touches to Kunde Hospital, the first medical facility in the Everest region. Kunde is a village of subsistence farmers who live in small, squat stone houses with walls and low ceilings blackened by wood smoke and large front yards of dust and rock, little stone fences to hold each family's yak. It's a bleak place to live, a tough place with a priceless view of the big mountains, the biggest mountain upvalley.

Kunde was home to the great Sherpa Mingma Tsering. Mingma was a high altitude porter on Dad's Everest climb in fifty-three. It was Mingma who worked for my father for more than thirty years on the school and hospital projects there. Over the years they became great friends. There's a portrait of Mingma hanging on Dad's living room wall. Mingma (no longer with us) was married to a woman named Ang Dooli, whom I consider to be my Himalayan aunt. They were people we considered as family, and who always treated us as family. We spent the Christmas of sixty-six with them. We'd made the journey with family friends, the Pearls. Max and Lois, their children. It was Max Pearl who dressed as Santa Claus, riding in on a yak instead of a reindeer. (Hence, my mother named her book about the trip *A Yak for Christmas*.)

The day after Christmas we walked upvalley in falling snow to Thyangboche Monastery, where we spent the evening celebrating my twelfth birthday. In the dream it seemed to me that we were near Thyangboche, not that there was anything concrete to support this feeling. I just wanted to look outside the tent to see the snow falling there.

Another day on we reached Pangboche, the oldest monastery in the Everest region. This was one of the places my father came when he was looking for the yeti, because the monastery was said to have a yeti scalp in one of its cupboards.

A few days on from Pangboche, with splitting headaches, we camped at the foot of Kalar Pittar at Gorak Shep, at seventeen thousand feet. In an attempt to lighten the mood of three children sickly with the altitude, Dad organized for him and the Sherpas to take us skating upon the frozen surface of the Gorak Shep lake. Using cardboard boxes as sleighs, our Sherpas—Mingma, Ang Tsering, Siku, Pember Tarkay, and Phu Dorje—pushed us around on the slick ice as we hooted and hollered.

The following day, Dad and our troupe of Sherpas towed Lindy, Mum and me up the Khumbu Glacier to Everest Base Camp. (Sarah had a headache and stayed behind.) After hours of staggering over the moraine—the rubble fields of boulders strewn across the glacial ice, where you can easily break your ankle in one of the booby traps of wobbly rocks—we reached a scruffy looking area that Dad identified as the site of his old camp from fifty-three. He wandered about identifying pieces of old equipment and rubbish from the expedition.

We were at seventeen thousand six hundred feet. I remember knowing you would die if a helicopter just dropped you there. You would die a day later because the air has only half the oxygen that it has at sea level. I remember my head feeling as if it would burst with pain, and I eagerly looked forward to the descent to richer air. Before returning downvalley, Dad took us into the lower icefall. As we walked among the ice pinnacles and the old crevasses, through a ghostly blue light, I felt a kind of wonder come over me, and that's what I remember.

✳   ✳   ✳

There isn't much I really remember from the first time I saw Everest, except how the sight of it affected my father. That was in sixty-two. I was seven years old, and the family was visiting Darjeeling, the pretty hill station in northern India, and the home of the great Tenzing Norgay. Anyway, we went camping in the pretty hills, on the Singulila Ridge. I remember one morning, it was very early, the sky was black blue, it was that first dilution of the night when my father took me in his arms and carried me out on to the ridge line. Then we headed up to about nine thousand feet, to look at Mount Everest, the top of it, where he had been with the great Tenzing, and where the sun would hit first and highest, eighty miles to the west of us, in Nepal. I remember some local porters carrying me and Sarah—all bundled in our sleeping bags and snuggled in bamboo baskets—on their backs. I don't remember for sure who was carrying whom.

(My mother wrote a book about that family adventure, too. It was called *Keep Calm If You Can.* They were warm and easy reads, my mother's books. They had her personality and voice—which makes them kind of hard for me to read these days. Anyway, she wrote an account of that very cold morning up on the ridge, although she and Belinda didn't come up with us.)

What remains clear to me, what I remember: we were all huddling to keep warm, waiting for the sun to hit the mountain. When it came, I spent more time looking at my father. It's something I've always done, always did as a child: watched how things affected him. But I always failed in dreams over the years to see what was happening on his face, and it would become the overriding anxiety of those dreams.

"What's going to happen, Dad?"

❄   ❄   ❄

In that subconjured world of dissolving moments, the pressure lamp came for a time the misted face of a flashlight, and later the softest moon, sitting small and distant in the corner of the green tent and then the tent not there, just the moon in a cloudy night sky and the clouds lit up in their bellies by city lights that lay beyond his view, for he was sitting in what seemed to be **the broad lawns of some botanical gardens with thick bamboo hedging along one side.** He was sitting on the grass with a boy he knew but couldn't name, yet he knew they were friends, and Hillary knew that he was a boy again too. The serious young stick—he was built like a stick—and sensitive with a tendency to brooding.

It felt as if they'd been sitting on the grass for some time, and then the grass and the gardens not there and Hillary following the boy through a big hall that had the feel of a museum, for they were suddenly in such a place, the moon traveling ahead of them to hang above an elevated stage where people were sitting in a large semicircle, five or six deep, facing into the corner, with musical instruments, an orchestra of shadowed figures embracing their instruments. "Your mother is here."

And there she was, looking very serious, seated near the front, on the right hand side of the orchestra. She played the viola, the lead viola in Auckland's Symphonia Orchestra. She was the support conductor when Maestro Juan Matteuccii was away. I remember many evenings after school sitting in the stalls before the stage at the old Auckland Town Hall while the orchestra practiced. Sometimes I watched and listened and other times I dreamed of places far away while I

waited for my mother to complete her rehearsal. (My sisters and I also played instruments for many years. Sarah played violin, Belinda the flute. I played clarinet.)

Then my mother walked over, walked past, and was met by a butler who summoned a tall and composed looking woman who now stood before my mother smiling. I could sense Mum's anxiety, and then watched her dropping into a rather elegant curtsy, bringing one foot behind the other, so they were lined up as she dropped.

The woman said, "That isn't necessary." And Mum headed back to the orchestra.

Hillary wanted to follow his mother, but the boy stood in his way, stepping to block his way no matter how he turned. The boy was talking very fast, chattering with the jackhammer sense of a squirrel, nodding his head with a squirrel's excitement, close and crazy, and when Hillary went to push him away, when he felt it all build up in his jaw and he put out a straight arm to the boy's shoulder, the boy said, calm and clear and considered, "Why don't you sit down? Do you want to sit down? Let's sit down."

Hillary looked around for somewhere to sit away from the boy. His mysterious friend kept standing very close, at his elbow, with his face in Hillary's face and talking very intensely, such that he became all mouth, yet drowned out by the barnyard cacophony of the orchestra tuning up. The more Hillary struggled to make out what the boy was saying and where he was at, the more the boy seemed on the verge of hysteria. Hillary told him they needed to sit down. He said he wanted to sit down and listen to the orchestra. Where the boy's voice was lost to the music, Hillary's voice was as clear and present as the tones of a radio broadcaster calling the highlights of a slow parade.

And then I remembered the boy's name. I started calling him Ferguson and he called me Hillary and that's what we prep school boys did. I'm not sure I remember Ferguson being as intense as he was in this dream. I am not sure he was like that at all. Indeed I remember him as a rather pleasant chap. He was the son of the Governor General, Sir Bernard Ferguson, the Queen's man in New Zealand. When Queen Elizabeth visited the country, she stayed at Ferguson's place. And when I was eight years old—eight years old!—the Governor General sent his official car for me, black and shiny, driver in uniform and peaked cap and the trace smells of pipe tobacco, perfumes, leather polish. He sent the car when school was done, to fetch me to the royal digs to play with Ferguson. It was around that time I'd asked my parents if I might go to my sister Sarah's school, instead of Kings Prep (which was actually next door to the family home), where I wore the blazer, the tie, the shiny shoes. It seemed to me that the people at Sarah's school were nicer than the people at my school. She had a wide circle of friends. She was happy. She's a lot like me, Sarah, but she had a pretty good time at school, as I remember it.

This was at a time when Kings Prep (and then College) was ruled by the rod, was modeled on the old British system of literally knocking boys into shape, from the time when Captain Scott had been a boy—before that, really. Hence, at Kings, Prep and College, in the sixties, modern educational approaches were considered whimsical and transitory and rather lower class.

There were a lot of bully boys and people pushing you around. You were taken out the front and strapped for spelling a word wrong or being in a daydream. I was always daydreaming. They'd stand you in the corner and ridicule you. I remember getting a report in late because I'd been away with my family, and the teacher got me up and had a great time laying on the ridicule. My mother wrote a letter, met the teacher and asked him to be more accommodating. The following day the teacher did it again—got me, put the boot in. As a boy of eight or nine you go "wow." It kind of blew my mind, really. I think Dad wanted me to stick out the jaw and bear it a bit more.

But it wasn't just the teachers who flogged you. The older boys, the prefects, the supposed good boys deemed worthy of authority at the college, they caned you too. I remember one afternoon we left a window open in the classroom. The following day, the prefects lined up the class, bent us over, divided up the backsides between them, and caned them. They loved it, the prefects. They carried on like malevolent gods. That was their right, indeed their duty, part of their education as masters of society.

A feature of the old school was the "fag" system, where you were made a servant of one of the prefects, who you called "fag masters." I was made a fag. My fag master was seventeen years old, head of the school's army cadet battalion. I toasted his sandwiches at lunchtime. I polished up his boots, his badge. I tugged my forelock.

Of course, it wasn't just the teachers or the prefects. Among your own fellows, the boys your own age, there were chaps who also used fear as a tool to higher social standing. I remember there were boys who filled their shoes with golf balls and they'd hit you with that. Or they'd carve the initials of their school house on the soles of their shoes, and they'd brand you with that on your arse.

By the end of my first year at Kings College, when I was thirteen years old, I'd grown to the size I am now. By the end of my second year, I started saying no to teachers, and no to prefects. I was a good boy in third form and fourth form. I took my work very seriously. But if I left my football sweater in my locker, they'd want to cane me. And I started saying no. It was pretty bad, really. I only got away with it because I was big. I wasn't a fighter. I liked wrestling but I wasn't very good at it. I just locked down against them, locked down inside. In the end, in my fourth year, I was asked to leave early, because

I'd said no to being punished for a prank I'd pulled with some other chaps. I'd said no because we'd already been punished, and they wanted to punish us again. I'd been saying no for a couple of years by then. I was pretty good at it by then.

I'm pretty good at it now.

❊ ❊ ❊

I remember Ferguson as a very nice little boy, a rather gentle soul, really. He had curly hair and he wore glasses. So I'd say Ferguson suffered mightily. We both suffered because we were the "sons of," yes, and because we didn't have the liquid social skills to thrive among our peers, among those little lords of the flies and their playground politics.

There was no "fitting in" with those people, I'm telling you.

Anyway, our parents put us together to play. And I remember my mother coming to take me home after such an engagement; how she was announced to the room and curtsied for Ferguson's mother. On that occasion Ferguson was his regular gentle self. But in the dream he wasn't acting like Ferguson at all.

Just as the boy was becoming the driver of that dream's intensity, Hillary banished him with a violence born from panic: from the big hall they walked a whirlwind tour of no place that stayed in the mind for conscious remembrance, each visit as long as a sleeping breath, emerging and returning then to the green tent where Hillary's sisters were playing cards. He asked them, "What is it?" He tried to get their attention, but Ferguson got in his face again, and there was an edge to it, and then a raw menace, for no matter how he twisted he couldn't get free of the boy to breathe. He felt as if he were suffocating. He felt pinned to the ground. He felt the insanity of one buried alive, that horror of revelation ignited; all pushing and tearing and wriggling and gasping as one futile spasm; that frightened jerky spasm of waking from a bad dream.

He fully woke in the lighted night, coughing up moss that had flowered in his lungs, his shoulders aching, his heart beating in the bruise of his ankles. He'd developed a cough in his chest that had thickened before he'd known it was there. The rattle in his chest was the only rattle to be heard. The tent walls still, no wind. The sun, hanging off to the side, burning a hole through the tent: a warming coal on his face in communion with his fevers, in defiance of his longing for a night of darkness. He keened his ear to the quietness, and there was only the quietness until the slow bellows of his fellows filled the tent, as a summer's night chokes on the raucous rant of crickets.

> "Hell is other people." The living and the dead, the loved ones and otherwise. Isn't that how it is for everybody?

Reaching for the pee bottle, he pondered his companions in their comas, with something akin to that bitter affection found only in the dark. Affection for a difficult child, for a marriage turned to malady. Less inspired than mustered as the right thing to do, that affection; and in the hope without conviction some curative lifebuoy might float into being by invoking it.

> I didn't want this trip to be about "the other guy." The self help gurus say that freedom from bad feeling lies in part with seeing how it is for the other guy. Well, I could see how it was for them. While I wondered how it was for them, in their heads, I could see their frustrations, and I could see our individual limitations rubbing against each other. I understand that it's how you deal with the other guy that counts. The gurus say, "Don't take it personally." I don't know how else to take it.
>
> This life, how one takes it. That's what this trip was really about. It's what all trips are about. I mean, it certainly wasn't about the Ulysses factor. There was no equal temper of heroic hearts.

Less a replay of Tennyson's "Ulysses," and more a sequel to Jean-Paul Sartre's *No Exit,* the one-act play about three horrendously self centered people locked in a room forever. The room is hell. Rather, the room is where hell happens. If the three people were able to cooperate, and give to each other some kindness and consideration, they might be able to make eternity bearable. Instead, they conspire in shifting alliances to ensure everlasting misery, suffered and inflicted. They are cursed by their inability to see anything but their own point of view, their own desires and resentments.

The play is most famous for its punch line: "Hell is other people."

This life, how one takes it.
Actually, the clearest definition of what the trip was about could be found on the tip of Peter Hillary's left ski, which was planted in the snow outside the tent, looking like a totem of happiness. There were ice creams and dogs and stick figures kicking a ball in a park drawn there on his skis, in indelible ink, by his children. On the tip of his left ski, his daughter, Amelia, had written a line from *The Lion King,* as spoke by a baboon: "The question is, who are you?"

Not that my thoughts went that far as I used the pee bottle. It was more like trying to give thought to a range of feelings, a few minutes trying to collect myself, so I could sleep again, so I could hopefully just sleep. More an earnest practical prayer for a little oblivion, really.

❋   ❋   ❋

I have no hope that you will accomplish all that you strive for. For few are the children who turn out to be equals of their fathers, and the greater number are worse; few are better than their father is.
      Homer, *The Odyssey,* the Richmond Lattimore translation

The dream ride in the back seat of the car with the little black dog on the dusty road didn't last very long; through the time I was half awake and gone soon after that, I suppose. It's a long

drive out to the Matuki Valley. Mingma Tsering Sherpa, from Kunde, made the drive with the family one year, the summer of sixty-four.

I was ten years old when Dad first brought Mingma to New Zealand. He brought him over to visit several times, because Mingma was Dad's sirdar, his right hand man in the Himalayas, because they were fond of each other, because Mingma and his family had shown Dad and the Hillary clan tremendous hospitality over the years, and because through Mingma, Dad wanted to show the Sherpa people that the Western world wasn't how it looked, from the outside, that he didn't have a bottomless pocket, and that he had to work hard to raise money for their hospitals and schools. In fact, over the years, Dad took Mingma on tour through the country to star at a number of fund raising functions for the Himalayan Trust. You know, a real life legendary Sherpa. He was a crowd pleaser, Mingma.

Anyway, I remember Mingma coming to stay, and because back home in Kunde there were no cars or roads, no television sets or electric light bulbs, life in New Zealand was very different for Mingma, and he found everything intriguing. I remember he loved mowing our lawns. And I remember Dad tried teaching him how to drive our family station wagon while we were in the South Island. Mingma was very nervous as he sat at the wheel with Dad beside him and we three kids in the back to witness the spectacle.

He eased on the accelerator so gently the car only crept forward.

"Give it more throttle, Mingma," Dad instructed.

"Yes, Burra Sahib," said Mingma. With that, he planted his foot on the pedal and our Holden station wagon surged out of the dirt driveway with the house on the other side of the narrow street filling the view ahead.

Dad yelled, "Turn."

Mingma turned severely and the car skidded a full one hundred and eighty degrees around and crashed back into the culvert beside our driveway where we all sat silently in a state of jangled nerves. That was the end of Mingma's driving lessons. I think Mingma knew Dad well enough not to take it personally. I remember it was around this time that Dad tried to teach me how to tie a bowline. It was his favorite knot, and he used it for just about everything. I'm afraid the lesson lasted little longer than Mingma's career at the wheel.

Dad's a doer. "This is how you do it, so . . . do it."

Mingma knew how to tie a bowline. Mingma was a mountaineer too. He made the first ascent of Annapurna III. And as a young man, in fifty-three, on Everest, he was one of the Sherpa heroes who hauled a lot of the gear to the high camps. Dad always said it was a team effort all around. "Everybody played their part." But Dad remained especially fond of Mingma.

When he came to stay in sixty-four, because the weather was wonderful in the Southern Alps, Dad decided that Mingma and he would take me on a climb of Mount Fog, an eight thousand foot peak at the base of the magnificent Matuki Valley on the west side of Lake Wanaka. The drive was long and rugged, and I remember it like a bedtime story. It's a drive I can take in my mind. The whole family came along. Mum, Dad, the kids, Mingma.

There were plumes of fine flour dust lifting from the wheels as they hammered like sewing machines over the ruts in the road all the way up the valley. The noise was awful, and the suspension often bottomed out with the hard knocking. The fine dust particles seeped into the car and turned to mud at the back of your throat. You could taste it there.

I can see the spot where Dad turned our trusty station wagon north, up and around a number of twisting bends and up onto a narrow section of road that became a precarious and narrow ledge around the western bluffs of Lake Wanaka. None of us wore seat belts. I don't think we had any. Besides, we all had absolute confidence in Dad. He changed down through the gears using the column shift and began inching the car forward and periodically pressing the center of the General Motors Holden's steering wheel to sound the horn. It didn't seem very likely out here, but there could be a farmer's son heading into town for the day, and it would be better not to meet him on a single lane blind corner, eighty feet in the air, above the deep green of the lake.

The road turned from the bluffs above the lake and we followed it west into the broad Matuki Valley, with its striking *roches moutons,* or rock sheep. These are bald rock hills that have resisted the great ice sheets that formed the valleys of the Southern Alps and appear smooth and round on the upvalley side, and plucked and broken on the lee. Elegant waterfalls plunged from the tussock clad flanks above us. Everything in the valley had a name: Twin Falls, Treble Cone, Cattle Flat, Black Peak, Sheepyard Flat, Wishbone Falls, Sharkstooth Peak, and our objective, Mount Fog.

On we went, hammering, Dad swinging the car from side to side to avoid the worst potholes, slowing only on the approach to the streams that we had to ford. From the bank above the stream we would all look forward through the windshield at the rushing water that tumbled its way over and around smooth stones and boulders. Dad, Mum and Mingma would walk out to find a relatively smooth route across, where we wouldn't drown the car in deep water.

"This way, good looking, Burra Sahib," Mingma would say.

"Yes, okay, Mingma. Let's give it a go."

Dad went back to the car and slowly approached the stream, easing the car down the bank and then pressing on the throttle to keep up the momentum. The blue station wagon jolted and slid over stones on the streambed. A big wave surged before the car; steam poured from the sub-merged exhaust. With a roar of skidding tires and the gush of water pouring from its doors, our wagon rose from the stream, climbed the gravel bank and came to rest on the far side. There were about half a dozen fords, and as we crossed them, we knew that they would be waiting when we returned.

The larger streams that came from the mountains above us had simple wooden bridges over them. They were just wide enough for a single vehicle, with two wheel boards to follow above the sleeper planks, so it was like being on a train track. Or walking a double wire. We all felt it was a good idea to keep our tires in the right spot.

And so we drifted across and up the road, and deeper into the mountains that grew around us. Ascending this great valley was like entering a geographic hall that narrowed and steepened and progressively overshadowed us, the farther we went up the grassy flats of the valley floor. You could tell Dad loved being up there. The more glimpses of craggy peaks capped with snowfields and creased glaciers, the happier he seemed to be. He started to whistle with his lips pursed and his cheeks flexing as he breathed. He liked to whistle cowboy songs, and he was whistling "There's a Bridle Hanging on the Wall."

The Matuki road is a one way trail that dwindles till you can go no farther, at a spot called Raspberry Hut. While the hut is painted orange, the name has probably more to do with a thorny creeper that grows as a noxious pest in these parts but each summer redeems itself by producing fruit. It's an old shepherd's hut sitting forlornly on its own upon the valley floor. We stopped there and had a barbecue dinner. Then, in the long twilight of summer, Mingma, Dad and I started up the great mountainside that towered above. We followed sheep and deer tracks through the bracken until we reached the golden tussocks at about three and a half thousand feet.

We ascended for an hour through these meter high tussocks, stopping when the light was getting low. We unrolled our sleeping bags among the giant gold tussocks on a ledge and lay back and watched the stars pierce the fading light. I was very thirsty, but the nearest stream was deep in a ravine that severed the mountain flank nearby. Dad and Mingma were sipping from a can of beer each, so Dad gave me his to try. It was awful. Why on earth do they drink the stuff? I decided there was absolutely nothing redeeming about the taste of beer at all, but I was so parched I gulped down several drafts and fell into a deep sleep.

Early the next morning we rose and began climbing again. We reached a rocky ridge line, which we crossed, and began traversing a vast snowfield beneath the summit pyramid. We had roped up with a white nylon rope, and I was in the middle. Dad moved steadily forward across the steep snow face, and I followed, stretching my legs from one great boot print to the next. Occasionally the fragile corn snow footprint collapsed and I would lose my footing. With a howl I would rocket down the slope on my side toward the valley thousands of feet below. With just a momentary delay the rope around my waist would draw tight and my father and Mingma would hoist me back up the slope and into the line of footprints.

I will never forget the confidence that they exuded up there on Mount Fog. It was a strange and exciting world, and they belonged in it. Late that afternoon we descended down the tussock flanks to the valley, where we could already see the car and some tiny figures wandering around it far below. The sound of my father's boots striding behind me, pushing through the tussock grass, stayed right behind me all the way down to the valley floor.

❄ ❄ ❄

In his dreams there were many faces, and as many stillborn conversations. Hillary had a question for all of them. But the questions were stillborn too, as a "sense of asking" half seen from many angles. From that subconjured world of dissolving moments he remembers best looking into the smiling face of a man named Peter Mulgrew, one of the Old Firm. He was to later think how odd it was to have dreamed of Peter Mulgrew, even for the length of a sleeping breath, because Mulgrew was the friend, the man he had thought of as an uncle, who had died on top of Erebus, the white volcano. It was a bitter business that always put a sinker on the happiness found in beholding that mountain. He hadn't seen Erebus for three days, given the blank.

> **A fanciful soul would say that Mulgrew turned up in the dream to let me know he was still watching over me. In a way I believe it was so. That's what your people do when they die. The ones who make a great impression upon you tattoo something of themselves onto your soul, and you carry them with you always. He was a good friend of the family—and for many years, Peter and Dad were close friends, equal sparring partners.**

Ed Hillary first met Peter Mulgrew as one of two candidates for the job of senior radio operator on the South Pole trip in fifty seven. Both candidates were naval chief petty officers, experienced and sharp. Hillary chose Mulgrew because the other man kept calling Ed "Sir" after being told to do otherwise. Mulgrew called him Ed, Mulgrew was Ed's man.

In nineteen sixty, Peter Mulgrew went with Ed Hillary to climb Makalu, the world's fifth highest mountain, without bottled oxygen. It was again on Makalu that Ed Hillary suffered a serious bout of altitude sickness, one of "six or seven episodes over the years" that would have killed him if not for the good people around him. On Makalu, Ed got up to a high camp, went to bed with a rude headache, and was found the following morning slurring his words and stumbling, unable to make any sense or coordinated movement. His fellows helped him down the mountain, and it was a good way downvalley when he came around. Having recovered his strength and faculties, and with no doubt that his bid for Makalu was over, Ed walked across to the village of Khumjung, at thirteen thousand feet, where he was looking to build his first school. Meanwhile, Peter Mulgrew was up in the death zone, going for the top, when he too collapsed, out of it in the killer cold, unable to be roused or raised. His feet froze solid as his fellows dragged him down the mountain. In one of Ed Hillary's books, there's a photo of Peter Mulgrew in hospital, wearing for the camera the eyeball smile of a man receiving an electric shock. Sitting bedside, his wife, June, smiling for the camera too, and his friend Ed smiling and looking sort of embarrassed that they're posing for this photo, given that Mulgrew has just had his legs chopped off six inches below the knee.

He had a lot of guts, Peter Mulgrew. Taught himself to walk with grace on artificial legs; sweated and swore through the razor blade withdrawal from addiction to the pethidine (a narcotic analgesic) that had been so beautiful when the pain had been too much. He got up. Successful businessman, competitive yachtsman.

Time passed. Louise and Belinda Hillary were killed in seventy-five. Peter Mulgrew flew with Sarah Hillary to Kathmandu when the terrible news broke. His marriage to June went west around this time and he began a new relationship. His friendship with Ed also ruptured (in part because Ed didn't take Mulgrew on the seventy-seven Ganges jetboat expedition, for reasons of team chemistry). Ed and June began keeping company. In the end, "we were the only ones left." They later married, in nineteen ninety.

The fate of Peter Mulgrew makes a pretty dark tale. It was certainly a dark and very sad episode in New Zealand's history.

In seventy-nine, polar pioneers Mulgrew and Hillary were invited to travel as commentators on a series of Air New Zealand DC10 flyover trips to Antarctica. They were to take turns, guiding alternate flights. A highlight of the trip, weather permitting, was a flight over Mount Erebus and the neighboring Mount Terror. Hillary was listed to play host on November twenty-nine, but found he had commitments in the United States, where he raised most of the money that funded the Himalayan Trust. Mulgrew flew in Hillary's stead, and the plane flew into a whiteout, off course and too low. Somehow the wrong flight plan coordinates had been punched in. Mulgrew was in the cockpit with the crew when the plane smacked into the saddle between Erebus and Terror. Two hundred and thirty people and a ball of flame, and later on the television a littered black smudge on the burning brightness.

> Planted around the smudge were many little green flags, marking out where the bodies had scattered. In ancient Greek myth, Erebus was the "darkness" of the underworld.
>
> I was at home nursing injuries from a mountaineering accident in the Himalayas. At first I didn't know where Dad was, and I nearly panicked. And then came the complicated truth, good and bad.

❋   ❋   ❋

He was very good to me, Peter Mulgrew. I remember when I was sixteen, Peter gave me a job for the summer at his window factory, never letting on when I introduced myself to my work colleagues as "Peter Hill." He understood where it was at, and I've always been grateful for it. I was in the middle of my standard issue adolescent identity crisis at the time, and finding it endlessly complicated by my public standing as the "son of."

When you're a teenager, it's difficult enough, struggling to find your own identity, to be recognized as an individual somebody. You're screaming to be seen for who you are, or who you think you are at the time. But I found that whenever I introduced myself as "Peter Hillary" to a group of people, it would always be met with "Oh, so you'd be Ed Hillary's boy," and everything would be different. They'd all be asking "How is he?" and "What's he doing?" and "What's he like?" If I was Peter Hill, I was just the sixteen year old pimply kid over there in the corner with the broom. "Tell him to do it." I enjoyed being that pimply kid, doing a job.

There have been other times when I've pretended to be somebody else, or have had other people pretend to be me. Mainly for a laugh, really. When Dad and I were on the jet-boat expedition up the Ganges, in seventy-seven, an old man got down on his knees, to put his forehead on my toes, because I was the son of "the great Sir Hillary." I was appalled. I was twenty-two years old. I hadn't done anything to deserve this . . . enthusiasm, beyond being my father's son. I'm not sure anyone deserves to have their feet worshipped. I had a few mates among the younger members of the team, and they'd take turns playing the famous son. As much as it made an amusing spectacle, it was interesting for me to watch someone else get eaten alive by all that misdirected adoration.

The "son of" business, I've got used to it. Most of it's pretty harmless, and much of it is kind of nice. In fact, there is a piece of "son of" theater that has become so predictable, virtually scripted, that I now take real delight in not only acting out the part, but anticipating the performance. To wit, every time I come through passport control at an Australian airport, the customs officer and I have the following exchange:

He looks at the passport, and the little photo. He looks up and says, "You're not related, are you, to Sir Edmund Hillary?"

"Yes, that's right," I say.

"Are you his son?"

"Yes, I am."

"Do you climb mountains too?"

"I do."

It finishes with the officer cocking his head and saying something like, "Well, how about that?"

It will be happening when I'm eighty-five years old. What do you do? I could get surly and scream, "Look! Damn you! I'm a person in my own right!"

If you need to scream such a thing, then you need to get a life.

❃   ❃   ❃

You know, it's a funny thing, because in nineteen sixty-six, when I was twelve years old, my mother gave me a book called *The Eye of the Wind,* the autobiography of Sir Peter Scott, the Captain's son. He was a champion fellow. Wildlife painter, conservationist, glider pilot, America's Cup challenger; he made it into some of the encyclopedias. It didn't occur to me for a long time afterward, but she gave it to me because she imagined that Sir Peter's struggles with identity might well be similar to what was in store for me.

"Peter, I want you to read another Peter's story," and she laid the book beside my bed. "Good night."

❃   ❃   ❃

So there I was at the summit of Everest for the first time, up on my fourth attempt, thirty-seven years after Dad and Tenzing made the first ascent. I was sitting up there with my friends Rob Hall and Gary Ball, also up for the first time after previous attempts. They'd been on the hill the year before too. There is no photo of us together at the summit and that's a mixed business. (Gary died in Rob's arms three years later, on Dhaulagiri. Two years on, Rob died famously on Everest, after

trying to assist a stricken client descending from the summit.)
But we had our great moment together, on May ten, nineteen
ninety. We hugged, we laughed, we were as scared as hell as
we needed to be, we sat out of the wind, huddled, like schoolboys sharing sandwiches or cigarettes behind the bike shed.
We made phone calls, patched through from the other side of
the world, via our satellite telephone at Base Camp. The first
call was for me. It was a journalist.

"Peter," he said, "how does it feel to follow in your father's
footsteps?"

I groaned to myself and thought, "Jeepers. Give me a
break."

To the journalist I said, "I have had a thoroughly good look
around up here, but I can't see my father's footprints anywhere."

Soon after, we were patched through to a radio program,
and we later heard that people had pulled their cars to the
side of the road to hear how it was at the top of the world. We
spoke with the Prime Minister of New Zealand. Then I had a
conversation with my father, who had just finished his lunch
at the table in the old family home. It seemed remarkable to
me. We talked about the climb and the conditions I had encountered and how they'd compared to his day. Dad didn't
jump in the air with excitement, but rather dryly reminded
me that the job was only half done, and that I had to get down
again.

He was right. Too often climbers put all their energy and
all their concentration into reaching the summit and have
nothing left for that all important descent to safety. I'd been
on the summit for an hour and a half, far too long. It had left
me in a pretty dreamy state. So I pulled my focus, said "see
you" to the boys, and started heading down. A few steps off
the summit, I felt I was suffocating. My oxygen supply had
run out.

On previous expeditions—to Everest, Lhotse, Makalu—I'd climbed into the death zone without using supplemental oxygen. As much as one can ever do so, I'd tailored my acclimatization to operate without bottled gas above eight thousand meters, where the air pressure is less than a third of that enjoyed at sea level. On this occasion, I was using bottled gas. You're not much more than a robot on bottled gas. Now the gas had run out, I was a robot whose battery had just gone dead.

I fell forward, driving my ice axe into the snow for security, and lay there panting desperately for air.

I thought to myself, "This is how it happens." These were the words that came to me.

And then, again to myself, "No. Not to this one, it doesn't." Sounds melodramatic, doesn't it? Well, these were the words I used to rouse myself as I lay there like a panting dog that had just been hit by a car.

I lay there and concentrated on my breathing. Deep, rapid, hyperventilating. Focus, focus.

It was raising the dead: getting to my feet. I got to my feet. I placed my boot with care and stopped to breathe, focus. Stepped again, stopped to breathe. Every move governed by the knowledge that it was fall and die otherwise. Fall and die. I'd seen it, didn't want it.

It

was

not

go

ing

to

hap

pen

to

me.

Focus, focus, all the way down, and then came the voices in my head. I thought it was Gary and Rob, but they weren't with me. It sounded like them. I ignored the voices. I gasped, I stepped, and that's all. It works well on the mountain, it is what is required; stripping your thoughts and actions to the dead bare essentials, such that nothing else exists but what's required to survive.

People often ask me do I want my own children to climb mountains. I can hear my father's voice as he answered this question in respect to his children. "It's up to them. In many ways I would rather they didn't. But if they do want to climb, then I will support them and I will want them to be absolutely passionate about their involvement in the game. It's an activity that doesn't brook mistakes or mistaken intentions. The one thing they must not do is climb mountains because their father did or, even worse, because their famous grandfather did. They must climb for the joy of it. They must climb for themselves."

But that goes for any pursuit, really. If it doesn't muster a little passion, then it is not for you. It is like falling in love. Different people are drawn to different men and women for many different and sometimes inexplicable reasons. So it is with pursuits that require passion and focus. The decision to climb and to keep on climbing is visceral and certainly intangible. In many ways you climb because there is nothing else you would rather do. And, like love, it is wild, it is difficult, it is marvelous and it can hurt terribly.

Yet here we are, Hillary and son. Just as there are family lines of doctors, lawyers, farmers, we became a small mountaineering concern. The first father and son to climb to the top of the world, actually. I am following in his footsteps, in many ways, and in many ways deeper and more important than our connection to the hills or the thrills. They are but the expressions of breeding and blood, not the full or even true picture of what we are about, as people. And as it goes for gifts and blessings, what works well in the mountains, under that constant threat of extinction, doesn't translate happily when applied to the regular life, to dealings with other people; emotional dealings, difficult dealings. But it's what we know.

I realize how I have absorbed the character of the man that is my father and laid it upon my own character, as he has absorbed the character of his father, Percival, the hard man of Responsibility and Righteousness. Dad's certainly pressed on me Responsibility, and a keen awareness that I have had, for the most part, a very fortunate life. Of all his achievements, what I admire most is how he listened to the Sherpa people when they asked for help. As he was building one school or hospital, people from far off places in the hills would come asking that they, too, be similarly blessed. He's piped fresh water to dry villages, he's planted trees, he's put in bridges, airstrips. Ed Hillary made a difference in the Khumbu. As a child, I was there when he was building some of the early hospitals and schools. Later I began working on them with him (and later again established a program whereby I lead schoolchildren on trekking trips through Nepal, to work on Himalayan Trust projects: painting, repairing, shifting rocks, fixing roofs, digging drains, giving of themselves). It wasn't that hard to be proud of my father, or to want to be a part of what he was doing.

The Sherpas are easy and enthusiastic with their affections and embrace of emotional truth, and it's always been easy for us to receive it from them, to respond to it, despite the fact that we share an awkward reticence, even resistance, to such displays. It's something I can defeat with logic in my mind, but am unable to turn around, such is the power of inheritance and example, such are one's limits, such is the color of my everyday fears.

Simply put, emotionally we Hillary men are cripples. Cap-

tured by our intellect and not our hearts and frightened to
take the ultimate journey. When my mother died, Dad sank
into grief. In the evenings he would knock back four or five
whiskeys. It seemed reasonable for a man to drown his con-
siderable sorrows and no one dared comment nor admonish.
It seemed like a reasonable role model, and justified, too, as I
struggled with my own slant on our loss. The wonderful taste
of wine and the warm fuzzy fur of a mind shutting down. The
easy retreat behind the firewall of the soul. And so passed
many evenings filled with talk of philosophy, evolution, cul-
ture, business, art, philanthropy and a ton of laughter, yet not
a whisper of feeling. Here lies our stagnant pool. Herein lies
the easy path to the bunker. Reach out and . . . what?

My father doesn't know how to do it. I don't know how to
do it.

"What's going to happen, Dad?"

While my father didn't go out of his way to encourage my
climbing (and indeed was more likely than my mother to get
grumpy as I explored in my youth various avenues of the dangerous life), over the years he's given me the occasional piece
of advice. One of the most important things he ever pressed
on me was to always make my own decisions, and stick by
them, regardless of whatever the rest of the group was doing.
The Hillary way, on or off the mountain. Whenever and wherever we find ourselves pushed, we dig in and hold our position, with no explanation or apology. We are masters at
putting up a wall, while not exactly enjoying the life behind it.
Reach out and . . . what?

Dad once said that I'm a chip off the old block, and I think
it's as simple as that.

CHAPTER FIFTEEN

Who is the third who walks always beside you?
When I count, there are only you and I together
But when I look ahead up the white road
There is always another one walking beside you
Gliding wrapt in a brown mantle, hooded
I do not know whether a man or a woman
—But who is that on the other side of you?

T. S. Eliot, "The Waste Land"

Day sixteen, it was so quiet. He woke from the dreams to the
chirp of the alarm and no wind at all, and the wonder of a beautiful sparkling day. After the three days in the blank, it seemed to
be the most sparkling day he'd ever seen. The sleeping coated
tongue was studded with diamonds, to all horizons glinting
under an immensity of blue with no cloud in it, nothing but
the swinging sun. Most remarkable were the mountains to the
north and the west, because there were ghost mountains playing above them.

Hillary coughed up the moss that had flowered in the last hours of sleep. He dressed with the manner of a bookkeeper deep in a ledger. He took his plastic bag outside and struck the pose in that grand privacy, beholding with a happy wonder the mountains, and the ghost mountains, impossible cliffs that rose from the feet of the true mountains and stretched above their peaks. They shrank away for a time, rose up again, from Erebus and Terror, and from the black finger of Minna Bluff to the west he saw them come and go. He'd seen it before, the mirage known as a fata morgana. A trick of the cold light, named for King Arthur's sister, Morgan le Fay, who lived in a castle half in the air and half in the sea. When Hillary dropped his gaze, he found bad news.

> **I'd lost an alarming amount of blood. A rather impressive spray across the ice.**

Back in the tent, he worked on his boot where the toe flapped about. With no workbench vise or electric tools, no helping hand for what was ideally a two man job, he found more frustration in his efforts than success. At one point, Hillary was holding the boot against his ribs with the crook of his arm, in the manner of a vet drenching slippery sheep. When he packed the stove and the bivvy sac, he did so with a heightened sense of purpose, with something akin to the wry affection that lost hunters bestow on their guns. He engaged in the necessary conversational exchanges with the removed focus of someone tying his shoes; over breakfast, during the long business of packing, as the tent came down, and when Philips, as was his habit now, approached to say he felt they needed to haul longer and harder and how there were various things he felt that Hillary could and certainly should do to pick up the pace. The younger man's voice may as well have been the shrill call of a dentist's drill for the enthusiasm it inspired.

> **As far as I was concerned, it was a beautiful sparkling day. There were mountains and ghost mountains. There was a**

bright spray of blood that inspired no mention, not even regarding its aesthetic majesty. Such a beautiful red. Anyway,
there was a feeling that morning that it was very much every
man for himself.

Hillary didn't know that Philips and Muir had started talking
about Hillary as being the problem. He wouldn't know for a year
or so until he read Philips' account of the trip: they'd apparently
come to this conclusion the previous day, day fifteen, when
Hillary had walked on the black beach with his mother (and
later overheard the unfortunate phone call). As they'd ambled
along together under cloud and snow, Muir and Philips talked it
over in fits and starts, walking on in between with their own
thoughts, meeting up again to share their reflections, talking
some more. At one point, they looked back to see Hillary hauling along without his ski poles. It was something he did from
time to time to relieve the ache in his shoulders, to work some of
the ache out of them. As they were watching him, Hillary began
swaying from side to side, as he did from time to time in the
whiteout, perhaps when he'd momentarily lose his sense of
what was up and down, perhaps as the sled had pulled back on
him. However, Muir concluded that Hillary wasn't in the right
"head space." Philips told Muir that he was so glad that Muir
could see it too, that they saw things the same way. They told
each other how glad they were to have each other along on the
trip, in what read as the earnest language of a schoolyard pledge.
They walked on to think about it all some more, keeping it to
themselves. And that was probably the beginning of Muir and
Philips together regarding Hillary as the other guy, when he became "the one."

Now, on the following morning, when Muir and Philips
locked in and leaned-to, Hillary dallied to let the others get
ahead. He wanted to be alone, to get himself right with being
alone, in a "positive" way. Mostly, he wanted to take in the new
world and be alone with the quiet.

I loved the incredible silence that came when the wind wasn't blowing. It made me feel that the mountains were listening to me. That they had stopped talking, or whatever mountains do, so that they could listen to the scrapings of the skis and the sled, the grunting. The others got ahead such that their scrapings couldn't be heard. I imagined the mountains couldn't hear them either. I loved the fact that Antarctica lets you listen like you have never been able to listen before. It's remarkable what comes to you when the exterior world is absolutely quiet. The first time I heard it, I was shocked. It was on Mount Vinson in ninety-one, with Graeme Joy. The others had gone to bed and I stood alone on the glacier in the huge, all encompassing silence. Suddenly I heard a helicopter. "Whop whop. Whop whop. Whop whop." I wondered how that could be. We were too far from anywhere for it to be a helicopter. We were out of range of helicopters. Then I realized that what I was hearing was my own heart.

He listened to his heart for evidence that he was alone, and that it was good to be alone and he determined to be alone from that point on, in the words that came to him, contemplating with a determined pleasure the mountains that had shrunk with the distance of three days' travel. The mountains were fading. Soon they'd shrink like drying boils to nothing and there would be no mountains to be seen, for some days, no more to the north, only the scything string waiting to the south. He beheld the fading Erebus, shrinking each day with the distance, throwing up ghost mountains now that pierced the sky.

When he moved on, the others well enough ahead, he thought about the joys of kiting. He thought about it cheerfully.

It was a beautiful sparkling day.

He wanted to think cheerful thoughts. And where he'd earlier struggled to find things to think about during the hauling hours, he found now an abundance of great memories and thoughts to be called into being. He was aware of this new abundance, and it

intrigued him that much of it would allow him the sort of reveries he'd hoped to enjoy in his dotage, that he otherwise hadn't
expected to see until that time when climbing a flight of stairs
was beyond him. Childhood memories, what had been for so
long the almost mythical "marvelous years," those that had run
in tandem with the less invoked "flogging years," the door was
open to them, to everything that lay a long way back, to just
about everything since it seemed. Friends, conversations, all
those great pieces of accidental comedy, the regular life, music,
dreams.

But he was keeping things simple. He felt it important to keep
things as simple as possible while he found his feet in his new
life. So he kept people out of his thoughts and kited much of the
day in his mind, flying across the ice with music playing in his
mind as the toe of his boot flapped about like a chatterbox friend
who'd lost his voice. During lunch, when he found the wolf fur
lining coming away from the hood of his parka, he made a
cheerful note to bring out the needle and thread that night. He
held himself that way through the day and into the evening. The
night, too, was quiet. It was quiet in the tent.

> **And that was day sixteen: a blue sky all day, clear and sunny
> and quiet, seven hours hauling, an extra half hour's haul on
> the day before. Twelve miles. Did my duties, made my calls,
> ate the food, drank the drinks, had mixed success with vari-
> ous repairs. Slept well.**

❄   ❄   ❄

Day seventeen, November twenty, the second day of his cheery
new life. The wall of happiness was holding. The silence was
gone; the wind blowing in their faces the taste of the longaway
mountains to the south, making it very cold. But the sun was out
and swinging through a deep blue void that seemed on the
verge of birthing stars and planets, nebulae. Togging up against
the wind with goggles and face mask only deepened the feeling

that he was no longer on the earth, but traveling through the universe as a castaway. The sky was everything. Seven hours hauling across the face of space, twelve miles and some.

The sky thrilled him. It was a good thing to think about in a fanciful way: the sky that threatened to carry him off, the cosmos. He made up a little story about it, a bedtime story for when he got home, for young Alexander. It was a simple story, about a little boy who travels through space on a free floating observation deck. That's how the day felt to Hillary, the place where he lived. It was simple and beautiful and after a while he brought Leonardo da Vinci into the story, to act as a kindly guide to the little boy in the story, and it was nothing to see the great Leonardo floating along on the space walk at his side, at the controls of one of his famous flying machines. When the going was good and simple, he could bring anyone and everything to life again.

> I tried to imagine what amazing things the great Leonardo would have dreamed up under the blessings of visual deprivation. I think he would have loved seeing that big sky. It was an inspiring sky.
>
> The great Leonardo was my childhood hero, and he's still one of my heroes. I was nine years old, around the time I was digging up the seabirds and threading their bones together, when I started reading about Leonardo da Vinci and decided he was the most extraordinary talented mind I had ever heard of. I loved the breadth of his genius: anatomy, aviation, architecture, military designs, and painting. Leonardo's designs for helicopters, water reticulation, anatomy and medicine all intrigued me. Where a lot of boys wanted to be Superman, I began copying many of Leonardo's sketches and pictures using charcoal and pencil, and I put them up on the wall above my bed with drawing pins.

There were so many questions he wanted to ask the great Leonardo under the big sky, but the rapture didn't extend to actual conversation in this instance. Instead, Leonardo floated by his side as a character in his story, saying the things Hillary felt he should say to move the story along. When the story was done, Leonardo departed, leaving Hillary wanting a big talk about deep things. His mind granted the request with the large serious face of his great friend Fred From staring into his own, talking to him.

> If anyone was to remind me of the great Leonardo, it would be the great Fred From. Fred talked the language of God: physics and mathematics.
>
> His name was actually William. His father's name was Fred. He had a brother named Fred too. But away from the family farm William was known as Fred. He was known in climbing circles as "Fred from the bush." And he was known for climbing barefoot on rock. I don't think he could afford boots in the early days of his climbing. And then it became what he was known for, and so he kept climbing in bare feet because . . . that's what he was known for. We're funny creatures, people. We need to feel we belong. Even the bright boys.
>
> Fred was a very bright boy. He had a Ph.D. in ionospheric physics. He had a huge future in front of him. He'd been offered fellowships in the United States and Germany. During our ten years as friends, Fred tried to explain to me the science of his work, what was involved, but I just didn't have the math (or the brains) to fully understand it. While this was a bit frustrating, and I suppose a little galling, I sort of enjoyed having to work to get the basics of his world. I found it exciting, because it was another world.
>
> Fred had a big bearded jaw and a very learned way of saying "Hmm."

For sixteen years, after that first try for Everest, Hillary hadn't been able to think of his great friend for any length of time without seeing again the frozen image of him falling to his death, the look on his face.

All those years he'd fretted and brooded on the fact that he hadn't gone down to see Fred From at the end of it. He'd just turned to climb up after seeing how young Craig Nottle had looked at the end of it when Fred came bouncing past.

> And I just couldn't go down to him. On the one hand, I probably would have been killed too, just trying to get to him. On the other hand, I didn't want to see my friend all broken up. But it always bothered me. Sometimes I've had the horrified thought he may have been in some way alive when he finally stopped bouncing and falling. I don't see how. And if he was, it wouldn't have been for long. I always felt he was disappointed in me. And any reverie of affection and longing I had for my friend always collapsed with Fred swimming through the air, with those desperate flailing arms and the look on his face.

But it didn't come to him on their walk together through the latter part of the morning. They walked and talked together, free of all that had happened, just enjoying the old deep conversations. He'd remember how marvelous it was, Fred being out there, walking across the face of space, rubbing his big, bearded jaw and saying "Hmm," talking about the cosmos and their place in it.

> The polar life, meanwhile, ticked by with the same meals, same drinks, same mutters that one must lift one's game, a new plastic bag, a new round of repairs, phone calls, including one at lunchtime to Amelia's school. Good to speak to my little darling. Didn't get to speak with George. George was at home sick with something, apparently. It's never simple with your children.

> Little George, cherub blond hair, built like a hopping mouse, very accurate with a football, very fast on his feet, not an easy chap to slow down. I wondered if George was living it up in front of the television set or if he was really laid out. After lunch, back in the harness, I wondered how it was all going

for George. He's a persistently cheerful fellow, and most of the time it seems to get him by.

I thought about George as I sat over the stove that night. I had to cook before I could attend to my repairs and there was the wind rattling the tent and that's all there was to hear, the only sound. It was all so very quiet. Slept well indeed.

❄ ❄ ❄

Most mornings now Hillary dallied to let the others get ahead, so he could have the place to himself. He'd get a little excited as he wondered what he'd think about during the day ahead. He'd plan to think of certain things, in the way one might plan a video movie marathon on the couch at home.

Sometimes, as he dallied, or as he hauled, he'd see the others looking back at him and then to each other and moving on again. Sometimes he noticed them, where they were, that they were there. Generally, when things were going well, once he'd found his rhythm with the sled and the skis, Hillary would be deep into whatever world his mind was projecting upon the emptiness, filling it up with beautiful pictures, with marvelous people he'd known, with colors, life. For to some extent, when he could keep it simple—and in the early days of his new self containment he figured that keeping it simple was best—Hillary was able to drive his mind like a car, taking in the view, taking to the roads and tracks he found most comfortable, and when it was all very good, music played in his ears, grand orchestral pieces or coffee shop songs strummed and mumbled, tunes that welled up spontaneously to feed the jolly mood.

Now and then the ruts in the road would take control of the wheel and Hillary would be driven down a road he hadn't planned on visiting. Still, he felt a new confidence, and he determined to walk the surprise dream lands with curiosity and patience, with all things of a "positive" persuasion.

More days than not, however, Hillary found he couldn't keep

it simple, and he'd be cast into places that made his heart hammer in his ears regardless of the scraping and the grunting and the wind blowing or not, as was the case on the third day of his new self containment. That was day eighteen, a Saturday, clear and sunny, no wind, absolutely quiet again, seven hours' hauling, not quite twelve miles.

He'd dallied in the Saturday morning quietness, listened to his heart for the kick of it, tried to hang on to it above the scrape of the skis, the heavy breathing, tried to feel that beautiful quietness that lay just out of reach. Then his mother turned up again, turned up out there, not in some place they had known together but out there, walking along beside him in Antarctica. It was some years before he could say how it had been for him, before he could tell out loud that it had felt to him more than living a memory.

> It was like she'd come out there to keep me company. It was like she was really there. Right there. In a way that was almost scary. Yet it seemed natural as anything to walk along talking to her. If there is one thing I know now, it is this: the people who reach out to others with the hand of kindness and maturity, whatever their age, become our champions. And this was my mother. She saw the best in everyone she met, and was an exemplary ambassador of the happiness that is there if you only care to look for it. A lover of music and life, open hearted without fear. She knew me absolutely, and she was the person in whom I confided as a teenager.
>
> "I want to try everything," I once told her, "so that I develop a wide range of knowledge." Like my hero the great Leonardo.
>
> She gently admonished me by pointing out that you need to judge whether or not the experience is worth the journey and that a little bit of everything doesn't add up to much in the end. We used to joke about the strange prospect of making a career out of dilettantism. Indeed, within a few short

years of her death, I'd tried a little bit of everything. Office toilet cleaner, pilot, ski instructor, mountaineer, author. I wasn't very good at any of them, apart from the toilet cleaning. They were good experiences, but what did they add up to? Eventually I had to decide to get serious with something, and that was climbing.

The thing is, it was my mother who encouraged me to get out there, into the adventuring game.

It was Mum who organized my first alpine climbing trip, to Mount Ruapehu, with the Alpine Club in the late sixties, when I was maybe fifteen. (Her father, Jim Rose, was president of the club in the fifties.)

And Mum was the one who signed the documentation that enabled a nineteen year old Peter Hillary to buy and own a Kawasaki seven-fifty triple two stroke, the most powerful motorcycle in its day.

(On the other hand, Dad passed me in the stairs at home without a word for two weeks, so strong was his disapproval. I understood he was worried I'd end up wrapped around a tree. And this was his way of saying so.)

The thing is, Mum saw I needed to go out on a limb; that I needed to challenge and express myself as a way of breaking out of my excruciatingly self conscious and awkward shell.

(I was one of those dorks who blushed when confronted by a member of the opposite sex. "I . . . I . . . I saw some interesting fossils yesterday," was my standard line of woo.)

Mum talked about the mountains and the motorcycle, and life choices generally, in terms of them being worth the risk.

"Ask the question and answer it honestly," she said.

Best of all, she had that faith in me, that I was making honest choices. If there was anyone who could give me a boost, and a dose of perspective, it was Louise.

There was no great surprise that she came to me on the ice, because she was my best friend, truly. And I could feel the outlying quietness as I told her about my children, the grand-children she never saw. She was excited to hear about them.

Then we talked a little about the last time I saw her alive.

❊ ❊ ❊

It disappoints me now how little of that morning I remember. Of course, I had no idea of its significance then. I've combed through it many times since, but I'm rarely able to do it with a cold eye. Rather, I have sifted through that morning with the prejudiced hopefulness of a pilgrim on a holy treasure hunt, finding signs of prophecy in the humblest recovered relic. I have remembered little lines of words spoken, fragments of mother and son banter that I have treasured, measured and interpreted beyond their incidental meaning. At the time, in the excitement of a looming adventure, the self centeredness of youth cast my anticipation only in terms of my immediate plans. I was twenty years old. The family had just set up home in a house in Baluwatar, Kathmandu. This was seventy-five. We'd come to live in Nepal for a year. And that morning, I was setting off to travel across India with an old pal, Simon Maclaurin. I remember the sun was warm as Simon and I enjoyed our breakfast upon the patio roof of the house from where we could look out across the rooftops of suburban Kathmandu past clusters of trees, tiled roofs, temple pagodas, to the Himalayas on the northern horizon. Such details are a blur, but I remember we didn't dally over breakfast and that it was my mother who ushered us downstairs to heave our packs, my skis and eventually ourselves into our Morris Mini utility for the drive across town to the bus depot. I remember huddling in the open tray of the mini with the gear, meandering through the narrow lanes of Kathmandu all lined with tall brick walls. I remember—or do I know them too well?—the holy cows wandering along the roads, foraging, and groups of porters carrying large baskets of produce on the back of their necks into the markets. Occasionally the road would rise over a simple brick arch that spanned one of the many creeks, or turn around a roundabout festooned with gods, a temple, and gigantic pipal trees growing right out of the monument. I do remember lines of Nepalis approaching the stone images and placing flowers and offerings of rice in leaf plates at the foot of the gods and daubing their foreheads with powdered vermilion. I remember explaining to Simon what the people were doing. Even the cows upon the road received blessings and thanks with a "tikka" on their foreheads. Their fly whisk tails flicking passers-by of all persuasions.

I remember the rushing air feeling cold around our ears and we huddled low in the rear of the utility. Soon we followed the broad boulevard that borders the Tundikhel, the parade ground, in central Kathmandu. Small groups of grass cutters squatted upon the lawn slashing the grass with sickles and placing handfuls into their baskets for their livestock at home. Opposite this broad green field lay the proverbial hole in the ground, the public bus depot, an acre of mud and potholes, of filth, dogs and chickens and the roaming eyes of despair. Scores of haphazardly parked buses were festooned with passengers pushing themselves and their baggage aboard, beneath the seats and onto the roof. The bus drivers strutted about like rock stars—I remember them.

What do I remember of my mother that morning? I remember she parked the Mini outside the depot, amid hordes of people and the din of squealing horns, yelping dogs. She walked with us as we hunted out the bus that would take us to the Indian border.

I expect—but don't really remember—that she was highly amused when a rather short local fellow walked up, tapped my very long skis in the manner of one knocking on a door, and asked me, "Is this the polo sticks?"

"They are very nice," he said, stroking them now.

Then he saw my plastic ski boots sticking out the top of my pack, bright yellow. "What is it? It is be-yoootiful."

Again he didn't wait for an answer. On a roll with his English repertoire, he looked at Simon and then to me, nodding, and said, "You are lovely boys."

Stepping carefully then past some excrement, he delivered his final compliment. "You are very fat." His eyes rolled and his head rocked from side to side, the jaw seemingly leading the cranium into a series of figure-eight rotations; the subcontinent's body language for a type of familiarity and undeniable supreme contentment. He followed all the way across the depot to our bus.

The vehicle had been cosmetically deified: draped with plastic streamers and tassels, images of favorite gods, a faded paint job of spectral circus tones. Mud caked the tires. Dogs with scabby wounds lifted their emaciated legs upon the wheels, releasing perhaps the worst of stinks. Kathmandu's permanent perfume of smog and burned human dirt was pleasant by comparison, as I remember it.

And Mum . . . well, Mum was just there. As mothers tend to be.

I remember, as the bus pulled out, Simon and I, taking ourselves very seriously, swiped at the air by way of hailing farewell, acknowledging but refusing to appear too interested. The bus belched a blue cloud, the driver trumpeted the absurdly loud horn, and with a crash of gears we were moving. Mum stood there smiling, happily waving, making broad sweeps with her arms, like a child making a tree in a breeze. I looked over my shoulder, saw her grow smaller and smaller, her arms still waving. Then she was swallowed by the surrounding chaos.

❄   ❄   ❄

"And how was that bus ride?" she asked me as we walked along together over the ice.

I told her everything I remembered. I told her how I had to cross my legs for a time because I'd drunk too much tea at breakfast, and how—when the driver pulled to the side of the road for a break—I told her how I'd bolted from my seat to find a bush to pee behind. On returning, I found all the other men on the bus lined up along the road, beside the bus, doing their business. The views out across the Mahabharat Ranges were magnificent and the air was reasonably clear.

I described the narrow plain of Nepal's terai, the receding image of the high hills to the north, and the road that led us to the border town of Birgunj, a small slum cut into quarters by the border running east to west, by the muddy road running north to south.

I told her—and I'd imagined at the time telling her of these adventures—I told her how we took a horse and cart from the Nepalese side, across open ground to Raxaul, where we passed through Indian customs. In the dingy dark shed—Customs and Immigration—was a rather dark and dingy officer who had obviously slept in his uniform for a month.

Like our friend at the bus depot, he was intrigued by my skis. "What is it? You are taking the polo? Where you go?"

He was only going through the motions, for without further ado he looked past us and gestured us by.

Simon and I wandered into town, sweating in the heat of the plains, under the weight of our packs. All the hotels—a motley collection—were full, it seemed.

"For polo players anyway," my mother chuckled.

Eventually we found an obliging hotelier, who led us to a store room by the faucet block—it contained two primitive hemp stretcher beds, a single tap, and a bucket. It was a hot night. It was very hot in the little room. No windows. Soon after lying down we were powdered with mosquitoes. In desperation we pulled out our "Everest" sleeping bags—rated to minus twenty degrees—and slipped inside. We'd tuck in our heads but it was impossible to keep them tucked in for long. By morning we were sodden, and our faces red and blotchy from the droning swarm. Without delay we crossed town to the Raxaul Railway Station and began the first of many long journeys on Indian Rail.

I told Mum how, on that journey, Simon and I had talked ad nauseam about religions and philosophy and moralities, the quandaries of life and death and the universe, the value of faith.

"Not that it was much help to me when I heard what happened to you," I told her.

❄   ❄   ❄

In the early afternoon his mother left him, and he returned to seeking the quietness of the world, the flat white disc under the dome of blue, the last traces of the mountains, not bumps, just glints in the distance. He figured they'd be gone by the end of the day and felt a satisfaction that the trip was leaving one world and moving into another. Talking away small waves of unease, he considered with a determined curiosity the idea that there would be no view now beyond the white and blue, for some days. He made plans for those days. After a time, he let his mind go with the vacancy of a kite.

So there I was, cranking along in a daydream of no focus, minding my own business, and then.

And then came a loud cracking sound that was traveling toward him from way off to the right of him, and then under him and away from him at a tremendous speed to the left. He veered sideways in his skis, sensing the ice beneath him sinking, and the sound traveled on until it was dead or beyond his ears and then all was quiet again save for his jackhammer heart.

When it came, as it was happening, all in that moment when fright took me, I first thought "Is it an avalanche?" because it sounded like an avalanche. Then, "Is it some huge crevasse?" It sounded like so many things that I'd heard before.

It was the only sound that ever made me get down on my knees and pray for a god, or whatever might be out there, to spare me and thereby win my faith and devotion. That was in eighty-nine, when I went back to Everest and I was nearly killed again coming down through the icefall—when an avalanche bombed off the west shoulder, and I'd run and hid behind a towering serac as the big wave came through and just prayed my heart out.

All these stories.

I've seen guys who were pretty good in the mountains end up sitting on bar stools, telling about the times they were nearly killed and how they got out of that one and another one and again until they've repeated themselves so many times they're beyond boring themselves, and still they sit there and talk. They'd been to the serious and desperate places until they couldn't go there anymore. All that was left to them was "and then there was the time . . . and then there was the time."

And then?

The sudden cracking and movement of the ice sparked an avalanche of "and then there was the time"—and my heart stayed hammering long after I'd made sense of what had actually happened. It was an event known as hoar slumping: the crunchy top layer of the shelf, inches to feet thick, had suddenly collapsed due to compression of hoarfrost crystals. It may have been the three sunny days that brought it on. It could have been the horror of the sleds in passing. It's always interesting when it happens.

In the late afternoon his mother returned. She stayed on for the evening, and perhaps the others saw him smiling to himself in that reverie. There were evenings when he saw happier places playing on the faces of Muir and Philips, but he'd lost the urge to say, **"Let's hear about it, eh?"**

❄ ❄ ❄

Day nineteen, seven hours, twelve and a half miles, under high cloud and a light cold wind from the south, and not even the glint of mountains remaining, just the flat white beneath their feet that went in all directions to the sky and meeting it, like the floor meets the walls of an aquarium. The clouds were the only view; long wisps, pieces of bleached lint, sugar grains scattered on glass, not gathering into mare's tails until later in the day, but making pictures instead of elegant birds and Cubist stringed instruments.

The making of birds, the conjuring of elegant birds in the sky, was a frequent fancy for Hillary. He was one of those people who momentarily lose all self consciousness and get red in the face and half lunge into the air when spotting a marvel on the wing. They had been his first and most uncomplicated love, birds. He loved their resilience, that they were out there at the mercy of the winds, that they remained so spirited no matter the conditions. He'd seen them high on Everest, up in the death zone. There were occasions throughout the journey when he was moved by the shadow of a cloud passing over to look up half expectant, for a wayward beauty. There were times he longed for the sky to fill up with them. He longed to see first the tiny black dot on the horizon, to watch it get bigger and thicker, then slowly spread into a fine black line, and there was a touch of menace in its mystery. Drawing nearer, the line would break up into dashes, no longer straight but shaped like an arrowhead, that's how he thought of the sky filling up with them. His jaw never failed to drop when they came over like that. And he re-membered it like that, from when he was a child, when he'd slung a pair of binoculars from around his neck and declared himself a birdwatcher.

Many of our summer holidays in the sixties were spent down in the South Island, at a little piece of land we had at Albert Town near Lake Wanaka. On the Clutha River side of the property was a large swamp that had been left as a nature reserve. When I was eight years old I built a hide down by the swamp using poplar and willow branches and took dozens of black and white photographs with my mother's old box Brownie camera. The photographs were invariably disappointing, as my subjects—white-faced herons and ducks—appeared as blurred dots upon a landscape of reeds, shrubs and water.

Being young and impulsive, I could only sit inside the hide for a short period of time before feeling the need to get out, and I remember always what followed—the sight of the heron's outstretched neck and the slow regular wing beats as it left the lagoon for a less harassed environment. I loved seeing them climb out of the water and into the air.

My passion for birds was fostered by some of the best birdmen in the country: Graham Turbott, an ornithologist and the director of the Auckland Museum, and one of my schoolmasters, Richard Sibson, who was one of New Zealand's foremost birdmen.

And of course there was my grandfather Jim Rose, who had been naming plants and birds to me since I could walk. I was eight years old when Jim first read aloud to me "The Rime of the Ancient Mariner" by Samuel Taylor Coleridge, the epic lyric that tells the story of a sailor who killed an albatross, and soon after lost everything. He read that poem to me many times, as a favorite bedtime story, and always out at Anawhata, with my grandmother Phyl sitting nearby. Jim and Phyl Rose, my mother's parents, used to live next door.

I remember one time Jim and Phyl telling me I could bring a friend out to the black beach, for the weekend. My best friend at the time was Nigel Lewis, an urchin of misadventure, redheaded. That was the weekend I heard "The Rime of the Ancient Mariner" read aloud by way of moral instruction.

Nigel had just been given an air rifle for Christmas, and he spent a lot of time shooting sparrows around the Lewis's suburban property, and no great outrage from the neighbors, apparently. The good old days, eh?

I remember visiting Nigel one day and being guided across a flower bed behind some hydrangeas where Nigel had assembled a graveyard of prodigious proportions—a pile of bird carcasses, mostly sparrows, in various states of rigor mortis. While it repelled me, in many ways there was something very exciting about the notion of being a hunter, pursuing the sparrow. You know: little brown bird pursued by two skinny legged boys practicing their man-the-hunter skills. And so when I invited Nigel to accompany me to Anawhata for the weekend, Nigel asked if he could bring the air rifle.

However, Jim was on the board of Tongariro National Park, the second national park to be established anywhere in the world, and it did not take him any time at all to deliver a blistering judgment on this request, by way of powerful argument. (Jim was, after all, a senior lawyer in the Auckland legal community.)

"There will be no guns at Anawhata," he said. "How would you feel if you shot a black-backed gull? Even if it was an accident?"

We meekly argued that we would only use the gun for target practice.

"No," he countered. "If you have a gun, you will probably use it to shoot something."

And in my heart I knew Jim was right. If we'd taken the gun on our adventures down through the rainforest and around the rocks, we would have had a grand time with the birds indeed. Equally thrilling and repellent, I knew it was true.

To quench our primal (prep school) bloodlust Nigel and I decided to go pig hunting instead. With the air rifle out of bounds, we taped an old blunt butterknife blade onto the end of a dried flax flower stem, dry and brittle and about five feet long, and with growing trepidation pushed our way into the tea tree scrub.

About one hundred yards into the thicket to the east of the little house, we came upon a very old pig rooting among the tea trees. A "pig rooting" being an area dug up by a pig, and not an actual animal. Already grass and small seedlings were growing out of the disturbed ground. The pig had been gone for months. But it had been there! This was just too much for our fertile imaginations. With a growing sense of panic we fled out of the scrub shouting loudly to Jim and holding aloft our spear with its butterknife blade.

That night, as the coastal wind buffeted the house, or "bach" (a New Zealand term for holiday house, derived from bachelor pad), Jim told us about wild pigs—the Captain Cookers, he called them—and how they had long, curled tusks that could disembowel a hunter's dog with one fearful lunge.

Then he read to us the dreadful tale of what happens when you shoot an albatross. And I made the firm decision to abandon hunting and stick to birdwatching.

Many years later, one of Dad's old climbing friends from the Everest days, George Lowe, told me that an albatross had been shot from the deck of the ship that was carrying Vivian Fuchs and company to Antarctica, in early fifty-seven. George was aboard the ship at the time. The beautiful bird was gliding in the air off the stern, occasionally veering off to wheel down and tip the water with its wing and glide up again to ride alongside. Then a crewman appeared with his rifle and BLAM! No more beautiful bird. George and I pondered with some malice the fate of that sailor.

❊ ❊ ❊

For a time the pictures of birds in the cloud put music in his head, some light orchestral piece that always reminded Hillary of misty green country. He'd never learned who composed the piece, but he always imagined it was by some English fellow, and for a time, in sympathy with the music, he saw Cubist stringed instruments half drawn in the sky.

For amusement, he conjured for his ears a lumbering version of Ravel's *Bolero*, the creeping anthem of desert caravans. He slowed the pulse of the music to match the progress and the lurching of the sled. It was a little joke he'd played from time to time, to pass the time. He was especially fond of turning the classic tunes of marching bands into dirges. But today time passed with gritted teeth through the hilarity of Ravel retarded. Then it got boring, and the music ran out with the abundance of memories. He'd found the abundance would come and go, and that was all right. But the boredom was a chore, and time passed with a determined blankness of mind that was beyond boring until he heard what sounded at first like the rasping drone of a cello.

It was a plane. He looked up and there it was, a big gray green Hercules transport plane passing overhead on its way to Williams Airfield from the South Pole. And then he saw it banking and coming down for a low pass to say hello and he got all excited and emotional and there was the pilot or somebody waving like an excited kid trying to get the attention of zoo animals. He was incredibly happy that the plane people were excited too, and he stayed with them as the plane glided past, banked around, flew over his head again, climbing, regaining the route home. How the others took it he couldn't say. He turned around in his skis, and saw them have a chat about it.

> I was a good way out in front of them. Jon was still ill with the flu, suffering with it that day. Eric had stayed back, to walk with him, cheer him on. I don't know if they were cheered by the sight of the plane.

Imagining and longing for birds in the sky; a lifelong habit, and never more richly felt than down on the blank. Music, likewise. And then along comes this musical bird. Not that I thought of it in such lyrical terms until later in the day. It was just such a shock and a surprise to see a plane, a plane with other people in it. It put tears in my eyes (which is never convenient in the sub zero).

It was so overwhelming it made me wonder if I'd ever really seen a plane before. It had that excitement. Of course it moved me.

I have to say it was also hilarious. It was like the civilized world playing a prank and making a statement: when it's moved to pop by, it does so.

(The next day we learned the plane's captain had sent us an e-mail, via the expedition website, in which he told how he'd flown Dad to the South Pole two years before.)

❋   ❋   ❋

In the tent that night: the men had a conversation, probably the first real conversation of the trip, and mercifully, perhaps, it wasn't about themselves. Or about the plane either. Rather, they talked about Captain Scott, because he seemed so very close to them. That day they'd crossed seventy-nine degrees fifty min utes South, the latitude where Scott, Bowers, and Wilson had lain down for the last time, two days' march to the west of where they were camped now.

I have a lot of admiration for the Captain. I certainly felt for him out there. And, yes, for his legend too. Why not? I'm sure he didn't feel very legendary as he lay there in his sleeping bag waiting for it. We certainly didn't feel legendary as we lay there in our bags, tired and sore and rubbed raw.

We wondered if we'd skied over them, given the creep of the sheet over the years. I said how at times I'd imagined spotting a piece of flapping brown canvas out there. And how

I'd occasionally stop and stare at the ground, wondering if I just started digging, would I find the Captain beneath my feet? Jon joked that if he found one of the Captain's freeze dried turds, he would get down on his knees and take a good long look at it.

We wondered how it was for them at the end, and how amazing it was that three of them nearly made it home. They nearly went all the way on foot. It boggled my mind. No dogs, no sails and certainly no possibility of rescue. The weather had been good to us over the previous few days, but we'd seen how wrecking it could be, how it all worked on a human body and mind over time. We could only half imagine Scott at the end of it, in those last days and weeks, withered and sick in the howling white, blighted with that crippling madness. We understood enough how it was that the Captain and his men weren't able to make that last eleven miles to the One Ton Depot. It was something we all remarked upon. And we wondered if we would manage as well as they did at the end of such a long journey. I think it put a shiver through all of us.

And as we talked, I imagined the Captain and his men looking out through their shroud of snow and ice at our young journey and wondering why on earth we were doing it.

It was something that had come to me a number of times on the haul, their wretched faces looking out at us, as I remembered them from the old black and white photographs. I can't remember if I mentioned this in our evening forum. It lasted only a little while, the talk, before Jon drifted back to reading *The Seven Pillars of Wisdom,* Eric was into Kim Stanley Robinson's *Antarctica,* and I set to writing my journal.

In the morning he remembered his dreams and everyone in them from a long time ago. He remembered dreaming with his eyes open, that he'd been half awake a number of times in the night, and that he'd lain there thinking while the dreams ran on.

Half awake, he felt sitting close his companion, his mother. It seemed that in partnership they called the dreams into being.

* * *

It's a confusing thing to be caught between waking and dreams, and it can be a little frightening too. It's a very frightening thing at high altitude, because it usually means that death has its hands gently around your throat by virtue of Cheyne-Stokes breathing. The alternating apnea and hyperapnea—no breathing followed by rapid breathing—of Cheyne-Stokes, and the accompanying dream state, is often part of how people die "peacefully," when they're worn out by an illness like congestive heart failure. Or just plain old age.

It comes on the cusp of sleep, when you desperately need to sleep. Just as that gorgeous drift into the netherworld drifts in upon us like cloud—gentle, soft, recuperative—your eyes roll back and your breathing slows, you feel heavy. Very heavy, very tired.

Your eyes roll back in your head, as your deep breathing expels all the carbon dioxide from the system and with it the desire to breathe slips away. You lie dormant. Still.

And then comes the dream. You could be swimming, diving, reaching for the surface of the water. The sensation of oxygen starvation wafts across your plummeting consciousness. You are drowning.

You are drowning.

Then comes the primal message: "Breathe. Breathe deep. Suck in the air. Suck at it."

If you're lucky, your subconscious is in panic.

You sit bolt upright.

In the regular life, you'll sit bolt upright in your hospital bed, or perhaps in your bed at home if your family is up to it.

You sit bolt upright, eyes wide open and your mouth sucking in the air. Heaving, hyperventilating. It's a horrible thing to see and to listen to. In the regular life it's a sign that it's time to call in a priest or the family, for the end is nigh.

At high altitude, you sit bolt upright in your sleeping bag, heaving, hyperventilating, desperate for the rarefied air. The horror of suffocation subsides. Your breathing settles and you look around the tent. It's rocking in the wind. It's roped to a little ledge on an ice face and it's rocking and you're happy to see it rocking.

You look at your climbing buddy and you listen. He lies there like a cadaver, pale and silent. Then suddenly he, too, lunges at the air with goldfish lips, with a long and loud gasp.

Then, as the panic subsides with the draining of the adrenaline, you each lean back into your sleeping bags, your eyelids become heavy again, and the hands slip gently around your throat again.

The dream awaits.

❆ ❆ ❆

"Do not grieve, even in death, Achilleus."
"O shining Odysseus, never try to console me for dying. I
    would rather follow the plow as thrall to another man, one
    with no land allotted him and not much to live on, than be
    a king over all the perished dead."

Homer, *The Odyssey*, the Richmond Lattimore translation

Day twenty, it was too cold to dally long in the morning with a miserable wind from the south and most of the sky wiped out with cloud. The haul was lengthened to seven and a half hours, with a gain of not quite twelve miles. Under cloud, navigating the blank slate was doubly tedious and time consuming.

The navigator, whoever was in the lead, had to constantly check his compass to ensure we were heading in the right direction. Everything looked the same, and there were no phys-

ical landmarks to get a bearing on. As navigator you looked
for a wedge of sastrugi or a group of sastrugi to march toward
for quarter of an hour or so. I spied a triangle of hyphens! Jon
saw a blob with twins. Eric saw one he called a "double
bump" which became a "bubble gump." And so on. Anything
to keep on track.

Obviously, when it was my turn to lead, I was out front. The
rest of the time I ambled a little behind. In the unpleasant
grip of day twenty, I wasn't able to keep it simple, because I
was too tired to try and keep it anything. It was one of those
days when there was no abundance of memories or cheery
thoughts or much thought at all, much of the time. We were
all cocooned in our caves against the cold.

The morning passed with barely a thought beyond the next hot
drink, until he took to brooding on the flapping boot and that he
was tired from being up late as the cook and why couldn't they
lend a hand fixing the boot, and damn the cooking, damn the
boot and on he went. Hillary was in the fugue's grim embrace
during the break in the bivvy sac and back in the harness where
it expanded to the darker woods of life in general, until he sank
to picking at the wounds he'd long defined as fatal to any true
peace and happiness. His mother and his sister being gone for
so long, and how they died, and how it had been for them at the
end of it, all light and glue gone with them, and into that hole he
went, loathing the grief with its dirty shameful shadow, self-pity.
Hence, it was an event, **the death of the family,** he generally
related with the language of an accident inspector. There was no
comfort of remove in doing so beyond the simplicity of stark
truth, of what was.

People like to think that it's all over before anyone knows
what's happening. And I think I swallowed all that dogma—
that it happens very quickly and without pain. I wanted to
believe it. Then I went away and did the math. I got my map
of Kathmandu and estimated the distances to the crash site.

I factored the takeoff speed for the aircraft, which for the single-engine Pilatus Porter was around seventy knots rising to one hundred. And then I factored where the plane had left the runway, because the Pilatus Porter is a STOL—short take-off and landing aircraft—which is what makes it useful for flying to the hills.

Anyway, I worked out they had forty seconds in the air before hitting the ground, and I've built up their last moments from there.

Mum was always frightened of flying, especially in smaller planes. She was always anxious. From the moment she buckled in, she would have been anxious. As the young New Zealand pilot started the motor and the propeller blurred to invisible beyond the cockpit windshield, she probably didn't notice that he failed to do his preflight checks. The family knew him. Did he look back at them and smile or even call out some words of bravado? She may well have thought about his recent accident in Saudi Arabia, where he had been rushed out of the country after he had hit and killed a man who stood upon a huge field to mark the extent of his aerial agricultural spraying operations. Perhaps she had wondered about his drinking at parties at our home in Baluwatar, Kathmandu. Perhaps she did. From full throttle to pulling back on the stick, to airborne and the young pilot's shocking discovery that his ailerons were locked and that the streaming red tape behind the wing indeed confirmed that the aileron guards were still in place. He would have been in panic.

From the passengers' perspective: they would have taken off, and Mum would have been relieved to have made it into the air, and she'd have told herself that it was going to be all right. Then she and Belinda and everybody else would have noticed the left wing was tilting and that it wasn't straightening up. They would have looked out the window and seen straight down to the ground and ended up arched onto their backs and into a dive. In a few seconds Mum would have gone from thinking, "this isn't right" to "something's wrong" to "this is out of control" to knowing this was it. I've figured they knew for a full five seconds that this was it.

I've gone through the business of thinking what the pilot could have done to save the day.

But as the plane climbed into the sky, the one option for re-gaining some control of the plane's movement around its lon-gitudinal axis, the one that controls the plane's ability to roll and turn to the left and right, did not occur to him: savage use of the rudder pedals yaws the aircraft around the central axis, and strong yaw, turning one wing into the wind and the other into the wind-shadow of the fuselage, creates greater lift on the windward side and causes the plane to roll and turn. This was his only option, and an opportunity lost, as it turned out.

Instead the normal instabilities of the air, tiny waves and eddies of turbulence and the twisting torque of the propel-ler wash, soon caused the plane to veer left as it accelerated to one hundred and twenty knots. At thirty-five seconds it banked steeply into a terrifying dive that would not have spared anyone from utter knowing terror. They plunged ver-tically into a paddy field near the sacred Buddhist stupa of Bhodnath. Amid the stubble of the harvested paddy was a small crater, three feet deep, from which smoke drifted into the air. I've seen it on video. The twisted wreckage lay around the impact site along with the silent forms of broken people. Among them Mum, Belinda, our friend Ang Gali Lama and his American wife, Barbara, and that young New Zealand pi-lot called Peter from New Plymouth.

How it helps knowing these things I can't say or argue with confidence. They're terrible pictures to carry around. I sup-pose there's the feeling that in some way you're there with them right to the end. The wanting to know—that I under-stand. I understand why my condolence calls and visits with

Mrs. Grant, mother of superman Bruce who died on K2, always included her questions. "What happened to Bruce up there?"

She'd read all the books she could find about mountaineering and the many ways it can kill you. She walked into K2 Base Camp looking for answers. Big Kim Logan took the whole family. It was a pretty hard trip on everybody. I hope they got something out of it, seeing where we'd been camped and the mountain above. Like, when I visited the Grants at home and she brought out all the old photo albums and put on all the old videos of Bruce performing feats of derring-do, I understood this was her way of hanging on to him.

We shared the business of being accident inspectors. More than answers, really you're searching for significant relics, those little emotional flags that you can grasp on to and keep forever, that keep those people alive. I understand it. For your own sake, you have to accept what is and suffer the pain. As I drank their cups of tea and looked through the photos, told them all that I remembered of my time with their son, I saw that I was giving them some of those little flags to clutch on to.

It's all about seeing what can be dragged back from my memory, because that's all there is. That's all there was for Mr. and Mrs. Grant. I felt for them.

Anyway, there were times on the shelf, out where there was nothing but the flat white disc, where the emptiness did its best work pulling my mind to pieces, that the wind on occasion reminded me of Mrs. Grant's voice. "What happened to Bruce up there?"

All she knows is he's disappeared into a black nothing and she wants more than that. He was the golden one, and she wants to know that he had Alison Hargreaves by the arm and he was dragging her down lowering her down as best he could, and then something happened and he disappeared.

But in the end none of that sort of matters. We're never going to know. You can't know. They're all dead. Every one of them. And that was the mood of day twenty. That night in the tent, as he sat over the stove, melting the ice and making the drinks and stirring the gruel, the dead friends came and sat with him, a gathering of many old comrades around him, in all their colors, and he took them as gifts from his mind, regardless of their questions.

"You're either happy or you're not. Which are you?" Later when he worked on the flapping toe of his boot, he surveyed his companions in their sleeping bags, their heads down the other end of the tent, their prisoner of war faces in black remove. He lay down missing his wife, wanting to be home, decided that was no good to him, because home wouldn't be the next thing for weeks to months to come. And with a determined cheer he built another wall of happiness. It was just another chore, an extra repair. As one emotional igloo melted, he put up another.

❊   ❊   ❊

Still, I hated to say yes, if for no other reason than that they felt I had to say it. If there's anything I like less than being pushed around it's being pushed around

Jim Thompson, *The Criminal*

It was like trench warfare, in a way. Periods of a heavy quiet— and then blam blam blam.

Increasingly came these confrontations out on the shelf, when I'd suddenly find Eric leaning in close to me, putting his face in mine, and my immediate thought would be, "Oh, what now?"

Because it was becoming clear to me that I could do very little right in the eyes of my young companion. These intense close encounters were his way of letting me know about the latest thing. My favorite was the time he walked up and said, "Are you a scruncher or a folder?"

I said, "What do you mean?"

He felt that I'd been using too much toilet paper, and he wanted to know if I scrunched or folded it, because then he'd know for sure. I said I was a folder. Apparently folders use more toilet paper. It was pretty unnerving, because he was just getting so wound up.

Bigger trouble lay with Philips first urging and then insisting that he take on some of Hillary's load, because it was Hillary slowing them down, and something had to be done about it. Hillary refused to countenance the opinion or the demand.

The whole thing puzzled me. Still does. They were faster than me, sure, but not that much faster. Whenever they stopped to have a chat, I'd be closing in on them pretty quickly. Then they'd look back and head off again. I didn't see how they could take enough of my load to make faster progress viable. And I wondered what it was really all about. We were hauling longer hours now. I was pulling my share. I wasn't injured beyond the various aches. The regular maladies of expeditionary life.

While Hillary couldn't see a problem in how he was traveling, he was fully aware by now that his companions did. It put a hole in his wall of happiness that he half patched with dark stuff.

Frankly, I was sick of it. I mean, these endless confrontations with this wound-up soul were starting to rattle my confidence, and that was the last thing I needed. But I started to feel hammered by these exchanges, day after day—and all I could do was dig in deeper. Regardless, there was no way on earth I'd give up my load. And that was largely a matter of trust.

Blam, blam.

❄ ❄ ❄

Day twenty-one, a Tuesday, three weeks out: a beautiful sparkling day somewhere in the middle of the coated tongue, the
other side nowhere in sight. Hillary's bowels staged another riot
in protest of the diet. They dropped back to seven hours, made
twelve and a half miles.

Too washed out to think, the sky made a good companion until his mother arrived. He kept it simple with his mother, as a
long walk taken in the most comfortable silence, simply taking
together the sun swinging in the cobalt void, where two delicate
feather clouds sat high together in the void, God's eyebrows
knitting a frown.

By day's end, Muir had broken his ski pole basket and a binding. Hillary's boot still flapped about, despite his nightly attentions. And as the men made camp, they broke the tent pole.

❄   ❄   ❄

Day twenty-two, November twenty-five. Under the blessings of
a northerly wind and another clear sky, a marvelous eighteen
miles almost. It was the closest they'd come to making their
original required daily average of nineteen miles, which had
long lost any relevance beyond the power of mockery.

Waking to the fresh northerly felt like Christmas coming early.
In fact it was just a month away, Christmas. Hillary's bowels
were still rioting and he was pretty washed out, so the promise
of sailing instead of snailing was very sweet to him.

> **In all the excitement Jon cut his hand at breakfast time while
> using a knife to separate blocks of muesli bar for our lunch
> packs. Blood everywhere, throughout the day: on Jon's down
> jacket, on my mug, through the tent, on the snow. Amazing
> how much blood there was. We closed it up with medical
> tape, broke camp as fast as we could, got out to the sleds and
> put the kites up. Jon crashed five times over the first hundred
> yards or so.**
>
> **Soon after, Eric tried pulling Jon's sled, along with his own,**

so Jon could sail without a sled. He abandoned the plan after he'd suffered numerous heavy crashes, and damaged his kite. Just too heavy.

Something must have moved inside Muir, because he improved over the morning and we covered about thirteen and some miles by lunchtime.

After lunch, the winds were lighter, requiring more precise flying. Eric and I took about one hundred and fifty pounds of gear from Jon's sled, on to our own, to make it easier to pull as he managed the kiting. With Eric and I pulling nearly five hundred pounds each, we flew another four miles. Both my number five and seven kites were damaged. A line ripped off the former, and a power cord broke on the latter. The sleds were just too heavy.

After making camp, we put in our second food and turd depot, with the snow block cairn and the bag of poo on the top to mark it, and our food and fuel in a pit on the north side of the cairn. We were two hundred and one miles from Scott Base, with another seventeen hundred ahead of us, another three hundred miles ahead on the shelf alone.

✳   ✳   ✳

Day twenty-three, twelve miles and some. With a cold southerly in their faces, no feeling in their hands, and the wind putting diamonds in the air around them while the sky above was clear. Midmorning they saw a giant parhelion, a spectral ring around the sun born from the swirling ice crystals.

It was a most beautiful halo, but it was rather overshadowed by one of the most astounding things I'd ever seen: a mock sun that hovered on the surface of the ice. It looked like a burning bush. I found it dazzling and kind of alluring because it was one of those wretched days when you had to frequently stop and bang your hands together to keep them from turning to wood. It was wearying business, your hands hurting like hell all day. And still there was nothing on the horizon, no matter where you looked. There was nothing to suggest we were getting anywhere. The burning bush was no signpost. It hovered just out of reach.

Moses wandered for forty years in the desert. Apparently his burning bush spoke to him. A talking campfire. That would have been all right by me. I was cook again that night.

❋ ❋ ❋

Day twenty-four, he woke to find the sky had fallen. The world was a cloud of drifting brightness, his companions blurred smudges for the seven and a half hours in the harness, his wall of happiness rickety with a stir crazy loneliness. It was waiting whenever he came down from the highs of his new life, in the hangovers of grief and longing that followed his rapturous visitations with the dead. Sooner or later they came, the hangovers, and little was good when they did.

There was no dallying when they locked in and leaned-to, and they held closer together, keeping a good pace through the cloud and that's all there was: drifting along the floor of the shelf and up into the sky and that's all there was: white on whites silvered to gray, a magnesium glare at the heart of it, no gravity.

The world dissolved, and I waited with mixed feelings for whatever was coming, and I knew it was coming when I started moving uphill and the blurred smudges ahead were above me and I was climbing toward them. And then the route went all over the place, from place to place as if I were dreaming, with that chaos. There was a logic to it too. We kept returning to a steep couloir, where there was no Jeff Lakes from K2 up ahead, just the blurred smudges on skis. The couloir was like the way station tent of my dreams, because the visions that day always began and returned there.

In the first instance we were heading up the couloir that came for a time a stand of winter birch that in turn bled into

the jutting roof lines of a cricket pavilion, that soon after bled back into the couloir. Time passed this way, hauling from one vision to the next, hauling as one place faded into another, never knowing what was to come. It was all right.

He'd been wondering who would come to him through the clouds, but most of the morning went by with the shifting visions populated only by the smudges ahead of him. He came to regard the smudges in the same way he regarded the speedometer on the dashboard when out driving the car, flicking his eyes over them by way of keeping himself straight. When the smudges turned to flickering shadows, he didn't pay any mind to it. And when the shadows were no longer made by his polar companions, when they began bleeding into the vague forms of long ago people, it took Hillary a time to catch on. Absorbed by the surrounding dream lands, relying on the smudges as an anchor, he shuddered with surprise as his eyes caught up with his mind.

Well, it was a bit creepy. Like in a movie, when you catch a glimpse of the bad guy lurking. Someone was there.

He'd come out of the couloir into a paddock of grass, thick and green, and here and there nesting boulders shaped like sheep and flaky with lichen, and over in the corner, off to Hillary's left hand but ahead of him, by the barbed wire fence, a child's swing set standing in a muddy patch and the eroding tracks of swinging feet, in the grass nearby some toy trucks. To the right of the trucks were the flickering shadows, closing on the fence line. Beyond the fence and all around, the grassy flat lands lay empty to longaway horizons, far above horizons meeting there bulbous cloud that sloped visibly upward like the wall of a tent, arcing over his head, brainlike in its massive folds, a mottled membrane of light and dark.

He knew the swing and the flatlands, for he'd returned to the Matuki Valley of his childhood. Hillary remembered looking across the wire fence to the alps keening north to south and in remembrance granted them the enormity and wonder of a child's perceptions. He remembered that view wiped out by cloud, leaving the feet of the mountains protruding below, like the feet of monsters otherwise hiding behind a curtain. When he returned his gaze to the swing set, ahead and to the left of him, he found instead a hay shed standing in its place. He also knew that hay shed, but it had never stood in that corner of the pad-dock. As he pondered this, the hay shed bled into a string of dog kennels, and that's all there was in the grass until the swing set returned, standing off to Hillary's right hand side now, the ken-nels staying in their place to the left, and dead ahead the flitting shadows, made not by his companions, he realized, but a man standing and facing him, with his eyes narrowed, wary and keen, like a gunfighter. Hillary knew this fellow. That is, he knew him in the way a child knows the bogeyman.

✳ ✳ ✳

We often visited the Matuki Valley. Through an old climbing friend of Dad's called Murray Ellis, one of the Old Firm, we got to know the Aspinall family who lived in the shadows of Mount Aspiring, deep in the Southern Alps. The Aspinalls ran the station at the end of the road, and they became good friends. Indeed, visits to the Mount Aspiring Station became highlights of those summer holidays in the South Island.

When we first got to know the Aspinalls, they lived in their original homestead on the north side of the great Matukituki River. To visit, you drove up the dusty road that leads up the valley and into the mountains, and at a lone hay shed you stopped. Inside, on the wall, was an old windup telephone splattered with bird droppings, with hayseeds stuffed in be-hind it.

I'd watch Dad wind the handle three times, put the phone to his ear, and wait. A single strand of wire stretched from the shed to a succession of poles, which led to the river and across the swift flowing braided riverbed and up the east branch of the valley toward a cluster of trees and sheds at the foot of the valley. Suddenly my father speaking into the handpiece, hanging up. "They will be here in about twenty minutes."

Eventually a tractor with a trailer appeared, moving rapidly across the green valley floor on the far side of the river. As it approached the river, it slowed down, entered the racing water, and slithered across the slippery boulders of the riverbed, the water foaming about the wheels. We'd see the machine emerge from the top of a steep cutting and, with a blast of diesel exhaust from the tall exhaust pipe, accelerate across the final grass flats toward the shed where we waited.

Jerry Aspinall was a tall, lean man with long wisps of hair strategically brushed across the crown of his head to conceal what was no longer there. He wore a thick wool pullover, woolen pants, and long black gum boots. On the trailer were his four children—his daughter, Julia, and his boys, John, William, Chris (who was my age and became a good friend), all with hair cut short back and sides. We clambered aboard and headed back across the river and out across the river flats toward the homestead. Paradise ducks called in the cold mountain air and huge Hereford cattle scattered before the tractor as Jerry impatiently drove up the track. I felt that this place was the greatest place on earth. To me the Aspinalls lived on the frontier and they carved out a living there.

While our parents sat indoors drinking tea and eating scones that Jerry's wife, Phyllis, had prepared, we explored the homestead area. Down to the wool sheds, past the dog runs, where lines of kennels stood with eight or nine working dogs chained to their little abodes, barking with excitement as they saw us coming.

Inside the gloomy light of the vast wool sheds there were things I had never seen before—shearing implements and old fashioned saddles and pieces of old rusting machinery.

The place was filled with the strong odor of sheep shit and urine and the pleasant smell of wool greasy with lanolin. Outside, hanging from the wire fence, was a row of dead keas—alpine parrots—that had fallen foul of Jerry's gun. There was a war between valley runholder and the occasional predatory kea. These beautiful green-brown parrots, with bright orange underwing plumage—the only alpine parrot in the world—have been decimated by the alpine farmers of New Zealand because they have been caught killing sheep on a few occasions over the past hundred years. They settle on the sheep's back and burrow with their powerful hooked beaks into the sheep's kidney fat, until this giant of agricultural intelligence is brought down and killed by a bird that weighs about one percent of its weight.

While to a young boy this epitomized the exciting Wild West–style struggle between man and nature, for me now it is another lamentable nail in the coffin of New Zealand's unique fauna. Regardless, it was absolutely thrilling to be there in the shadow of the great glaciated peaks of the Southern Alps, the sparkling fresh air and residing at the raw alpine outpost of the homestead.

Life at the homestead was different too. While the Aspinalls had electric light, the electricity was generated by a mini-hydro plant up the hillside. If it stopped—usually when it was raining or snowing—someone had to don a coat and clamber up the mountainside in the rain or snow to unblock the intake pipe and reset the machinery. Also of interest: the Aspinall children received their school lessons by correspondence. There was a small classroom in the homestead. They had their own play area that was really a corner of a paddock, the small swing set and the half dozen toy trucks and beyond spread the enormity of the alps.

Christopher and I spent hours running around the farm and all the while we made plans to explore the valleys and the mountains around us. Years later we made a long day trip up a peak opposite the homestead. We ascended through the beech forest and into the tussock and then along a series of narrow interconnected ridges that led to a series of sharp slippery summits that had the form of the serrated edge of a bread knife. I found these sorties invigorating. The clarity of the air, its coldness as you sucked it into your lungs, and the youthful power of our legs as we hiked higher and higher along the ridge lines. From up here you could see the summits of mountains spreading to the horizon. I wanted to visit them all.

A farmhand called Dave lived in a caravan near the house, had lived on his own up there for about ten years. Apparently Dave loved to hunt, loved to be alone—and to a boy's mind Dave was a mystery figure of some darkness.

It was Dave the farmhand standing ahead of Hillary, between the remembered swings and kennels, his back to the illusory fence.

I don't know why he was there. I barely had time to think about it. Dave remained under my conscious gaze for a startling moment only. Later, in the tent, when I thought about him, I wondered if Dave was still in a caravan somewhere, if he was anywhere at all. And I wondered if he still loved being alone, how that was for him.

❋ ❋ ❋

From the Matuki Valley the route wandered into a supermarket and across the deck of a sailboat, then upward again and into the couloir and upward until he was walking flat through the drifting cloud on the shelf with the smudges of his companions in front of his nose.

But soon after getting my bearings with physical reality, the route started wandering again, and again I'd get caught out by the flickering shadows, and the faces they made. It always

felt as if they'd been watching and waiting for me to see them there. Startling stuff.

It was in the late afternoon, as he was skiing up the couloir again, that he started meeting up with old friends, and in the other places that he wandered through to the evening he saw them, and everything being good with them, it was all good again while they were there.

The late afternoon was always popular with the dead friends. If they only came once through the day, it was in the late afternoon, taking the place of the sunset, giving voice and form to the feelings that belonged with the sunset, and that he generally resisted articulating.

Hillary and company made thirteen miles over that crazy visionary route, through the drifting brightness, through all those walking dream lands, their longest haul on foot to date. What route the others had taken in their minds he didn't know. Someone remarked how warm the day had been.

❅   ❅   ❅

The cloud was gone in the morning, day twenty-five. There was the flat white, the swinging sun, the big blue void, and a northerly at their backs that blew steady but slow. They put up the kites, wheezed southward. There was no feeling of flying, rather that heaviness that comes from sitting in a car as it's pulled out of a bog. They traveled as if on the verge of something dramatic that never came.

Everything went into the arms and the eyes to keep the kites in the air, the body postured right. All the while Hillary was willing the wind to pick up, to get a little pep in it and blow him south to the mountains. The others made similar prayers during the breaks, the hot drinks.

Later in the day the winds moved around to the southwest quarter, meaning they had to fly across the wind and progress was slowed then to inching, and the strain on the arms was akin to holding up barbells for an hour or more at a time. The kite lines were similarly stressed. When he surveyed the others on their slowmo drag, he chuckled at a dark joke that he felt but couldn't articulate. It was Fred From who was able to say it. His face was there, full of gentle mischief.

"Aw, Hillary," he said. "What are you doing?"

Fred thought it was hilarious too. He was that sort of fellow. When he asked how things were, it was because he wanted to know, and he always took the right tack. He was gruff, but he was very sensitive, and he was someone with whom you could laugh about the awful things. He had some of what my mother had.

I remember in those last years Fred was living up in Queensland with a lovely woman named Judy Gemmell, who had two children from a previous relationship, and how Judy said the children had very fond memories of Fred. Which says a lot about him.

One of them was a little girl named Jodie. A pressure lantern had exploded nearby when she was a baby, causing burns over forty percent of her body. I remember Judy telling me about it after Fred died, how he had never noticed, or showed in any way that he noticed, Jodie's scars. He just focused on her and seemed to really enjoy this parenting cum guardian role. Judy said how Fred got really excited when they were walking one day to meet Jodie's bus after school, and how he ran up to the bus, and as Jodie came down the steps, made her stop there so he could get a photograph of her. It made Jodie feel really special.

So, you know, Fred was one of the good guys. And he was someone I kept thinking about down there. Like how great it would have been for him to be there, in flesh and blood. Instead he'd come as a ghost, two or three times now, in the same way my mother kept coming, to keep me company. Even when I tried to work through these events with the

thoughts of an accident inspector, looking at them cold, I remained boggled by them, and by the way I'd submit to them
happily.

On day twenty-five, inching along with the kite, wanting
nothing more than the wind to get some guts and blow us
somewhere, because we weren't anywhere out there, we
weren't getting anywhere, and I was hungry to see things
that would tell me we were getting somewhere, it suddenly
seemed so hilarious and there was Fred From wanting to
know how it was going. And when I had a good rant about
how it was all going, he seemed bemused by it all. He looked
kind of sad and serious too. Fred was one of those people who
could talk about anything without getting emotional.

"Hillary," he said, "this might be the end of the world
... but it's not the end of the world."

With the kites up they did a good day's hauling. That is, they
made fourteen miles. When they put up the tent, the wind was
still coming from the north, a gentle breeze only.

※　※　※

The breeze died in the night, and they woke to the silence of the
moon, day twenty-six, November twenty-nine, a Sunday clear
and mild when they started out. They did a little better on foot
over the seven hours, making fourteen miles and some, and
Hillary's boot flapping about throughout with an unprece-
dented palsy. It had been flapping for nearly two weeks, the gap
filling with compacted ice. It was falling apart.

After dallying with the boot, willing it to behave, Hillary got
the urge to sprint. And as he hauled off, he started running in his
mind, loping along through the parkland at the back of his
house, where sheep grazed among the big trees and the green
ground sloped upward to a peak named One Tree Hill, where
there was an obelisk, and a famous old tree that had several
times been vandalized by indigenous protesters. It was one

hundred and twenty years old when they put it to the chain-
saw. As he ran, he remembered the tree, and the tree was there,
and from the top of the hill he looked for a time over the city. He
was invigorated by running, could feel it as a boost through his
body as he carried his cross, the horror of the sled, still the best
part of four hundred pounds, and on he went running down the
other side of the big hill and down to the fields and out to the
street and along the sidewalk that ran along the parkland fence
and along to another set of palace gates and up into the fields
again and up to the slopes with the sheep and to the hill and
down again and on under a big empty sky and the shadows of
trees. And then the blue sky disappeared.

> **One of the extraordinary things about walking on the shelf
> was the often and sudden transition from one world to the
> next. And so it was that afternoon when a sheet of stratus slid
> away the blue and the horizon disappeared with the sky, and
> there we were on a flat sheet of typing paper again.**

And still he kept running uphill, because that's how it felt now,
and on he ran through the parkland that came for a time different places, beautiful places, and it was toward the end of the day
the trance broke with a vision that made all their hearts hammer, the three of them: a blue glowing crack in the dead flat white
to the south. The crack contained mountains—not the full, scything string of the TransAntarctics, just a few little jagged teeth.

> **Like ships appearing on a watery brink at sea, really. Little
> sail shaped points in that window of horizon. And we only got
> a glimpse before the cloud closed over again, but what a great
> moment, and what a relief. Four weeks on the shelf and there
> was the other side. The TransAntarctics finally in sight! And
> behind the mountains was the plateau with the Pole at its
> heart. Not that you could see it, but you knew that it was right
> there. The mountains were very very small. There was still a
> long way to go, but now it felt like we were getting some-
> where. There was a view.**

And there was a softening, if not a lift, in the community mood, and a fresh cheer in the stove's chuffing as Hillary melted the ice, stirred the lard. He had work to do on his boot and that wasn't good, but he consciously filed away the darker thoughts until he got to the boot, and built up a happy campfire with old friends from the mountains.

He'd seen the mountains to the south. When he first beheld them, he'd shivered with the same disbelieving happiness that had come with embracing the dead friends and their companionship, as if the mountains, too, were a vision beyond belief.

❊ ❊ ❊

Day twenty-seven: they dallied in the morning as Hillary continued working on the boot. The mountains were there, under another blue void, and the others took in the view of those little teeth on the horizon to the south as he labored. After two hours the boot still wasn't right, and it was a job nursing it through the reduced haul of six hours and keeping a good pace. They made twelve miles and some.

He figured if the boot got much worse, then the trip would be over. Outside a successful repair, the only option, and not an easy one, was to have new boots flown from France to Christchurch to McMurdo and out to the shelf, a pair for all of them. But he figured his companions would resist the resupply, in the name of protecting expeditionary independence and integrity. From heel to toe, the boot was trouble. He decided to lay it out like a map of the world, and in the tent that night he told the others that their future as polar adventurers lay with his boot—restoration or demise. He had an idea how to fix the boot, but it was a big operation best achieved with many hands, so how about it, boys?

> It was a hell of a job. I had to release the front of the sole away from the boot, cut out the broken shanks, and then cut out blocks of plastic from my sled. I stuck them in and bolted

them together. It was pretty difficult to do with a penknife and a simple little hand drill. I stayed up until nearly midnight, and it still wasn't done. The others were sleeping, so I went to sleep too.

❉   ❉   ❉

Day twenty-eight, December one, four weeks out: Hillary worked on the boot over breakfast. Time passed with no view of the mountains through the bleached rags and spindrift to the no horizon. It wasn't a great day out there, but it was ticking by, the opportunity to cover some miles. And so it was that Muir and Philips pitched in with the boot. Then they hunched for six and a half hours into a buffeting blindness, blurred smudges in close formation, bones chilled and shaken, all faith in the compass, making not quite twelve miles, and their clothes choked with ice at the end of it.

Later in the day Eric apologized to me for his niggling and nagging. We shook hands.

Jon mumbled, "Thank you, fellows."

In the diary that night I noted, "Things should be better now."

I wasn't writing much about the others in my diary, beyond recording incidents of illness or events related to the work and the rest of it. Otherwise, it had become as if they weren't really there. And then out of the blue, the handshake.

I didn't know what I felt about it at the time.

"Things should be better now."

All right.

And then out of the blue, and I remember it was around this time, in those early days of seeing the mountains to the south, that Eric began talking about the young brother he'd found dead and cold on a bed, the previous year. He talked about it at some length one night, and in a manner that suggested it had been playing on his mind out there.

Our estrangement was such that I didn't consider the meaning of his sudden need to talk, at that time. It just came out of the blue as the next surprising thing. I mean, I'd been wondering if the others were being haunted, but it just didn't click at the time that Eric may have been suffering. One of the quandaries of a siege, I suppose.

CHAPTER SIXTEEN

"My nerves are bad to-night. Yes, bad, Stay with me.
"Speak to me. Why do you never speak. Speak.
"What are you thinking of? What thinking? What?
"I never know what you are thinking. Think."

I think we are in rats' alley
Where the dead men lost their bones

"What is that noise?"

                        The wind under the door
"What is that noise now? What is the wind doing?"
                        Nothing again nothing.

                              "Do
"You know nothing? You see nothing? Do you remember
"Nothing?"

I remember
Those are pearls that were his eyes.
"Are you alive, or not? Is there nothing in your head?"

T. S. Eliot, "The Waste Land"

The quandaries of the siege were many as Hillary and company crawled across the second half of the shelf. It was a long time drifting to shore, and Hillary's cravings for company in the flesh returned as a physical gnawing, like hunger. He felt squeezed from both sides, by the living and the dead. He wanted a breathing somebody with whom he could walk and talk and talk and talk—his wife, kids, friends, talkative strangers, anybody with a winning smile. There was no such face to be seen, despite the flashes of goodwill. He felt squeezed by the living, the two with whom he slept and ate and toileted. They were right there, but utterly out of reach. Hillary didn't believe he would have been as lonely if he'd made the journey solo. The loneliness would have been terrible much of the time, he reasoned, but it wouldn't have been so cruel. The others were there but not there and nothing to be done about it.

Meanwhile, he was truly struggling now with the dream life, no matter the unfailing rapture enjoyed in those visitations, for the hangovers that followed were accumulating with the bodily aches and the tearing. They soaked into his bones with the chill, stirring the familiar fear to walk sentry in vain against horrors it didn't fully recognize, stirring fears he'd regarded as long lost to walk again with their no good purpose. Still, the dead friends weren't easily abandoned, and they always came in the late afternoon, even if it was simply as a quality of mood at first, and then in all their colors, and he was generally grateful to see them called into being. There was nothing else going. Save for the dead friends, and for the occasional reverie uncomplicated by ghosts, everything else and everywhere else in Hillary's head now fed the loneliness: the regular life, the marvelous years, the bedtime stories, music, all of it led to a longing, a bodily hurting that confounded him. For this was not simply a return to loneliness, as he'd known it in the long-ago life, as a mood that came on for periods of time under particular external pressures. Hillary was on a tour of loneliness complete, that known to the castaway, the marooned. And then he was amazed to find there was more to it, his deepest dread, something like the loneliness of the dead.

Or the brain dead.

Increasing in length were the times when Hillary couldn't think of anything to think about. Now, when they came, he was beyond thinking about thinking, in a void beyond thought. It amazed him that hours at a time were lost to this profound vacancy of consciousness. And it was to these cursed times he gave the name **"episodes of absolute emptiness."**

> It actually annoys me that there are those holes in my life. All those heartbeats spent for nothing but a lousy few miles, because that's all that was happening. It was like I had the consciousness of a mule pulling a cart, and I may be selling the mule short.
>
> Pull.
>
> Hot drink.
>
> Pull.
>
> So what if the mountains were there? What does a mule care about the mountains?
>
> In those empty stretches there was nothing in the world to my mind beyond hauling and drinking the hot drink. I didn't think about the hot drink when I was hauling. I didn't think about it when I drank it. I just drank it. There was nothing. And I didn't know if the nothingness was an alternative to the hangovers, or the consequence of them.
>
> Meanwhile, in the tent, peace talks had broken down before they'd really begun. The mountains more than two hundred miles away still, the Pole so much farther it was best not to think too much about, and Eric in deeper—and I suspect darker—communion with the numbers, with each passing night. The numbers were clear. And lo he began cracking his whip with a frantic renewal of purpose. But, you know, who ever really got anywhere whipping a mule?

And lo the community mood returned to the simmering stew, day twenty-nine, December two, with wooden fingers in a brutally cold wind from breakfast to lunch and then fine to hot in the late afternoon.

Yes, hot.

The sky cleared, the wind died, the lovely mountains came out and the sun beat down with surprising gusto, a vicious glare that bounced off the blue windblown ice and into their faces. Bathed in the reflected solar radiation, it was hot work hauling. When they stopped, for a drink or to adjust their gait, the sweat in their long johns turned to frost.

> **We did an interview at midday for a television news service and, you know, I can turn it on no matter the mood. On darker days I might be somewhat crisp, but I'm on. It's easy enough because there's a formality that goes with it, a certain degree of formula, really. And after the formality, you hang up the phone and go back to where you were at. Later we got out the video camera, to record our haulage through the summer afternoon.**

They made thirteen and a half miles, the boot flapping throughout. **(The repairs had failed.)** The boot had to wait until late in the evening because Hillary was cook again. He brooded and muttered to himself through the first round of drinks, because he openly hated it now, the cooking. He consciously cooled the volcano by making wordless fun of his bitching. The stove was cheerily chuffing, and he was sick of the dark halls. Even so, as he built up his campfire for the night—I **still loved the stove**— he lapsed into damn the cooking as a rhythm to groove on, as he considered who to make his companions for the night.

He hadn't always hated cooking. Once he'd cooked a fruitcake over a fire; when he'd gone to the mountains to show **the old bastards of the game** a thing or two.

> **I hadn't quite turned seventeen years of age, and my father was very keen on my going to university, and for me to be**

making plans for a proper and sensible life. Instead I went to the storeroom under the house and grabbed some of his climbing gear, including his best pair of crampons. I was off to the hills with Nigel Lewis (my old friend with the air rifle and the grisly pile of dead sparrows). Nigel's mother gave us her car for the trip. I'm happy to say Nigel's still walking and breathing, in Toronto these days.

Anyway, Nigel and I went down to the South Island, for about six weeks, on a truly great adventure—and an undeniable odyssey of idiocy. We traveled first to the Nelson Lakes National Park area, to warm up with a few smaller peaks—like Mount Travers and Mount Hopeless, about seven thousand five hundred feet each, and of no great technical difficulty—before we got into the serious stuff. We had a good week in those modest mountains, camping at their feet, carrying on like heroes.

We'd bought brand new Thunderbird ice axes by mail order from America. The Thunderbird was a most inappropriate axe, designed not for mountain climbing, but for trekking. However, inspired by the alarming literature in the mail order brochure on the horrors of falling, and not being able to arrest a fall, we signed up for the Thunderbird, whose claim to fame was its efficacy as a self arrest tool. Besides, we both liked the woodsman's axe head pick on the Thunderbird, which we mistakenly identified as a great design. More than anything we liked its Day Glo orange color.

Anyway, at week's end we got lost on the walk out to the car, which we'd left at the road end by Lake Rotoiti. It was a six hour walk through thick beech forest, and we'd started out too late in the day. It got dark, and we were so tired from the big week and our ridiculously heavy packs that we'd sit down together at the side of the track and just go off to sleep (and that's how it almost always ends out there, with some bastard with an axe or whatever, that's what we were thinking. I mean, that's youth for you). Lying among the beech trees, we'd hear a few morepork owls, and we'd get a bit scared, and stagger on, with that fear that comes from being in the dark, and it was black night under the trees, and we'd start wondering about home and nice beds and doors with locks on them. In the end we crashed at the side of the little track, freaked out but just too tired. In the morning we found the car a mere two hundred yards on.

It was on the drive south to our first peak of real note, Mount Aspiring—the Matterhorn of the Southern Hemisphere!—that we stopped and camped at a family camping ground by the sea, and I cooked a fruitcake over an open fire, in two tins, one inside the other, the embers nicely spread, and other campers coming over and saying, "You watch that fire, you boys."

"Do we know fire? We know everything." Anyway, my shirt was holed with flying sparks and the cake was a bit burned. We threw away a charred hunk from the bottom, but the rest of it was pretty good. Then we moved on to the bigger mountains and were nearly killed on several heroic occasions. That we survived was all to do with plain dumb luck. Some of what I remember best is how excited we were.

❊   ❊   ❊

Day thirty, a Thursday: clear and fine, and hot on the haul, Hillary and company stripping down to longjohns and gloves without the over mittens. For seven and a half hours, they made fourteen and a half miles, and still the boot flapped. The views to the mountains, however, were excellent.

They were a great tonic, the mountains. As we inched south, their sail-like points rose into tent shaped peaks separated by flat white horizon until the mountains grew above the horizon with increasing complexity that progressively joined and interlinked into a range, a barrier of formidable proportions.

Steep, white, ice streaked with rock spurs and faces, and so the mountains became recognizable on our maps and the deep clefts between them became the great breaks in the barrier that led famously to the Polar Plateau. Not that you could see these glaciers leading all the way to the plateau from the shelf. It's just that we knew that they did, or hoped that they would.

Scott and Amundsen simply headed due south, faithfully following the longitude line they started on, hoping they would find a way. For them it truly was the unknown. I never saw Amundsen down there, but the Captain kept turning up from time to time.

He saw the others up ahead, too, from time to time, one of them stopping to point something out to the other. He'd wonder what they'd seen. He'd think about catching up with them, to the conversation. Sometimes he'd try, nearly get there. They'd hear his scraping approach and off they'd go. Time passed that way until he dropped into the mule, vacant with laboring in the heat and the mountains so far away, **and the rest of it.**

His mother brought him out of it, and he was moved to leave the ice for a time and take her home to meet his wife and children, to the house with the parkland out the back. They had a marvelous time, cups of tea. They all got along. It was something he occasionally daydreamed in the regular life, as thoughts there rather than the detailed conversations lived out on the ice amid conjured props of familiar armchairs, pictures on the wall, bookshelves and such.

The hangover came on as he worked late into the night on the boot: a flu of savage grief that welled up and twisted into a cry that he strangled with fear that was familiar but no great friend. Sometimes in the regular life it welled up like that, and he'd sink into himself and watch his wife get anxious, and nothing to be done about it, he'd take the drive out to Anawhata and sit in the little hut and hear the western squalls wailing, and he'd wail along with them. Looking out at the black-backed gulls tossing and lurching and the sun coming in red through the window and those old red drapes and the smell of everybody that had ever been there and the little kid paintings on the walls, he remembered all those times he'd been out there and all those people lost to him over the years—how they'd all taken him out to the little hut on the headland, safely removed from the living and from the well meaning things they may or may not say. Away from anyone and everyone, it was a good place to howl it out. And now there was the red light coming through the wall of the tent, and it was all welling up. He remembered those evenings, and it was all welling up, but there was no way—**no way on earth**—he'd let it out in the tent. He gave himself fully to the broken boot instead.

> **I tried a new strategy: using my crampon toe strap as the polar equivalent of string (and some webbing from my harness to reinforce the cracked inner sole). If I'd been suddenly dropped onto a park bench somewhere wearing nothing but my long johns, as I essentially tried tying the wayward sole to the rest of the boot, people would have taken me as some poor homeless wretch at his ablutions, I'd wager. Was this really any way for people to spend their lives?**

He was skinny and ragged and rather wretched to behold. In the video footage from this point in the expedition, the three of them were all looking wretched and worn and strung out, and with an almost hostile self consciousness under the camera's eye—the faces of men in a soup kitchen, shyly sharing their turkey dinners with the evening news, reluctant recruits to peace and goodwill to all men.

❊   ❊   ❊

> **Nigel Lewis and I had a movie camera with us, on our teen titan adventures in the alps, a weighty sixteen millimeter unit that actually belonged to my father, and had as sensible a**

place in our packs as our canned food—all testimony to our naïveté, really.

After cooking our fruitcake, we drove down to the Matuki Valley, over the rough ruts to where the road ran out, and for two days we trekked through the grasses and the grandeur and up to the snowline, hauling those heavy packs, and how they remind me now of the sled. We spent a night on an exposed ledge in one of Dad's little Sears Roebuck backpacking tents. It was a pretty scary night too. Ferocious Nor'wester gusts blasted down the steep ravine adjacent to where we cowered in that little orange tent. We cooked food as best we could on a small petrol cooker while the tent was frequently collapsed inward upon us. This was our first serious sortie into the big mountains, and we wondered what would come next.

The next morning the wind had eased and we collapsed the little tent and continued up the steep slabs above the rumbling creek that tumbled over the boulders in the back of the steep gully. These were old glacial slabs, and the ice had cleaned and shaped the rock to be smooth and scarred. The slabs were too steep for any loose rocks to accumulate upon them, and so it was only on shallow ledges that any morainic detritus piled up. Occasionally we would spot a squat rock cairn and would climb across to it with some pleasure, for these cairns indicated where we should go, or where someone else went when they were lost, where they perhaps perished. (Just like those little bunches of flowers you see at the side of the roads now.) One of the cairns led us out on to the huge steep faces above the head of the Matuki Valley—one slip and it would all be over, fall and die—and so we gingerly made our way back across the fingery terrain to the slabs near the plunging stream.

Steadily we climbed higher on that gray day toward Hector Col, which straddled the watersheds of the Matuki and

Waipara valleys. Near the pass we turned up the rock slabs to a small snowfield, where we roped up in case of crevasses. We plugged a long and tedious dotted line up the glacier to Bevan Col, and from the deep crescent of the col we looked north-east across an even larger glacier to the most beautiful mountain I had ever seen: Mount Aspiring, rising in the evening light like a beauty, the Matterhorn of the Southern Hemisphere.

I think I fell in love. Elegant ridges rose at an exponential rate to a delicate summit, all snow clad and glowing, nearly ten thousand feet. This was why we'd come to this place, to climb the beautiful but serious Aspiring.

It was late in the day as we looked out onto the broad expanse of the Bonar Glacier and spied in the distance a tiny orange shape, a mile and a half away, Colin Todd Hut, sitting at the top of the Shipowner Ridge where it joins the Northwest Ridge of Aspiring. We were tired, it was getting late, and we didn't want to spend another night in the tent. We were desperate to make it across the glacier to the little shelter.

The shelter wasn't named for a man whose life it saved. Colin Todd didn't make it across; he didn't make it. That's why they named the hut after him. So many of the huts in the Southern Alps are memorial huts—named after people lost for good—and all standing as good reasons for why you don't want to get caught out.

The snow was deep and wet as we plowed our way across the glacier, avoiding suspicious hollows that indicated snow bridges, winding around open crevasses. As the sun sank behind the peaks across the western valleys that separated us from the Tasman Sea, we staggered up onto the rocky knoll of Colin Todd Hut. The simple corrugated iron hut was small in stature but big on appeal. Robust and weatherproof, painted orange so it would be easy to spot for weary or perhaps desperate climbers. At just eight by twelve feet it was small and nestled in a collar of large rocks to prevent the ferocious winds of the roaring forties lifting it up and tossing it away.

Ten years later that is precisely what the elements did to Three Johns Hut in the Mount Cook area. With three people inside it, a savage Nor'wester blew the hut from its foundations and over a thousand foot bluff nearby. All three died. Suddenly New Zealand's mountain huts began to sport huge steel cables spread across their roofs and bolted to colossal boulders or bedrock. The authorities decided they needed to know more about these storms, and they placed anemometers near some of the huts. When they checked back after a few storms, the anemometers were broken. The last recorded reading was one hundred and forty knots.

* * *

Day thirty-one, December four, one month out: hot and sweaty again while man hauling. They tried kiting in a gentle northerly, but it petered out. They lost time trying to make it happen. For the seven hours they made **the dreaded** twelve and a half miles, most of it hauled.

When they put up the tent that evening, they were three hundred and thirteen miles from Scott Base. When they put in their third depot, with the usual cairn of snow and the thirty pounds of turds on top, Hillary was wondering if they'd ever make it back to that spot, to camp there again and eat that little cache of food. He wondered if the others were figuring similar doubts.

* * *

Day thirty-two, a Saturday, seven and a half hours, fifteen and a half miles and Antarctica once more a tanning salon. They were down to their longjohns again, not enjoying the heat because it gave them a thirst they couldn't fully slake, restricted in their refreshment by the daily ration of fuel for melting ice, making drinks.

> We began to dread these days, as they sapped your energy
> and drained fluid out of your body like a tap. Sweat, sweat
> and more sweat. The view, however, was magical.

While the sky above their heads was clear, the sun swinging like
an assassin on a rope, there was cloud drifting over the mountains, casting moody shadows and colors and textures that
they'd seen similarly cast in other places, and in memory had
taken on a quality of fantasy, such was their estrangement from
the beauties.

> Time passed between beauty and oblivion, boredom and
> bone weariness. And hunger too. My body wanted more
> food. There wasn't any more food to be had. We had our daily
> ration, and that was all the body could handle, anyway. The
> Captain and his men wrote about being hungry. There were
> nights they went to bed with nothing more than a biscuit and
> some weak tea, only to get up the next morning and haul a
> full day. I imagined that at the end of it, when they were lying
> there with their thoughts, I imagined they could hear their
> stomachs growling above the wind. Does an empty stomach
> keep growling all the way to the end?
>
> Often toward the end of the day of hauling, when I was feel-
> ing particularly hungry, I could hear the groaning and
> squeals of my stomach. Because our food was of low bulk
> and high calorific content, our stomachs shrank. Because the
> food was all reconstituted and most of the calories were in
> the form of fat and oil, there was no need to chew. Oh, how
> I longed to chew on some delicious meat, chew long and
> hard on a crust or a toffee bar, crunch my teeth through a
> celery stick or a carrot. Chewing is a large part of satisfy-
> ing your hunger. Like dogs, we should have brought bones
> with us to chew and salivate over and swallow and chew
> again. If we had had something like a bone to chew on, we
> might not have spent so much time chewing away at each
> other.

There were many repairs that night, and it was for a time very quiet. They were all up late nursing various bits of gear back to life.

At about ten p.m., Jon Muir leaned over toward me, holding up a small cube of Styrofoam about the size of a thumbnail. It was used as a safety block for the emergency switch on the Argos beacon. And it had written on the side "1.15 kg."

"It's heavier than it looks," said Muir with a grin.

This was the joke that sparked the one big laugh of the trip. We both erupted into shrieking laughter. Out of control shrieking that was amplified by the big silence of the shelf. I don't know what people would have made of it if they'd suddenly had a window into our world. It would have been pretty frightening, I'd imagine. I don't know what Eric ever thought about it. He never made a sound, never said a word. And the shrieking went on for a long, long time. Jolly good stuff too.

❄ ❄ ❄

Nigel Lewis had long red hair, and his face when it laughed was quite crazy to behold. He wore everything on his face, and I remember him looking tired and then so excited as we made it across the glacier to Colin Todd Hut, and coming out of his skin as we shoveled the snow that had piled up against the battered wooden door, and as we unbolted the door and stepped inside, he was excited. I was excited too.

These mountain huts are powerful places. A beam of light shone in through the small westfacing window and through the open door. The floor was peppered with the incisions made by many crampons, by the old bastards of the game. Along two walls were tiny single bunks. They had old dirty looking kapok mattresses upon them and some coarse gray blankets pushed to one end of the top bunk.

Beneath the window was a bench covered in aluminum, and at one end a clutter of old cooking pots, half burned candles, an empty bottle of port, and some leftover food. There were a handful of trashy novels and, most valuable of all, a hardcover journal filled with the handwritten intentions and observations of the visitors to the little shelter. If anything went wrong, this was where the rescue party would come to read our last written intentions, our last will and testimony. It all seemed very heavy. And then entertaining. The jottings in "the hut book" were sometimes poetic, sometimes absurd, lurid, philosophical, and even embarrassed records of failure, distinctive by their brevity.

We dusted down the bunks and spread out our sleeping bags, excited that we had the place to ourselves. We spread out our gear; Dad's film camera, our climbing gear, and all the food and cooking utensils we had brought with us. The wet tent and climbing rope we hung from hooks on the walls to drain and dry, and as the light was going down, we struck some matches and lit several of the old candle stumps that were left on the bench and the soot covered windowsill.

It has always amazed and delighted me how a hot mug of soup or tea changes the atmosphere of even the most miserable situation. And so it was for us as we cradled hot drinks in our hands and joked about what extraordinary heroes we were. It was classic teenage foolery, using strange sounding accents and pulling stern "adult" faces.

Nigel: "So where have you guys been?"

Me: "Oh, we have just been up the south face, new route, never been climbed before."

Nigel: "How long have you been climbing?"

Me: "Oh, couple of weeks, I would say."

Nigel: "Oh, there you go exaggerating again, Hillary. It will be ten days tomorrow."

And we'd hoot with laughter, open and crazy. We stayed up late laughing despite our exhaustion from the long day's trek. So it was a late start the next morning, by mountaineering standards. At about eight a.m. we left the hut with the sun already lifting well into the sky on a reconnaissance for the Northwest Ridge of Mount Aspiring. We just kept going—slowly, cautiously—and late that afternoon, much to our surprise, we reached the summit.

Our anxieties about descending the steep ramp of snow that sidled down off the ridge were replaced by a growing confidence in our newfound techniques for traveling on ice. Suddenly we thought we knew everything. We knew nothing. We'd done a bit of rock climbing, worked with rope, put belays in, but limited experience, really. Instead of analyzing the day's climb, and learning from it—looking for what we'd done wrong and where we'd been lucky—our summit success convinced us of our natural genius.

When we returned to Colin Todd Hut that night, we found we no longer had the place to ourselves. Instead we met two young Wellington climbers, from the "rough and tough" (by reputation) Tararua Tramping Club. These two seemed so much more worldly and confident than we were, even though we were about the same ages. They didn't have orange Thunderbird ice axes. Rather, they had wooden shafted tools with curved picks, the choice of the current crop of climbers, the Chouinard Frost Piolet. (Designed by the Californian gurus of clean climbing and alpine style. But we hadn't heard about any of that . . . yet.)

One of the Wellington boys was Warwick Attwell, a fellow who I would see from time to time as our lives crossed over the years. Waka, as Warwick liked to be called, went into the film industry and later joined Dad's Ocean to Sky Expedition up the Ganges as part of the film crew. Unlike Nigel and me, Warwick and company weren't wildly impressed with our climb of the Northwest Ridge. Rather, they had their sights set on the elegant, steep, and much more difficult Southwest Ridge.

I guess in a way unspoken they raised the bet. We would wait and see how they went and then who knows what we would do. They headed up the next morning.

It was a rest day for us and we enjoyed it to the full, under glorious weather on the edge of the Bonar Glacier, above the world of valleys and rugged country that fell away below. We made a number of Monty Python–like movies, up on the Shipowner Ridge, striking manic poses as hard men of the mountain. One of the films ended with Nigel attacking the cameraman. It was pretty sophisticated stuff.

When the Wellington crew returned from the summit triumphant, Waka proceeded to intimidate us by doing extraordinary gymnastic feats. Like, rising from a sitting position into a handstand and then doing vertical pushups. We were thinking, "Jeeesus. Is that what it takes to climb the Southwest Ridge?"

Nigel and I had decided that we'd give it a go.

❊   ❊   ❊

Day thirty-three, December six: sixteen miles and some in a cool breeze under a blue dome painted with high cloud; a mixture of sugar grains, fish scales, loose and lumpy cigars, and ragged sheets of dilapidated gauze draping to the horizon across the falling face of the sky, reaching behind the mountains. Hillary and company could see the Beardmore Glacier now, the grand entrance to the riddled road that the Captain and company had taken up to the plateau, where Evans was buried.

Already the entrance to the Beardmore looked hazardous. We could see the broken ice in the severe crevasse fields just above its broad entrance, which was ringed by steep sided peaks. The scale of these glacial entrances is immense. The Beardmore is nearly twenty miles wide at its base, down there on the beach, so to speak, at the foot of the TransAntarctics. Twenty miles wide. That's equivalent to the length of New

Zealand's longest glacier, the Tasman. And yet in Antarctica the Beardmore is a midget among titans.

Most splendid to behold was Mount Kyffin, a giant sentinel standing to the side of the entrance to the Beardmore. In the clear air Mount Kyffin seemed so close. It's like that at high altitude, when you're looking across at neighboring peaks; through the thin air, they're right there, under your nose. The TransAntarctics were to continue looming with similar magic, but I think Mount Kyffin was the first to do so, and the experience fresh and profound, something akin to being born again.

Other expeditions were on the Antarctic ice that season. It wasn't something the company cared to think about, or talk about in their media interviews, but there were other people out there: a Dutch trio, who were **planning a traverse via the Pole and descending to the Ross Sea,** and a solo Japanese skier also seeking to cross the continent.

In a phone call with Scott Base we learned that one of the Dutch had been evacuated, because of a ski pole injury or a crampon injury—it wasn't made clear—and now the remaining pair's sleds had broken up and they were waiting for new ones to be flown in. What a nightmare start for them. The solo skier, Oba, from Japan was going well, and had covered nearly three hundred miles in the last eight days alone.

I thought, "Jeepers! The winds must be very good on his patch of ice."

Oba had set out from the coast to the west of us, on the South African side of the continent. Three hundred miles in eight days. We'd covered about three hundred and sixty miles in a month and two days.

Despite an abundance of repairs, including the nightly ritual with the boot, I gave myself an early night, and was asleep by ten.

❋ ❋ ❋

Day thirty-four, they mixed drinking chocolate with their morning coffee because the powdered milk had run out. After breakfast, Hillary washed his feet and changed his socks for the first time since leaving Scott Base.

In all the years of picking expeditionary cheese from between his toes, Hillary couldn't remember his feet ever smelling so much like death. He'd known death in his breath for some years, as all men in their forties are cursed in the mornings to taste their slide into decay. But the socks, peeling away from his feet like old mold, reeked with the terrible sweetness of someone in need of a summer's grave. His bare feet, likewise. With the stove packed away, he crawled into the vestibule and washed his feet in the snow. Then he washed the rotting socks in his eating bowl, in the princely luxury of three hundred milliliters, or three easy swallows, of warm water he'd saved from the cooking pot.

> Pretty disgusting, but then we are unkempt smelly men now and a little of our own sweat and stench left as a residue in the bowl and mixed in with tonight's slurry of stew, butter and oil is unlikely to do me any harm. Perhaps dead sock liquor will provide tonight's dinner with a pleasant pungency reminiscent of garlic, a lasting piquancy like chillies (not to mention a microscopic life of its own).
>
> I was hungry just about all of the time now—I think we all were. I craved food, real food, fresh and with real flavors. Lard doesn't really have flavor. In phone calls with friends, I'd ask them to describe the salad dressing they were having, the grilled fish and lemon sauce that went with the salad, the crisp white Sémillon that went with the fish. On the one hand, it was torture. On the other, my capacity to "make real" the things in my head allowed me to flavor the lard with whatever treats that my friends had shared with me. Those little conversations on the phone were like sharing a meal with someone.

In the tent that night, Eric scraped the cooking pot to remove all the porridge and stew that had built up, inside and out, and on the base, over the past weeks. I assumed he tossed them out, but as we ate the meal, it became evident that the month old scrapings were mingling with the stew and butter and oil. With the sock liquor, it was a special meal indeed. A little extra something.

They all deserved a little extra, having hauled eighteen miles and some. Cool and clear conditions, no sweat, the boot still flapping but the community mood buoyed with the feeling that **nothing can stop us now.**

※   ※   ※

It was snowing in the morning, and a little windy, so after breakfast they toileted in the vestibule. Hillary made the first visit, found the tearing had worsened, and when he was done, the snow was stained red. Muir went in next, saying nothing of the blood when he emerged. Then Philips went in to put on his boots. He, too, said nothing. It was all so very quiet.

It was unpleasant outside, day thirty-five, a Tuesday, eighty-three and some degrees south, with wind blowing the falling snow in their faces, the sky wiped out by bellying cloud, cold hands. And Hillary choking on his self containment now, haunted and isolated by his mother's visit, welling up as she walked beside him, welling up as he regarded his companions, something giving way, inside and out.

Muir broke his second binding, so it was a shorter day of six hours' hauling. They made **the cursed** twelve and a half miles.

※   ※   ※

In this game, you learn by going in over your head. That's a good part of the game itself, even when you know what you're doing. Nigel Lewis and I knew we were going in above our heads when we struck out early the following morning for the Southwest Ridge, leaving the Wellington boys in their bunks.

I wonder if we'd have gone all the way had those boys not been there. There was a certain smile on their faces we didn't want to see.

So up we went, "crunch, crunch, crunch" across the glacier. And then the occasional "Uh!" as the snow crust collapsed without warning and we sank up to our knees, our hearts hammering in the hope that it was only a snow crust subsiding, not a snow bridge straddling a yawning chasm.

As the dawn swept her rosy fingers across the pretty snow peaks of the Southern Alps, the white arc of the Southwest Ridge swept above us to a narrow ice notch and then up to the tiny summit. We were really going out there. The route required sound technical skills—knowing the vagaries of ice and snow, knowing how and where to place your ice screws—and we didn't have them. We were learning as we went along, really pushing ourselves now.

"Keep the rope tight. I am going to cut up the face to meet the ridge up . . . there," Nigel declared, pointing high with his mighty Thunderbird. And with that, he swung the ice axe into the frozen snow above his head, kicked a cramponed boot into the slope, then the other, swung the ice axe again, higher now, and then again kicking for footholds. But when you are green, you tend to overdrive your ice axe, and you don't feel sure about your crampon setting on the ice. It all takes a little longer and feels less secure. These are the skills and knowledge that come with time and experience.

In this manner we swung leads up the face to the knife edged ridge line. I remember our toes feeling wooden in our leather boots, and the boots bending beneath the balls of our feet, our calves aching with pain akin to cramp. From the ridge line we followed the steeply ascending crest of the spur, rope pitch after pitch, to the ice notch that leaned out above us. This was going to be the test piece, and we both felt anxious about it. Fall and die. We climbed on.

A steep ten foot step of ice, tilted about sixty degrees, led into an ice polished couloir. The couloir led in turn to an exposed finish where the ice cantilevered out over the world below, and up which we had to gingerly climb, swinging our ice axes and hugging the face. We pretty well excavated the slope cutting bucketlike pigeon holes in the ice for the toes of our boots. There was nothing under our boot heels but thousands of feet. With some relief and a growing excitement, we climbed, one by one, over the crown of the ridge above and up onto the tiny summit. We were out of our minds with joy. At that moment we knew the rapture.

Top of the world, Ma.

Aspiring stands above all the mountains around it, and from the summit we could see the long string of the Southern Alps reaching north toward Mount Cook and south to the naked walls of Fiordland—a veritable Milky Way of summits, a forest of lonely snowy places that can only be visited by putting on your boots and tying on to a rope. To the west we could see all the way to the Tasman Sea, blue and clear to a distant bank of mares' tails, the jet stream indicator of an approaching front, the weekly Norwester, and a force to be reckoned with.

We had lunch up with that beautiful view and then climbed down the steep summit flank to the gentle rampart of the Northwest Ridge, following our crampon impressions from two days before, and those of Waka and his climbing partner. The ridge is like a broad arterial skyway, with plummeting cliffs on each side (that would quite scare me some years later when I made the first ski descent of Aspiring). Well down this broad ridge a steep rock buttress rises, obstructing the route, forcing one to descend off the ridge and onto a section of the mountain called the Ramp, a diagonal snowfield flanked above and below by large cliffs. This exposure means that the Ramp must be traversed with great care, as a fall would result in tumbling over a cliff face and flying into space above the fractured Bonar Glacier.

Two days before, we had cautiously belayed each other down the Ramp, rope length after rope length, pegged to the slope. But with the Southwest Ridge under our belts we decided we would try moving together down the face, roped up but not pegged to the mountain—just like the big boys of the alpine game. This technique requires experience, teamwork, extreme caution, and a short rope—certainly a much shorter rope than the one tied between us.

Plunging over the edge of the ridge, we reversed down and across the Ramp, facing into the mountain, kicking our crampons in below us, placing our Thunderbirds into the thawed snow above. The hot afternoon sun had turned the crisp frozen snow to a crystalline porridge, which tended to ball up in our crampon points, making precise foot placements difficult. By swinging the distinctive adze pick above our heads into the slope, we tried to secure ourselves as we moved. I had a coil of the rope in one hand and planned to pull it around my secured axe for greater protection should the need arise. The more we moved across and down the Ramp in the hot afternoon sun, the more relaxed we became. We felt we had it in the bag.

Suddenly, above me, amid a cascade of snowballs and sliding crystalline corn snow, Nigel shouted, "Hold!"

Then he tumbled forward and came rocketing down the snow slope, shooting past me at alarming speed. I rammed my Thunderbird into the snow, but I couldn't get the deep purchase I required. I put the coil of rope around the handle of the ice axe and held on tight. A couple of seconds and the rope pulled tight, ripping my axe out of the snow. The jolt lifted me from my crouching stance and dragged me violently down the slope, the dynamic climbing rope stretching between us like a thick elastic band.

Nigel managed to stop himself.

Until I screamed past, hauling him from his perch on the slope. The terrifying elastic yo-yo tore us down the slope toward the bluffs. Each time, as I slowed myself—with the self arrest magic of my Thunderbird—Nigel would shoot past and off I'd go, sliding again, just rocketing.

By some grace we both stopped ourselves sliding at the same time, about thirty yards from the drop straight down, a dead way down to the glacier, clawing at the snow face for purchase, kicking platforms for our feet, trembling, savoring survival, and not a little in shock. The only sound was the "sh . . . sh . . . sh" of snow rolling down the short slope below us, and disappearing over the edge.

We got our breath and continued across the Ramp, with renewed care and plenty of anxiety, trembling and then not, and down the mountain we went. By the time we made it across to the hut, we were feeling very pleased with ourselves. But the hut was empty. The Wellington boys had gone.

While it would have been very sweet to blow our trumpets at the Wellington boys, we had a great time doing so when we met a few people coming up to the mountain as we walked out and downvalley. These were people who'd been trying to climb Aspiring for years, but had always been robbed by the weather. And the weather was already changing when they meet these two young upstarts. We carried on like champions of the world.

"Oh, we had gorgeous weather. We climbed it twice in three days."

It was all a bit much for them. "You're bloody joking!" they said.

It only made our heads grow bigger.

❄   ❄   ❄

Day thirty-six, December nine, the sky was slate gray with heavy cloud, with the shelf glowing white like a fluorescent light. The horizon was blurred to invisible where the sheen of the ice soaked into the bellies of cloud. They were walking inside an empty ball, as big as a planet—but hollow, and with unusual rules of gravity. From time to time, jagged peaks of mountains came into being, dreamy glimpses only, majestic but ghostly, haunting as they receded. And from time to time, various places Hillary had known came into being, landscapes and streets unbidden and splendid, neither ghostly nor brief in their articulation, but dreamy, yes. Everywhere he went was so very quiet and still and no other person to be seen.

From the middle of the main road, down the street from the family home, the home he made with his wife, he could see cars approaching from both directions, from a good way away but never coming closer. He listened for the sound of traffic, for the distant hum that all cities sing. It was so quiet. He looked across the street to the shops, but couldn't see anybody in them. Through the big glass windows everything was blurred. The telephone wires were kinked as if held by the wind. But there was no wind.

Striding along the flat lands of the Matuki Valley, feeling small against the mountains, his feet making no sound as they slid between the golden tussocks, Hillary crossed a small twinkling stream that looked to be flowing but was frozen, not as ice, but in suspension, in time. Everywhere he went, the world had stopped. He was the ghost in those places, and he felt them fill up with the sadness he brought to them, painting them with emotional graffiti.

As you do. Time passed, haunting the past.

It was later in the day that I talked to Fred From about the possibilities of the world and its clocks stopping. Time, stopping. He reckoned it was possible to do it on paper, with the numbers. How clean and full of potential is the world in the abstract, we pondered with dry wonder.

By the time I met up with Fred, the cloud had withdrawn like a curtain and a brilliant blue sky smiled down on us and our twin tracks across the shelf and the colossal glacial barrier of the TransAntarctic Mountains filling the western skyline.

Eric was having difficulty warming his hands. He had frost

blisters on his fingers, and his fingernails were going black. During breaks it was Eric's habit to remove his mittens when performing various fiddly tasks, like attending to his thermos or adjusting the straps of his harness. If the wind was blowing, spindrift would catch all over his gloves. When he put the mittens back on his hands, the ice particles melted into the gloves, through to the fingers, where it would turn again to ice. It was now catching up with him.

At the end of the day we got out the video camera and filmed a typical setting-up of camp.

They had put another sixteen miles behind them. Meanwhile, Hillary's other boot was breaking up now. He worked on both of them until late in the night, welcoming old times, the ghosts of old times, peopling the tent with them, sitting among them in a quiet suspension.

✻ ✻ ✻

Day thirty-seven, a Thursday: the wind was at their backs in the morning, hard and fast and faster still as the morning passed with the kites up. The kites looked pretty against the belly of the cloud, through snow falling lightly, and the snow traveling in sympathy with the kites. The cloud wiped out the mountains, the sky, and the horizon. And there were pieces of cloud dropping to the ground around them—in tumbling swarms that slid around their shoulders and legs as they were whipped ahead by the wind, in the swooping fashion of wraiths passing through, passing through their bodies as they sailed through white on white, traveling at some pace, all eyes on the compass, for there was nothing in the world to make their bearings.

With the poor visibility and nil definition, it was easy to believe you were flying through a cloud soaked sky. The only suggestion otherwise was the clatter of the sled skittling across the crests of sastrugi and wind ruts. And it was quite a clatter because we traveled fast—only to be slowed by frequent cable breakages on the kites. It was difficult and very cold work repairing them in the field, with the strong winds. And it was tedious to be wasting time like that.

In all we traveled nearly twenty-four miles, but got a little off course due to the poor visibility and wind not conducive to the required line of travel. At lunchtime Eric found he'd lost his watch and went back to look for it, to no avail.

It was a big day's work for the arms, and I was happy to stop at seven p.m. and set up camp. Soon after, I began repairs to my number five and seven kites, ski poles, sled harness, and, yes, my boots.

At three a.m. I woke feeling nauseous. I knew it was probably the large quantities of olive oil that were in the evening stew. I tried to keep it down.

"I don't want to be sick. I need this food."

But no, and suddenly I vomited it all out the back vestibule. I was famished at breakfast, and the butter soaked porridge looked very appetizing for the first time in thirty-seven days.

✳   ✳   ✳

Day thirty-eight, fourteen miles and some under cloud: the world was a flat sheet of typing paper to behold, but a rough and ragged place to haul a sled. They'd run into a dense field of sastrugi they couldn't see, a highway of clumps and razor ridge lines that remained invisible until they were right on top of them. They followed the compass all day, the three of them swaying about, trying to keep their feet as the sleds pulled back with the ceaseless rhythms of an idiot pulling on a church bell rope.

The ghosts came to Hillary in glimpses only, but he enjoyed unbroken conversation with them, regardless. His eyes were generally locked to the spot before his skis, his mind obliging him clear eyes for the stumbling terrain. In the whiteout came again the feeling that he wasn't getting anywhere, made pro-

found under the tearing labors, the horror of the sled's violence
and the will to keep standing. He didn't want to break an ankle.

(Mike Stroud, in ninety-three, broke an ankle on his walk
across Antarctica with Sir Ranulph Fiennes. Stroud kept on
hauling, his ankle strapped. That's where the bar was set.)

> At lunchtime I called Mount Macedon Primary School. I
> spoke with my little darlings, Amelia and George, and some
> of their school friends. The call was covered by one of the
> newspapers.
>
> And then we returned to hauling over the invisible clumps,
> following the compass—and it was all welling up as the
> ghosts talked to me. I would have been thankful if the cloud
> had dropped around us.
>
> It was all welling up, and I truly hated cooking that night. I
> hated trying to repair my broken boots and making no great
> progress. I hated the smell of the tent and the sounds the oth-
> ers made sleeping. I hated having no one to talk to. I hated
> the nagging. I hated the bickering. I hated being part of the
> problem. I hated feeling . . . being made to feel that I was a
> burden. Oh, yes, I know the therapist line: that one must own
> one's own feelings, and that nobody makes us feel anything.
> What a load of crap. I've found that you walk along with your
> sadness, fears, vulnerabilities, all your open wounds. . . . -
> and . . . well, you do so at your own peril. I've always hated
> that. It was in this mood that my imagination wandered to
> dark places. I thought of murder. Of being murdered.

❊ ❊ ❊

Day thirty-nine, December twelve, through a blizzard. It was a
late start in the morning. For three hours Hillary worked on his
broken boots, with help from Muir and Philips. Huddled over the
boots, they had to raise their voices to be heard over the screams
and the rattles of the tent, the walls cracking in their ears like a
bullwhip at close quarters. Under falling snow and heavy cloud,

with freight train winds blowing the snow in their faces, they made a direct line for Depot Five, having decided not to put in Depot Four. They followed the line as blurred smudges. They would need the depot food up on the plateau. As they followed the compass, pieces of cloud came down in steady bombardment, a ragged gauze haunting that swept their faces, whistling. When Hillary's mother came to him in the late afternoon, he wept—howling in animal communion with the storm. The clouds passed through where she stood and she was there as his goggles filled, and what bled from his eyes turned to ice.

Then, as so often happened, soon after she left, there was mercy by way of grandeur.

> Just before seven p.m., when we stopped to make camp, the storm abating, we saw the base of mountains ahead—their looming feet that through cloud or not always look like the feet of giant beasts. We were so close to them. These were the peaks that flanked the Shackleton Glacier. They were close by, but not as close as they seemed. Where the immensity of the bare white plain sapped my spirit, the feeling of immensity invoked by the giant feet had an intense restorative power that held me well and good through the night. In maybe three days we'd be free of the shelf and its psycho monotony.

With the late start, a shorter day of six hours, not quite twelve miles.

❄   ❄   ❄

I remember it was a journey of twelve miles that Nigel Lewis and I made to humility. There's no doubt that some of the old bastards had a good, long laugh about it.

Now, my parents didn't really know what Nigel and I were getting up to, beyond some camping and tramping. They certainly didn't know we were climbing Aspiring, by any route. I think they knew we had some plans, but not as ambitious. Well, our ambition was out of control after our near fatal triumph on the Southwest Ridge. After trekking out to Nigel's mother's car, we drove up to Mount Cook Village, Base Camp for the big boys of the game. We now honestly reckoned we were going to show those old bastards a thing or two.

Arriving in the village—a no frills ski resort to the eye—we set ourselves up at the New Zealand Alpine Club's Unwin Hut and waited, as you do at Mount Cook, for the weather. (This was where I met Fred From, a couple of years on.)

When the forecast sounded good and the sky was largely clear, we drove the short distance to the airport. Our plan was to fly into the mountains, and so make the best use of the good weather, rather than walk in under blue skies only to see the next front swing in from the west as we were about to go for a summit.

We had our eye on Mount Cook itself, at twelve thousand three hundred feet the highest mountain in the country. We were aware that a good many people had perished on its slopes over the years—and, despite our bravado, our brush with death had left us a little more fragile than we were prepared to admit to ourselves, or to each other.

So, as a gesture of humility, we decided not to try for Cook straight away. Instead we'd warm up by first knocking off the country's second highest peak, Mount Tasman, eleven thousand five hundred feet. To our thinking, it was shorter than Cook, therefore it had to be easier.

In fact, Mount Tasman is one of the most difficult mountains in New Zealand. (I would later climb Tasman by its most difficult and dangerous route with Fred From: up the two thousand foot Balfour Face, a sustained near vertical climb through ice bulges and steep rock gullies choked with seventy degree ice.)

But to Nigel and me, "second highest" meant "second hardest."

Anyway, out at the airport, there was a sign listing the various places serviced by the little ski planes of Mount Cook Airlines.

"So where do you young chaps want to go today?" asked a mustachioed pilot with many gold bars on his lapels.

Among the names on the list was Tasman Hut (actually called Tasman Saddle Hut). We figured Tasman Hut would be at the foot of Mount Tasman.

"Tasman Hut, please."

He stood there looking at us, in all our pimply faced boyishness. Then he called over a young pilot with rather fewer gold bars.

"Denis, can you take these young men up the Tasman for me?"

Soon after, strapped into our seats, with the propeller wheeling, the pilot mumbling into his microphone, we taxied for the runway, beholding the broad valley around us with the excitement of five year olds on a sugar binge.

And then we were airborne, flying over the boulder chaos of the braided Tasman River and on over the crumpled contours of the Tasman Moraine to where the white ice of the glacier appeared in streaks and facets.

"That's Mount Cook up there," shouted Denis the pilot, pointing steeply to a point above the left side of the little plane.

"That's Plateau Hut down there." He pointed, banking the plane to the left to bring the hut into view.

And we're going, "Great, great. . . . That's great."

"And that's Mount Tasman," he said, pointing dead ahead of us.

"Where's Tasman Hut?" we both chorused, looking around the base of the great white peak that Denis was now turning away from.

"What was that?" he shouted back at us.

"Where is Tasman Hut?"

He pointed to the north, toward the head of the Tasman Glacier.

"But isn't it at the foot of Mount Tasman?"

Denis shook his head. Tasman Saddle Hut was twelve miles away.

"But . . . but . . . we want to go to Mount Tasman," we wailed.

Denis began mumbling inaudibly into his microphone. He wouldn't look across at us. He wouldn't meet our gaze. He was nodding his head. He was obviously conferring with the senior pilot, who obviously said something like, "If these guys don't know where the hell they're going, don't take them to Plateau Hut."

Plateau Hut, the true launchpad to Mount Tasman, is in very big country, similar to Himalayan country, Western Cwm country without the high altitude; huge crevasses hundreds of feet deep, frightening, fantastic, fall and die, no place to miss a step. They weren't taking us there.

Instead they decided, "We'll take these greenhorns up to beginner's country."

Which turned out to be Tasman Saddle Hut, at the head of the mighty Tasman Glacier, the ride we'd paid for.

I remember the skis cranking down beneath the wheels and Denis turning the Cessna in toward the névé—the snow at the top of the glacier that hasn't yet been turned into ice. He throttled back, and we glided in with flaps down and flaring above the rushing surface of the snow, the skis just brushing. We slid and bounced a line of tracks down the glacier—and then Denis pushed the throttle to full again and we flew up and away. Now that we had marked the field for a landing, we would commit to an uphill approach.

The little plane glided in, pushing a bow wave of snow as we planed with the tail wheel still flying, and as the speed dropped off, the tail of the plane came down to the snow. The main skis sank into the soft wet snow, and Denis pushed the throttle for more power so we could taxi up and around at the top of the glacial basin. He pulled the mixture and cut the engine. We all jumped out, and Nigel and I just stood there. We knew we were in another world altogether—far bigger and more savage than Aspiring, and greatly more serious than our benign scrambles in the mountains at Nelson Lakes.

"Jeeeeeezus," we chorused.

This was bigger, farther out there, more serious than we had ever dreamed. But it was beautiful and we were there.

❊   ❊   ❊

Jesus suffered forty days in the desert, and at the end Satan appeared with all his temptations, and at the end the angels appeared with all their ministrations. For Peter Hillary, day forty on the shelf passed in like company, under an overcast sky that stole the horizon at their backs and to the east, but tightly framed a wide and intimate view of the mountains and the glaciers tumbling down their flanks, giving a glimpse only of a blue void over the plateau. Beckoning them was the wide open mouth of the Shackleton Glacier, yet there was the feeling of walking through a great hall toward a gargantuan mural or diorama of a place longaway, of no true destination. The mountains were painted with diorama colors.

"Forty days and you're still on the shelf. How does that make you feel?" said Satan.

"It's not the end of the world," said Hillary's mother.

No. It wasn't the end of the world. Not yet. Not for many more weeks. For nearly six weeks now we'd been inching across this lump of ice, and we still hadn't reached the other side. I skied along that day with this boggling thought, amazed and humbled and rather emptied out by the sheer scale of things in that place.

We moved pretty well, however, putting in five ninety

minute sessions with our customary three tea breaks and one
lunch break with hot chocolate drinks, chocolate, muesli bars,
Propel bars, salami and cheese.

Was it God or the devil who put the taste of lasagna and red
wine in my mouth as I hungered for the lunch break?

Just before camp we crossed a series of baby crevasses—
nothing to worry about, but we were still thirty miles from
touching the mountains, and we could only wonder at the size
of the holes in the Shackleton Glacier.

For the seven and a half hours, seventeen and a half miles.

❄   ❄   ❄

Day forty-one, a Monday: the jaded fugue of living under cloud
for too many days in a row continued. When Jon Muir unzipped
the door of the windward vestibule in the morning, the world
was a bellying cloud with snow in it; no face of space, the mountains wiped out save for spooky glimpses, and that's all there
seemed to be. But as Muir stuck his head out of the tent, he
shouted in joyful surprise, "Birds."

Hillary's head soon followed.

It was true. Two strong and stout skuas had been nestling on
the snow close to the little red tent. How long they had been
with us, who can say? By the time my head emerged from the
tent, they'd lifted off the ground, and were gliding casually—
effortlessly—to the west of us, landing on the snow about one
hundred and fifty feet away. They nestled down to survey us.

Why on earth were they four hundred and eighty miles
from Ross Island, from the sea, food, anything? I wondered if
perhaps the katabatic updrafts along the TransAntarctic
Mountains were a skua flight path to the Weddell Sea or the
eastern Ross Sea. Maybe these two Antarcticans just wanted
to look around.

Perhaps the birds were surveying the occupants of the tent for
their potential as breakfast. In its repertoire as a bullying oppor-

tunist, the skua can make like a vulture or crow, raking and pecking at the eyes and tongue and other exposed delicates of an incapacitated animal, including a human. (On the other hand, according to the field manuals, skua breast meat is apparently very tasty, but only in an emergency as all Antarctic wildlife is protected. Also, one needs to trim off much insulating fat to get to the meat.)

The Captain and company called them "skua gulls." They are a sort of gull, but at twenty inches or more in length, they're quite a bit bigger than the variety that generally swarm for crumbs at beaches and city parks. And they have a large, hooked black bill, for the efficient pecking and tearing of delicate morsels, and powerful claws for catching fish, pulling young birds and eggs from their nests, and desecrating the near dead.

They're rather dirty looking birds too—a rufous brown color that pales at the breast, with pale flecks on the nape and the neck, and white markings on the primary feathers that become evident when the bird is in flight. With broad, powerful wings that taper abruptly, skuas are built for both long distance hauls and accelerated sprints. Aggressive and agile on the wing, able to twist and turn over the waves like fighter planes, skuas habitually commit outrageous acts of piracy—chasing down other seabirds, even bigger birds, even the mighty albatross, seizing them by the tail, harassing them until they literally cough up their dinners.

Isn't nature wonderful?

It was a wonderful boost to the spirit to see them out there. As I noted in my diary that night, "It's a good omen and it uplifts us all. There is life out here. We are not alone."

And while it was a miserable day hauling under falling snow, with cloud falling in pieces and drifting, the better mood prevailed, with some excitement later when we could see rocks—rocks!—sticking out of the ice. And now and then we'd see the mountains looming through the cloud, truly above us, for we were crawling at their feet now. Their shadows moving about: the earth was moving.

On the downside, my shoulders were in a lot of pain from the repetitive action of working the ski poles and the sled still heavy at about three hundred and thirty pounds now. I took an anti-inflammatory tablet, and Jon gave me a shoulder rub while I was sitting on my sled.

During one of the breaks, in an interview with a Melbourne radio station, Hillary talked about seeing the dead. Later in the day he told a newspaper reporter that his head was being done in from walking too long in the company of the dead. If the others thought anything of these declarations, they never made mention. Nor did anybody make the obvious jokes when they camped that night at the foot of Mount Speed, having made not quite fifteen miles.

It was all so very quiet. And I was tired cooking dinner, wasn't moved to build up a campfire beyond thinking about the skuas visiting our tent—what were they up to now? And I thought about leaving the shelf—we were about to do it. Sometime tomorrow we'd be at the entrance to the Shackleton, and there would be many beautiful things to see. Otherwise, it was really quiet in the tent, and I was in bed as soon as I could manage it.

❋　❋　❋

I often had the feeling that Leonardo da Vinci wanted to be a bird, to be blessed with their gifts. He wanted to fly, of course. Who doesn't want to fly? But I think it's the resilience of birds that I admire most, that grounds my affection for them. The terrible places they choose to play in, the daring and joy.

No matter what the weather on the steep ice of the Lhotse Face—on Everest, at between twenty-two and twenty-six thousand feet—you always see the marvelous yellow billed choughs. They are the greatest fliers of all birds in my opinion, certainly when it comes to the tricky turbulent conditions on high altitude mountains. And they appear to enjoy it, riding those murderous gusts and vortices, up there where men choke on their dreams. At the end of the day they tuck their wings back and descend into the gloom of the valleys below like black darts, curbing the speed with a roller coaster flight path, like skiers on a slalom descent.

On the South Col, at twenty-six thousand feet, we had plenty of yellow billed choughs (and small flocks of mountain finches) scavenging about our camp for tidbits of food. As we staggered about and our mountain tents quivered in the strong winds, the birds got on with looking for opportunities. Choughs will eat rice scraped from a cooking pot, biscuits dropped by exhausted climbers, and they have been seen scavenging on the bodies of dead climbers too. On one occasion I saw choughs at twenty-seven thousand five hundred feet—and I have no doubt that if a chough thought there was any food on the summit of Everest, they would be up there too.

I have also seen the large Gorak ravens up at the South Col, but only singly. They appeared to struggle with the conditions more than the nimble choughs. Feathers would lift from the tops of their wings as they fought with the turbulence coming off the ridges. They didn't appear to enjoy it, but they are never what you'd call a happy looking bird. So who knows?

❄   ❄   ❄

Day forty-two, December fifteen, six weeks out, their last day on the coated tongue: they set off with the mountains right in front of them, and above them, but they couldn't see them through drifting cloud and snow. They couldn't see anything save for the compass, so the going was slow and tedious for most of the day, inching blind. Welling up in Hillary now: the all is spent impatience of waiting for a ship to dock, the hunger for the arms of the old sweethearts waiting there.

Through the falling snow and under the shifting shadows of

the mountains, his companions looked like charred stick men, black and twisted, the animated remains of witches. When they floated above him under the power of whiteout, he shrugged it off as a magic trick he'd seen too many times before.

Still he was drawn upward, along a walking track into an orchard of spindly peach trees, naked in their winter, and a glimpse only of his great friend Roddy McKenzie there among the trees with a set of pruning shears, and dressed in tweed clothes.

They'd once worn tweed together, McKenzie and Hillary; they'd walked all the way to Everest Base Camp in tweed suits, pretending to be Mormon missionaries. That was in eighty-nine, the year he prayed for his life in the icefall. The tweed suits took a beating, although they never went above Base Camp. What Hillary couldn't figure were the pruning shears, and why one of his living and breathing pals had taken the form of one of his ghosts. The quandary of the shears only fueled his impatience, and on he went brooding for a short time and no more Roddy or orchard to be seen. There were practical things he needed to think about now, expeditionary business. He needed to think about how to raise them with the others. Pressing matters. And still he was impatient, wandering next for a while up a red clay road and a single telephone line making hammocks between the old rotting poles, gray and flayed, standing some distance to the left of him, running parallel to the track that reminded him of many places he'd walked. It had the feel of many places he'd known. He wasn't moved to think too much about it. He was drawn upward and along, and still he was impatient to touch the other side.

> Eventually we reached the ice sheet below Mount Speed on the western side of the entrance to the Shackleton Glacier. I was in the lead, and the happiness of leading up onto this ice, approaching a long finger of rock that descended from the peak. It felt like climbing out of a breaking sea and onto a certain shore. There was no music playing, no emotional strings,

but the sky began to clear, and there were jigsaw pieces of a beautiful blue and the light polished and golden on the fraying edges of the cloud and the mountains on top of us, with breathtaking views up toward the steeple of this gargantuan altar, the thirteen thousand foot Mount Wade.

But it was so like coming ashore. The relief is an ecstasy. And then you realize you're hungry and tired, and so you worry about those things, thereby diluting the ecstasy.

As we made camp and set up Depot Five, we sorted the gear in our sleds and recalculated the amount of food we had left, and the distances yet to travel. It was going to be very tight, I told the chaps.

As I wrote in my diary, "We may need a food resupply at the South Pole. And Peter Cleary may feel that if we can't get back to Scott Base by February seven, then lifting us out earlier may be a safer and more face-saving option for Antarctica New Zealand and for the Americans, who would have to do the evacuation. I am very concerned about all this and will ponder it tomorrow as we trudge south up the mighty Shackleton Glacier."

Well, it wasn't like we were going to have a party or anything. For the day, our last day on the shelf, we made a rather creepy ten and a half miles.

PART FOUR

MOTHER'S LOCKET

CHAPTER SEVENTEEN

Do not wander aimlessly hoping to find a landmark. You will cover a lot of ground and become far removed from your destination, or fall over an ice cliff. Sit down with your back to the wind and THINK. Try to remember your movements and discover where you went wrong. You may be able to retrace your steps. If you can't do this confidently, do not attempt to.

Plan your next course of action.

Take note of the wind direction, it is your reference point for subsequent movement. Try a square search in the immediate area, but do not be tempted to move too far on the first attempt. Proceed up wind ten or twenty steps—you may have to crawl. Then move across wind left or right the same distance, then downwind and back to your starting point having completed a square. You may not be at exactly the same spot, but should be near to it.

If nothing is found and you may not have regained your bearings go upwind the same distance again and complete a square in the other direction. This process can also be repeated downwind of the starting point. The distance covered this way obviously depends on visibility. When you are sure you have covered the four squares repeat the process with larger squares. Do not panic if the first efforts reveal nothing, after all you have covered only an area of forty metres square.

It is important not to exhaust yourself.

From a government manual for Antarctic operations,
regarding a lost individual in a blizzard or fog

From the lore: there was a certain explorer from the early Antarctic days who knew personally all three of the greats; Amundsen, Scott, and Shackleton. How well he knew them, and to what extent his opinions were corny reflections of their legends, who can say? Regardless, this fellow, for some reason, was one day moved to declare, "For organization give me Amundsen. For science give me Scott. But when all hope is lost, get down on your knees and pray for Shackleton."

Or words to that effect.

Those boys of the sea, they loved Ernest Shackleton. They love him still. Unlike Scott or Amundsen, Shackleton lies in a hole in the earth at a fixed point on the map: in South Georgia, the jagged tooth of rock and ice in the Southern Ocean where he'd walked with ghosts and ascended to legend. And if you visit Shackleton's grave, you'll see what Hillary saw when he later made his visit: sailors who go there to have a drink with the great man, to pour a glass of rum over the cold ground. They fancy it sinks to warm his bones.

> **It's like something you might see at a rock star's grave, given the reverent irreverence—a humble familiarity—that accompanied the ritual.**

It is a rock star's grave. And it was a rock star's death, at forty-eight, while on the road again (sailing to his fourth polar expedition), from a heart attack following a heavy friendship with hard liquor. Whisky, women, and wild singing—Shackleton loved them all, much to the distress of his wife, no doubt. He'd promised her that he'd go south no more, always promised that such and such a trip would be the last. And was that why (beyond any gesture of returning a god to his Valhalla) Lady Shackleton sent his body back from Monte Video to a hole on faraway South Georgia? Floated by drama and passion, even as a corpse, Shackleton was the true rock star of the polar game.

He was what people call a character.
All that Irish blood, knighted by the English, dressed up in a bear suit and stood on a London corner collecting funds for one of his trips, **always got good coverage in the papers,** funny and charming and wild at heart, wanted to be a poet, pulled a gun on one of his men by way of attaining obedience, nay, loyalty, always loyalty; hot headed with the loyalty of a caring father, Shackleton, deaf to sensible suggestions and shadowed by no forgiveness hotly held against all who rejected or abused that loyalty, threatened to shoot at least one other man who wavered, nursed his men through their bouts of madness and visions and their deaths of spirit. Mostly they loved him back.

> **My father respected him immensely. Shackleton was one of his heroes. I remember hearing the stories, how Shackleton lost his ship in the ice but not a single man. I grew up hearing how he was a man of exceptional leadership and deep responsibility, how he made his most famous decisions under great duress and stuck with them—and so in that way Shackleton was part of my life education, the part handed down.**

The thing is, Shackleton wasn't a particularly good operator, in that his expeditionary plans were as half baked as those that killed the Captain and company. His ambitions were founded on passion and dreams and will, more than the all good sense required, at one with big reality, and the reality was that Shackleton's mighty excursions always ended the same way, with Shackleton and his men staggering in, "at the end of their tethers," more dead than alive. However, while the Captain fossilizes in the history books with his lyrical voice, Shackleton looms larger than ever as the hero. From his colder heart Hillary might say that Shackleton **was simply doing his job. Even so, he did it heroically.**

The hero he was, no doubt. Indeed, for all of Roald Amundsen's stunning achievements at the ends of the earth, it is Ernest Shackleton who gets the popular, sentimental, human vote as "the greatest of all polar explorers." And Shackleton never saw the South Pole.

What does it mean? What does that stuff about "the greatest" ever mean?

It probably means that Shackleton's story was bigger and more entertaining (more pleasing) than anybody else's. Broadly, it follows an old Hollywood formula: man gets himself and his fellows into outrageous trouble, then does many heroic things to get them home alive. In the detail, in the moral fabric of the yarn, it's a classic—an epic up there with *The Odyssey,* and with a happier ending too.

❄   ❄   ❄

A land of darkness, as darkness itself; and of the shadow of death, without any order, and where the light is as darkness.

Book of Job, 10: 22

From the mouth of the Shackleton Glacier, it took Hillary and company another forty-two days to reach the South Pole. Eric Philips would later and for some years glumly and very publicly ruminate about how and why "we did so badly." Mainly, he said, it was Peter Hillary's fault. And so for a time Eric Philips generated headlines.

Time passed, and Philips backed off from his position publicly, naming the "failing" of the expedition as "team chemistry." But he nonetheless tends to a cold silence or a hot bark when challenged by an alternative viewpoint, especially that voiced from the perceived Hillary camp. It will always be as he remembers it.

Likewise for Hillary, whose blood seems to crawl whenever Philips is mentioned out **of the blue.** On occasion, privately, Hillary refers to the shorter man as **"my little bête noir."** It's doubtful that much would be gained, ever, from talking to one about the other. In that way they're cursed and blighted by the other, by where they stand. Muir is similarly stranded, by his social makeup, and by his probably complex alliance with Philips. Like Hillary and Philips, Muir can provide no healing insights. Whereas Dr. Mike Stroud and Sir Ranulph Fiennes, following a restorative stretch in the regular life, sort of patched things up, Hillary has not spoken to Philips or Muir for some years.

> It remains as it was on the ice: huge egos, bitter resentments, nobody willing to blink, various states of emotional gangrene and incompetence.
>
> Hence, when my children ask me, "Daddy, who fatally wounded your South Pole trip?" I'll tell them, "We did it together, my little darlings."

❄   ❄   ❄

What became the most famous polar hatred in the lore was born out of the first serious attempt to reach the South Pole, in nineteen oh three, on what is known as the *Discovery* expedition (the *Discovery* being the ship that carried the company to McMurdo Sound). The heroes in waiting were Robert Falcon Scott (newly promoted from lieutenant to commander then, but already "the Captain" to his men), Scott's great and loyal to the end friend Dr. Edward "Bill" Wilson, and Ernest Shackleton, the outsider.

There was also a support crew that went part of the way across the shelf, and a string of dogs that were all killed as the food ran out. Even so, it was a miserable trip to nowhere, very slow going through much soft snow under too many beautiful sparkling days in a row that sent the men snowblind and the dogs dawdling behind; the men pulling the sled in a frigid sweat under the swinging sun because they didn't know much about dogs. Of course there were blizzards too, and they tended to wait out the worst of them.

After barely inching for two months, they reached eighty-two degrees South, the farthest south man had trod, about three hundred miles across the shelf, and their limit. They went no farther than the middle of nowhere. Mad with hunger and the blindness and the frostbite, their dreams a torment of beautiful banquets, the men turned for home. Shackleton by then sick with scurvy too, the odd man out bleeding from the mouth, rotting. He was taken onto the sled, hauled by the others. Shackleton never forgave Scott for later portraying him as a burden, and for treating him like a weakling. Scott never forgave Shackleton for being Shackleton, his own man, with his own rival cult of personality, even when traveling "alone." It was probably a good thing they carried no gun. The three of them were half in the grave from starvation and exposure by the time they made it back to base—barely made it.

"Hell is other people."
Invalided home, Shackleton immediately determined to redeem himself, avenge his honor, as they called it then, by somehow getting south again, by somehow raising his own expedition with his own men and going for the Pole. He determined to claim it. It took years of charm, hilarity, grandstanding, and dramatic eloquence to raise the money. Meanwhile, Shackleton and Scott kept the grudge alive by badmouthing each other, carrying on like tiresome divorcees.

It tore a rib out of Scott when he heard that Shackleton, in January nineteen eight, had made his wintering base at Cape Royds on McMurdo Sound, because Shackleton had promised to steer clear of that part of the Antarctic coast, because Scott had claimed it as his own. Four years on from January nineteen oh eight, the Captain would be dead, and through those years and a good part of the polar walk that killed him, the dead diaries say the Captain bitched and brooded about his rival right to the end—that bloody Shackleton.

❉   ❉   ❉

While Peter Hillary didn't get down on his knees and pray for a Shackleton, he found on the glacier named after the hero a timely restoration of spirit and confidence; a boost of morale that the great man himself might have provided had he simply wandered to Hillary's side. (He never turned up.) It came instead as a familiar friend, the restoration; it came as it always did with a return to the mountains, and his mind sucked greedily upon the scenery, feeding on the sense of place, the sense of time passing, the evidence that the world was still turning.

> I was delighted to be entering the mountains and the unknown, a place of features, moods, colors and changing shadows with the rotation of the day. After being nowhere for so long, this was somewhere, the best sort of somewhere. I was also freshly motivated—excited—by the fact that we were now engaged in true exploration, in a featured landscape.

But not of a place completely untouched, or untrod. The Shackleton had been visited and partly explored by scientific field parties. Hillary and company actually found a remnant of one of those visitations, a bamboo pole sticking out of the ice a little way up.

> In Arthur C. Clarke's and Stanley Kubrick's *2001: A Space Odyssey*, a tribe of ape men one day discover a black stone monolith standing in their wilderness. Some of the apes get angry; others are intrigued and excited. That's how it was for us; that's how we reacted when we found the bamboo pole. Eric kind of stamped around angry and disappointed that the "explorer" experience had been polluted; Jon squatted down to take a close look. I thought it was amazing. We went up the Shackleton and we found a bamboo pole!
>
> We saw many marvelous things up there, and we were the first ones to see a good many of them: the Shackleton had never been traveled from bottom to top, and we were the ones to do it.
>
> We did it in six days, from the shelf to the plateau, we

knocked the Shackleton off. "Yeeha," I said at the time. It was howling at the time. We had good weather the first four days on the glacier, and then as we approached the plateau, the sky darkened, the wind picked up; it was colder those thousands of feet above the shelf.

Shackleton never saw the glacier named in his honor. He never got that far east. I think he would have enjoyed it more than the Beardmore, however, from what I've read of that riddled road. If he ever comes by for a chat, I'll tell him how his glacier was a marvelous place to be, and a mostly reliable route—save for the odd mishap or obstacle.

Indeed, on the day they moved up onto the Shackleton (day forty-three, December sixteen, a lovely sunny day) Philips and Hillary on separate occasions fell into small crevasses, to their knees. The immensity of the place invoked a similar prostration, but of wonder as well as vulnerability.

The scale of the Shackleton was so vast; we were always diminished to a tiny speck, a flea's footprint, by the sheer size of it. On that far flung shore of the Ross Ice Shelf, the mouth of the glacier—where we entered it—was ten miles wide, an immense plain of ice fractured with crevasse fields and fringed by towering peaks. From the shelf, it wound its way through the TransAntarctic Mountains for ninety miles till it rose to the Polar Plateau at an altitude of nine thousand feet.

While the glacier narrowed and steepened as we ascended farther up, it was never closing in around us or giving you that claustrophobic feeling of having mountains towering above you. They were for the most part a fair distance away up rambling side glaciers and beyond subsidiary hills coated as always in ice. Beautiful mountain scenery. The dream of climbing among them filled many of my hours hauling upward. My mind took it as a gift of respite and succor, walking among the mountains.

For the first fifty miles the rate of ascent up the glacier was not very obvious. This did not mean it was easy, or simple. Periodically we would encounter a fold in the glacial sheet that produced crevasses in broad bands, and we would wind around the affected area and on up the glacier. At times we would pull the sleds over successions of crevasses, leaning into our harnesses and straining to lift them up over the lip of the steep sided ice fissures. On occasion, my companions and I were beholden to each other, when the sleds had to be picked up and carried, over broken or steeper ground. For more than sixty miles the snow had been scoured off the ice by the fierce polar winds and we had to wear crampons on our boots to gain purchase on the polished green and ancient blue glare ice, hard and old as hell, almost frictionless. This was often scalloped by the sun and transparent for six, ten feet into the heart of the glacier. At one frozen lake we were able to gaze into the depths of the clear water ice at large bubbles cemented into the ice in wonderful shapes and colors.

Throughout it was hard work, with the jarring of the crampons on the hard ice, the weight of our sleds on the steep ground. (I slept hard.)

Here and there great morainic boulders littered the glacier, and at the fifteen mile mark we encountered the extraordinary Swithinbank Moraine, a heavy thread of garbage rock that hugged the true left side of the glacier—for forty miles!— and effectively divided it in two.

Sooner or later we would have to choose which side of the moraine we would travel on, because crossing it with our sleds still weighing three hundred (and some) pounds would be very difficult. In the end we chose the true left side as the moraine rose into an impressive spine of huge boulders. The Swithinbank is fed from a giant rock mine where the Shackleton Glacier has undermined a rock outcrop called Matador Mountain, the remnants of a once substantial peak. The result is an almost inexhaustible supply of rock for this distinctive medial moraine.

At eighty-five degrees South we found open water. Water flowing in defiance of the deep sub zero.

But before then, before we saw the lakes and streams that emerge from the Shackleton Glacier like rabbits out of a hat . . . before all that, we saw the patch. This was at Thanksgiving Point, where we made camp on hard smooth ice and used ice screws to anchor the tent, where we found nearby on a north facing granite face a patch of green algae. It was twenty below zero at the time, and in the winter it would be dark and around seventy below zero, yet here was life. That it was so beautiful to behold had everything to do with place and time; where it was, where we were, and how long it had been, how long it seemed since we'd seen something fresh and green. It was a greater miracle than even the skuas. Because it was like we'd discovered life on Mars.

These were interesting times. As I wrote in my diary, for day forty-four, December seventeen: I am cooking tonight, and the stove isn't working well. It smokes and flares so I turn it off and in an increasingly bad mood strip the stove, clean and repair it, and put it back together again.

But his good friend the stove would keep acting up, blowing black smoke, chewing through the fue!. It would take many days of wondering **what the hell** as the fuel went up in smoke, many frantic phone calls to Scott Base before the problem could be named. It wasn't with the stove. The fuel (white spirits) had been contaminated with diesel when it was decanted back at Scott Base. The dirty fuel was their second "Evans," their second potentially lethal mistake. They were already feeling the first one: the ten days' food they had taken off the sleds on the eve of their departure.

Certainly, Hillary was getting anxious about the food supply, if it would see them through to the Pole. He wanted the Pole. Increasingly he was **thinking about the Captain,** about what the Captain was thinking when the food started to run out. **It sickened me.** He held little to no private hope they would make the return journey, and so he fretted about making the Pole, about not making the Pole. It almost moved him to prayer, because they simply had to make the Pole. It was welling up.

❋   ❋   ❋

On October twenty-nine, nineteen oh eight, Shackleton and three companions left their wintering hut, and with Erebus as their view, they made for the shelf. On December three, they became the first men to cross the coated tongue, to be astonished by the mountains they met on the other side. They were the first to see the glacier they named the Beardmore, and the first to take that riddle road to the plateau.

On January four (nineteen oh nine), Shackleton and company were camped in the belly of a rabid dog at about nine thousand feet, eighty-eight degrees and some south, just one hundred and nine miles from the Pole. **So close.** But his men were suffering then with the various polar plagues, their dreams haunted by a growing fear of starvation. To lift the mood, Shackleton read aloud to his boys, *The Merchant of Venice,* the story of a man collecting on a debt, one pound of flesh. Shackleton wanted the Pole, ached for it as he did his sums, surveyed the situation. All the ponies they'd set out with were dead. They had food enough to bag the prize, but it was clear they'd die on the way home. Shackleton wanted the Pole, but he turned, got his men home—sick and starving, hideous with scurvy, worn out but alive every one of them.

Upon returning home, Shackleton was knighted, hailed as a hero, and no doubt satisfied that his rival the Captain was back in the shade, his nose bloodied, declaring he'd investigate Shackleton's claims of eighty-eight degrees South because he for one didn't believe it. They carried on this way. Scott had won fame but no knighthood, and he didn't get one until after he'd died. And still the feud was to continue with Scott's martyrdom, and then later when Shackleton died, too, it continued, strangely, spookily.

❅   ❅   ❅

Day forty-six, December nineteen, the weather still good, we ascended the glacier above Thanksgiving Point and reached the side of the Swithinbank Moraine. A short way downvalley was a clear break in the moraine, which I felt we should have crossed to reach the eastern side. We continued on up, however, on blue glare ice. It was like hauling on tilted glass. At Mount Heekin broken ice forced us into an ice gully on the true left, which led through frozen lakes, narrow ice gullies and beside bone dry moraines and rubble peaks. Climbing over an icy ridge near the base of Mount Heekin we searched for a place to cross the moraine. It looked as if a long and very arduous portage of gear and sleds awaited us. Then, ten miles south of Matador Mountain, adjacent to the Baldwin Glacier, we found a frozen lake with a swift little glacial stream, a flowing stream at eighty-five degrees South, an icy corridor through the moraine for us to drag the sleds and a snowy spot on the east side of the Swithinbank Moraine to pitch our tent for the night. I tried to jump the stream and nearly fell in, to my horror. But the running water made a nice change from melting snow and ice for drinks.

Day forty-seven, December twenty: The mountains disappeared into cloud and lightly falling snow, and it was heavy going over bulging blue ice and foot wide crevasses, the sleds tilting and catching and nowhere good to step to sort it out; the sleds needing to be lifted and wrestled and rolled and out they'd come until they caught fast again on the steep and broken ground. Moving up this way, they discovered the Shackleton, where it peeled off the plateau, was one diabolical crevasse field, and no way through it. The Shackleton wouldn't take them all the way to the top. (Bit like Shackleton himself—almost got there, not quite.)

It was here, high on the glacier, just below the plateau, that Hillary asked if he might travel with his companions on occasion. The answer was no. At the end of his tether with the situation, he wept for a time as the others skied off together.

> **Black clouds hung in the sky to the west, letting shafts of sunlight gleam on the icy peaks above the glacier. There was very little snow, so we tied the tent down with ice screws and leapt inside. I was cook again.**

Day forty-eight, December twenty-one. Minus thirty degrees, stiff southerly at twenty knots. In goggles and parkas, they made a line for the Zaneveld Glacier, one of the major tributaries at the head of the Shackleton. The Zaneveld was their detour to the edge of the Polar Plateau.

> **We traversed through a broad glacial basin adjacent to the massive crevasses that barred the route up the Shackleton. Then the route meandered up along the side of the Everet Nunatak, with its layered golden strata topped by crumbling red rock. With a final push we ascended a long crevassed slope, gingerly crossing many huge snow bridges, to the southern end of the Everet Nunatak. Here we put up our tent and looked out at the wonderful view back down to the Shackleton Glacier, the mountains to the west and glimpses of the Matador and Vickers Nunatak to the north. We'd done it. We'd got through. It was after I put blocks of snow on the tent flaps that I let out my "yeeeha!"**

The next morning, day forty-nine, December twenty-two, at the edge of the plateau: the wind was blowing forty knots, and one of Peter Hillary's fillings fell out, from his upper right premolar. He asked Philips for help fixing it, but Philips said he wanted to use his "fingers to take a shit first." Philips' thumb was the color of old dried blood, cracked tar. His frostbite was becoming of great concern to the others. Muir was getting sick again. Aside from the accumulated aches.

> It was a terrible day, but we went out anyway. It was terribly cold and the conditions were frightening. It took over five hours to get ready. The wind was screaming, spindrift racing, blinding. After five miserable hours—and a gain of about five miles—we blindly searched out flat ground to pitch the tent. Inside we and our gear were covered in snow and ice and frozen breath and dribble. The tent looked like a snow cave. When the stove didn't work properly, giving off smoke, fumes, and little heat, we all became depressed.

> Some time after eight p.m., the storm rages, the phone rings. It was our public relations firm in Melbourne, calling with our Christmas media list—people we needed to call, interviews we had to give, the "public" to entertain. I didn't feel entertaining. "Great God. This is an awful place." The wind shrieking, the tent flapping with astonishing violence, and frozen condensation snowing down upon us and our spirits.

> My eyes were stinging from the fumes, and from the cold.

The next day, day fifty, the world was still shrieking. They stayed in the tent, sat together through the day, made phone calls, no miles.

> Outside the wind blew more furiously than ever, fifty to sixty knots, I estimated. The sun cast fleeting shadows of spindrift blasting across the sunlit nylon of the tent, and I felt thankful for its simple shelter.

Day fifty-one, the world was still shrieking, but they decided to head out anyway. As Hillary packed up the stove, Philips and Muir returned from packing their sleds.

"We're stayin' here," said Muir.

Their hands and feet had turned to wood in the little time they'd been outside. They stayed a second day in the tent, still at the lumpy edge of the plateau, not yet quite upon it. It was Christmas Eve. They came out of their trenches and had a few laughs. 'Twas the season.

The next morning, before packing up and moving up onto the plateau, they sang a few songs over the six a.m. porridge and coffee. Eric had written humorous poems for his companions, one each. Muir presented Hillary with a tiny card from Yvonne, and a miniature bottle of whisky that she had sent along as a surprise, to be shared by all. A teaspoon each, a sip of communion.

❉   ❉   ❉

Time passed in a place where boiling water turns to snow when thrown into the air. They saw another bird up on the plateau, the day after Christmas, a skua. They saw another halo around the sun, during a grand moment when the sun came out over the dimpled plain of hillocky white waves, and there was much sparkling. Mostly there was chaos; shrieking and buffeting, mad rags and slivers in gunshot flight. In occasional quietude, the gentle breezes came to their faces as dancing flames. Time passed in the deepest sub zeros, another world of cold. From their hairy chins and nostrils Hillary and company grew beards that looked like translucent ice cream cones, and flourishing ice moustaches. When they tore off their ice beards at the end of the day, hair and sometimes frozen flesh were torn off too. They grew plates of ice on their clothes. Everything was choking with it. Minus forty degrees. It sucked on their strength.

Between Christmas and New Year they lost another two days—tent bound, no miles. One day lost to the chaos, the other because Muir couldn't move. He was ill with some kind of flu, and then desperately ill after taking the wrong combination of medicines. For one long day he exploded, dropping his long johns on the march and baring his legs to the acid howling from the south, washing him out. One evening Philips cut his hand badly while separating frozen muesli bars, splattering the kitchen utensils with blood. **Blood everywhere.** Hillary was feeling sore all over, craving sweeter sleep. As they lay still in the tent, the cold seeped into their bones. One evening, about two

hundred and forty miles from the Pole, Hillary figured how fast
the world was turning: about a thousand miles an hour at the
equator; a little more than sixty miles an hour at the spot where
they were lying under siege. The stove still blowing black smoke,
chewing through the fuel. The fumes from the stove gave them
headaches, nausea, lethargy. Philips eyes were bloodshot. The
food store was shrinking. Too much time had passed, was passing.

> Those first couple of weeks on the plateau—that ice aster-
> oid—were very tough. We'd make a few miles and get pinned
> down again.

Day sixty-one, January three (nineteen ninety-nine), minus
twenty-five degrees, zero miles: they were sitting at nine thousand feet, in the belly of a dog tearing itself to pieces in one un-
ending shriek of horror, seemingly so. In fact the shriek ended
four days later. This was the first of those four days, bunkered in
the little red tent, glued to the spot, eighty-six degrees forty-six
minutes south. It was over those four days they decided to abandon the return leg of the journey. It was Peter Cleary at Scott
Base who raised the issue in a phone call. He put it to them as a
request, that they accept a plane ride back to McMurdo Sound
from the Pole. And so, as they sat on that spot, for many reasons,
they were finding a deeper communion with the Captain than
intended, hoped for. From Peter Hillary's polar diary:

> The New Year has not been good to us so far. At the end of
> cooking, I measure the fuel used last night and this morning.
> We have used eight hundred milliliters, which is three hun-
> dred milliliters more than allowed for in the daily ration.
> Consequently we have as little as twelve days' fuel left, with
> just fifteen days' food, and a fifteen mile per day average in or-
> der to accomplish the dream, the bottom line dream of reach-
> ing the South Pole.
>
> Clearly this is in the balance. The Pole is two hundred and
> fifty miles away. Outside the blizzard rages on and we are un-

able to leave the tent. So another day lost to the weather, a situation that is now almost the norm for us on this wretched Polar Plateau. A high, cold ice plain of raging winds, spindrift that flows like sand from one side of Antarctica to the other and more often than not a sky blotted by cloud and snow and devoid of any definition. Perhaps that sums up our lot: lost in an icy void, with an unreliable and fuel-guzzling stove, fumes that burn our eyes, a dwindling food supply, one of my companions floored by ill health, the other suffering frostbite, my own body battered and drained, the vagaries of brutal weather. And yet, we can sit in this bubble of shuddering nylon and telephone our loved ones, the media, Scott Base. We can communicate our situation, our fears, our logistical nightmare to people who feel for us but cannot reach this most remote place. I feel very lonely here.

UNCERTAINTY. That's what we came for. We got it now!

Peter Cleary at Scott Base has been discussing our fuel and food and weather predicament. The delays! We can still make it, but we need good weather. We need a resupply of fuel and food and will now certainly be flown back to Scott Base from the South Pole. They won't bring a plane out into this. And this could go on for who knows how long. Here, now, it is so awful. You can only be here to comprehend how awful it is. (Isn't that the apology for a lame joke? "You had to be there.")

Going outside the tent is not an option. We toilet in here, sleep in here, eat and cook in here, read, wonder and feel weepy eyed at the interminable separation from those that we love. I think everyone's wondering now. Will we reach the Pole? How certain that seemed once, that we'd get there, and now with the storm outside and the stove misbehaving inside, it seems so uncertain. We'd have to be very unlucky to die out here, but now that's a genuine part of the uncertainty too, and I don't like it. Poor old Captain Scott, I think I have an inkling now; sitting in the sleeping bag, writing these thoughts and worries, enduring all that Antarctica hurls, as it does, each day so intensely and so completely. "Great God. This is an awful place." Great God, how does the Polar Plateau fit into your grand plan? We have all lost a lot of weight and I realize now that I haven't eaten a fresh vegetable or fruit for two months. We haven't washed or shaved either. We live in filth. Each other's filth. And yet we go on this mad unnecessary quest that proves nothing. Only that we were able to endure the pain and discomfort and uncertainty of the passage, that we found the Shackleton Glacier to be a navigable route to the plateau and that for some unfathomable reason we shall as individuals feel better, stronger, worthier for the experience—but much of that will be in retrospect and right now such words are inappropriate. Now I feel frail, easily tearful and shaken by the immensity and power of the natural world that most of us do everything in our power to avoid. Now I am indubitably in it, I can't get out of it.

I dream, I muse of being elsewhere. Of rolling in the grass in our backyard with little Alexander. Of having a lovely hot bath and feeling my frost nipped toes and fingers smarting (they are pretty good really, I've done well) and hugging Yvonne, feeling loved. I think of Amelia and George and time with friends but mainly family and home. I could barely be further from them now and I do not feel proud of that. The absentee husband, the neglectful father, the reckless man. Perhaps Amelia's contribution to the tip of my ski says it all: "The question is, who are you?"

All I know is I desperately miss my family.

❄   ❄   ❄

"He was just a word for me. I did not see the man in the name any more than you do. Do you see him? Do you see the story? Do you see anything? It seems to me I am trying to tell you a dream—making a vain attempt, because no relation of a dream can convey the dream sensation, that commingling of absurdity, surprise, and bewilderment in a tremor of struggling revolt, that notion of being captured by the incredible which is the very essence of dreams."

He was silent for a while.

"No, it is impossible; it is impossible to convey the life-sensation of any given epoch of one's existence—that which makes its truth, its meaning—its subtle and penetrating essence. It is impossible. We live, as we dream—alone."

He paused again as if reflecting, then added, "Of course in this you fellows see more than I could see then. You see me, whom you know."

Joseph Conrad, *Heart of Darkness*

Time passed, with Sir Ernest Shackleton ahead on points in his rivalry with the Captain, enjoying a couple of good years of being "the one" who almost got to the Pole. And then Captain Scott sailed south again. And then came word that Amundsen had bagged the Pole, and that Scott was missing, and then yes that he was dead but had seen the Pole. That was nineteen thirteen, the year Britain wept for its polar dead, and complained about the bloody Norwegians. Shackleton was back in the shade. But not for long. Realizing there was no better time to promise the (emotional) nation full restoration to glory and honor, and thereby inspire it to make a donation, it was in a spirit of outrageous opportunism that Sir Ernest Shackleton started work on the expedition that would lead him to a true heroic grace, his true greatness.

He promised greatness. "The greatest polar journey ever attempted," he said of his plan to make the first crossing of Antarctica, from the western to the eastern side, touching the Pole on the way through. Again, his charm and sense of drama inspired the public to dig deep, and for many young men to offer him their services. Five thousand volunteered, and twenty-seven were taken.

Most of the others probably went to the European trenches a year later instead.

❄   ❄   ❄

In December nineteen fourteen, Shackleton and his men entered the pack ice of the Weddell Sea, under steam and sail, aboard the beautiful whaler *Endurance.* By January the ship was frozen into the pack, held fast and drifting. The men sat and waited for the winter, drifting through the winter, the wooden hull groaning in the dark. Nine months passed this way.

In October nineteen fifteen, the *Endurance* started leaking. It was being crushed, broken up. The men began taking off stores, lifeboats. On November twenty-one the wreckage of *Endurance* sank to the bottom of the sea. Dragging their lifeboats with them, the men hauled across the pack toward the open sea, the ice often splitting and separating beneath their feet, where they made camp. One evening Shackleton spotted one of his chaps floating in an open lead of water, in his sleeping bag. As he pulled the fellow onto the floe, the ice closed over again. There's film footage showing some of the men walking in a long line during this time, each with his right hand on the shoulder of the man in front of him. **These were Shackleton's team building games—to keep his polar family together. In fact, after a time the haul to the sea proved too arduous, and they stayed put upon the vast plain of pack ice as it drifted imperceptibly north.** They lived on blubber and seal meat. Four months passed this way.

In April nineteen sixteen, the pack ice disintegrating now, they got into the boats, made for Elephant Island, beyond the tip of the Antarctic Peninsula; ten days thirsty and freaked out on the churning monsters of the Southern Ocean, a good number of the men going to pieces during this time. (Hence, Shackleton kept it quiet when they drifted wildly off course at one point.)

The hysterical happiness of reaching the island soon turned to a quiet panic. Elephant Island was a lump of rock and ice, and only limpets to eat when the penguins departed. It was a place where they'd freeze to death if they stayed too long. (It was here that one of the fellows had his gangrenous toes cut off, one by one.) For months now they had been living in an uncertain state of survival. Now winter would come, it was coming, the darkness.

Two days after landing at Elephant Island, Shackleton called for volunteers, for a rescue mission. His plan was to rig up the biggest of the lifeboats, the twenty-two footer *James Caird,* and sail for South Georgia, where there was a whaling station, seven hundred churning miles away. He chose five men on the basis of their seafaring skills or their optimism. (The party included Tom Crean, who four years earlier had nearly starved to death with two companions on their desperate retreat from the Polar Plateau—one of the last three men to see the Captain and company alive.)

It's all in the lore, how it took them sixteen days of roller coaster desperation to reach South Georgia, days swallowed and spat up and swallowed again by the chaos of the great Southern Ocean; spat off course, spat all over the place in gales that lasted for days and how they found their way, the story goes; the navigator Frank Worsley said to be some kind of natural genius, with the instincts of a seabird, no matter how he hallucinated castles and other wonders in the bergs and rolling boulders, "growlers," the makers of smithereens, how they slipped them and the invisible murder of the night; and how they got through with their swollen tongues, with half their fresh water polluted with sea water but always two hot meals a day and all the while Shackleton urging his fellows to keep their chins up, or to sleep, and all the while they watched him turn into an old man with worry for the men he'd left behind.

They came ashore with smithereen violence, on the unpopulated side of the island, with an unexplored mountain range between, and no way to the whaling station but over the mountains, and all too exhausted to make a start straight away. It's all in the lore. After resting in a cave for a number of days, Shackleton headed up the steep glaciated slopes, taking with him Crean and Worsley only, stopping only for meals, every four hours, and otherwise moving for thirty-six hours straight they worked to find a route across and down the mountains that wouldn't kill them outright, and how they moved, how it was they moved with their minds strung out and swinging between an emptiness and visions and all the months of desperation and anxiety walking them at the end of their tethers. For thirty-six hours straight they pushed on, made the other side of the island, made the twenty miles to the whaling station, nobody blinking when they walked in as filthy rags, told their story. After four attempts with four different ships, Shackleton returned to Elephant Island, counting the heads of his men, the wretched huddle on the distant shore, finding them there, every one.

❄ ❄ ❄

It was after they had entered the glacier that Hillary began hearing voices of the living in his head, except they sounded there with the stark intimacy of a sudden someone talking close to his ear in what had seemed to be an empty room. His wife mostly, talking to him, calling to him. She came unbidden, another gift from his mind to assuage the agonies of loneliness. Where on the shelf his diary had been largely kept as a public education document, on the glacier he began writing about the emptiness of living with the others:

> I long for conversations and good long expressive talks. I think such a long period of being deprived of such interactions is one of the hardest things for me to deal with. There is a loneliness in only talking with oneself.

All comfort was found in the mountains, and in what they evoked in his determined daydreams of climbing upon them;

good company in the living and the dead from all those years in the mountains, and no difference between them, they came to him as bands of ghosts, the old friends, the greats of the great times, they came to climb with him, they went on new adventures together in the TransAntarctic Mountains. And there was nothing in their coming or the mood of their visitations to suggest that Jeff Lakes or Ken Hyslop or Mark Moorhead or Bill Denz or Rob Hall or Fred From (or any of the others who happened to be dead) were dead, just as there was nothing to suggest that Roddy McKenzie or Kim Logan or Geoff Gabites or Merv English were any more alive than the dead friends. They were just friends, mixing it up.

It was in the wisps of black smoke that continued to flow from the stove that Hillary saw clearly who had come home alive and who had not and why and where and how it all happened. All those stories, telling themselves in the hypnotic malevolence of the stove, demanding to be heard, remembered, what he had known firsthand, the old imaginings of things he'd been told, the mountains and what he'd found there.

How he'd found his colder heart.

It wasn't until high on the Shackleton that the story of Ama Dablam began telling itself to Peter Hillary. It was a story that lingered as he sat on the plateau with the southerly shrieking. It was a hell of a story, and he remembered how beautiful it had all been, how hard and scary and very beautiful it all was, no matter how they rubbed up against one another with the stress of going right up the middle, and the feeling that yes it could all come down on their heads, the most beautiful mountain in the world.

"Ama" means "mother." A "dablam" is the silver plated locket box that a Sherpani wears around her neck, containing her prayers. Hence, "Ama Dablam" translates as "Mother's Locket." However, when Hillary went to the Khumbu to climb the mountain in seventy-nine, it rubbed his raw soul a little when a friend in Kathmandu told him she thought Ama Dablam actually meant "Mother's Arms." There was something to it, given the mountain's shape as an eroded sphinx, with two elegant ridges indeed descending as arms for eight thousand feet.

Where the sphinx's arms touched down, there was a grassy meadow, where yaks were brought to graze and where Hillary and three other young climbers set up their Base Camp. There was his old friend Merv English, who had climbed with Hillary in the Mount Cook area for some years. There was Geoff Gabites, who Hillary knew less well. Indeed, Gabites, who was a little older and married and ran an adventure equipment store, initially suspected he'd been invited along to outfit the expedition cheaply, "at mate's rates." Ken Hyslop, a friend of Gabites, was a shy and quiet and pleasant soul whom Hillary didn't really know at all, beyond his reputation for daring on the hill.

> **But I quickly grew to like Ken. I enjoyed his company, and his dry sense of humor.**

They were planning to make the very big time on Ama Dablam, twenty-two thousand five hundred feet. The mountain was first climbed by a team led by Ed Hillary, up one of the sphinx's arms. His son was planning on a more direct route.

Peter Hillary had spent a good part of that year looking at Ama Dablam's mighty West Face, the sphinx's bulging bosom of hard, shiny ice, five thousand feet of derring do. He was twenty-four years old, watching a bulge of ice to see if it moved, avalanched, collapsed. His idea was to climb the mountain as a fly on the wall, right up the middle, from under and up and over that bulging face, never been done, **one of the most daring and spectacular routes ever attempted;** five thousand feet of steep to vertical technical climbing, every step and movement critically computed, nothing under the balls of their feet. This was rock star climbing.

"And then we would have been heroes." All the old bastards of the game would have had no choice but to say, **"Jeeeeezus."**

Ed Hillary was in Kunde at the time, staying in the home of his old friend Mingma Tsering and his wife, Angdooli, working on Himalayan Trust projects. He didn't want his son to climb Ama Dablam, not by that route. It was too far out there. The black hole in the family, four years old, was eating them both alive.

❄   ❄   ❄

I remember from our Base Camp on the grassy meadow, where the sphinx's arms touched down and where yaks came to graze, from the meadow we climbed up this little glacier to a rocky outcrop where we set up our advanced Base Camp, at about seventeen thousand six hundred feet. From there the West Face just went straight up above us. Foreshortened, a route so steep that we couldn't see very far. It was scary because the locket jutted out above our two little tents. We talked about the weather, and how we were excited. We were all scared as hell but we kept it to ourselves.

A couple of days before, they had soloed up a lower ice flank, and with Hillary leading, they traversed across a rock band, putting a fixed rope on the route that led right into the core of the gully that sat in the middle of the West Face.

We wanted to put in ropes to make it quicker. The rock band made it hard to get into the gully.

On the first day of the climb proper, leaving in the early dark, headlamps on, making good time over the fixed rope, they found their groove and swinging their ice axes above their heads, fly walked up the gully to a second rock band at twenty thousand feet.

Before the day got too warm, they called a halt to the climb, moving out of the gully slightly to the right, on to steep snow ice cut into fine runnels, like teeth on a comb, they moved out on to the face and hacked out tiny ledges, six feet long and one foot wide, barely big enough for their backsides, and they tied themselves on for the night, taking hours to climb into their sleeping bags and sort out the cooking gear, everything done in slow motion, handling each object as if it were a toxic test tube, not wanting to drop anything because there was no way to get it back, passing drinks along the ledges and just hanging on, they all had their own ledges because it was so steep and Hillary could reach up to Merv, and there he was sitting above him but no thought to conversation; men at work.

> It was a bit like being on the South Pole trip that night, in that we were all cut off from each other; focused on not making any mistakes, not dropping anything, not falling, checking and checking that you're tied on, everything is tied on, melting snow and ice and drinking and drinking. We had two little stoves. Merv and me, Hyslop and Gabites. Four's a good number, I reckon.

> No one had been on the West Face before. No one had even tried it.

They all slept lightly, were easily roused. It was cold but still, perfect conditions. It would have been all so very quiet if not for the **dinking** sounds coming down the mountain, little bits of ice, little bits of rock, speeding bullets. But it was clear and there were stars out there.

Next morning, in the dark, boiling water, making drinks and everything taking a long time because they're at altitude and half their backsides are hanging off the ledges in the dark. It took four hours to put on their boots and crampons, put away their sleeping bags, the stoves, from four a.m. to eight a.m. just getting ready and having their drinks and making sure they didn't fall off, feeling the altitude.

> We moved on, traversing and diagonaling over to the left, to get up and over the second rock band; climbing up steep runnels, up to seventy degrees on very hard ice, climbing in two sets of two swinging leads. I was on a rope with Merv. Ken was on a rope with Geoff. In effect, I was leapfrogging from belay to belay on a rope with Merv. Ken was doing the same

with Geoff. We climbed through the vertical rock band and out on to very steep ice—and then the angle started to ease a little, back to fifty or sixty degrees. I'd led up through the rock band and it was just starting to drop back a bit and the idea was we'd stop early, around two in the afternoon.

I called out "belay on" and Merv came up, collected the tool box—the various screws and pins and nuts—and up he went while I held a belay stance on a ripple of ice I'd cut with my axe, just wide enough for my boot, holding the rope pretty tight so if Merv falls he's not going to fall too far—because the farther he falls the harder it's going to be to stop him falling, and the greater the chance that he'll pull out the protection, pull both of us off.

When Merv called out "belay on," I felt secure enough to pull out my small camera and snap off a couple of shots of my friend at work further up. I figured we'd finish the day after my next lead. We'd traverse off to the side, get off the central face, and spend the afternoon in the sun, on a sloping ledge, just fifteen hundred feet from the top.

It was a beautiful sparkling day and we had completed the most daring and difficult part of the climb. We'd spend a good night and knock off the summit in the morning. Things were going to plan.

On Everest, just below the summit, there's an obstacle forty feet high, a cliff of vertical rock sticking out of the ridge. It's called the Hillary Step because my father was the first to climb it. It was known in Dad's day as "the sting in the tail." I've often found the sting in the tail often comes as you are most excited and thereby open to surprise.

Hillary put his camera away, thinking happy thoughts of victory, and then thinking only of the belay of ice screws he was pulling out. He called "Okay, climbing."

Geoff Gabites was on belay, tied to the mountain about sixty feet above Hillary, and out to the right of him, with Hyslop climbing the ice above—when there came a mighty cracking sound.

Somebody cried, "Oh, fuck."

A chunk of green ice the size of a car had broken away from the locket, was falling their way, breaking up into armchairs, and then television sets, books, and cameras, and Hillary hugging the face, tucking his helmeted head, leaning in now and thinking **Here it comes, here it comes.**

And then it came, pounding and pulling on him, the beating of a mob, that chaos and violence. He was being stoned to death, the horror of a hundred slingshots. He felt himself falling, he felt himself hanging, broken into wild angles, drowning in the ice clouds brought down with the avalanche.

It was still coming down in dribs and drabs as he found himself hanging, twisted over on his right hand side, his ice axe gone out of his hand, one of his crampons gone, right ankle smashed, a smashed finger, his ribs broken on the right hand side, his left arm broken in two places just above the wrist, both bones in the forearm sticking out rudely through his jacket, but all he could wonder was why his chest was being crushed, why it was so hard to breathe. A little time passed when he realized that there was another rope **sawing into my rope** where it came off the climbing harness, sawing into it just like in the movies.

Geoff Gabites and Ken Hyslop had fallen past, on each side of him, roped up together. It was their rope caught by his rope. Hillary was the hook on the line. His friends were dangling below, hanging from his body, sawing through his rope. He looked down and saw Gabites in a bad way about fifty feet below, hanging against the ice face. Hyslop was about a hundred feet farther down, over a bluff and out of sight.

The first thing I did, with my good arm, was clip an ascender above where the rope was being sawed through. I'm thinking that if the rope rope snaps, I'm not going to fall with the boys.

They were all hanging off a little aluminum stopper that Merv English had put into a crack in the rock. English hadn't come off the mountain. He was the only thing linked to it.

> Merv was a bit knocked around, but otherwise in pretty good shape. He was the best we had. Geoff had taken a pummeling, and had suffered a very deep and long spiral cut by the rope that had been wound around his forearm. He was hurting all over. Ken we couldn't see. Geoff kept calling to him. They were pretty close friends, and he kept calling out, but Ken didn't answer.

Everybody was pinned down or seemingly unconscious, but Merv. So Merv has to come down the rope, to see what's happening with the rest of us.

It took some hours for English to get them all pegged to the mountain, to fold away Hillary's arm—a bottle of smashed bone and blood—by cutting a hole in his jacket and tucking it in, before they got to see how Ken was doing, what had happened to him; the massive head wound, the tortured form hanging half upside down, silent.

Then came the short conversation about who would go down and cut Ken away, who would cut the rope. Gabites insisted on tending to his friend, English following him a part of the way, and then stopping; English and Hillary watching Gabites miserably disappear over the bluff, down the now secured rope. The rope was taut. And then it hung loose. Hyslop went all the way to the bottom.

> Ken had to be dead. Surely. It had stayed with us, the terrible thing, the fact that we couldn't say under cross-examination, we couldn't say one hundred percent that Ken was dead.
>
> Ken's family couldn't understand why he wanted to climb and most of them have accepted what happened, that it wasn't anybody's fault. But there was always the sense of why couldn't it be someone else, why couldn't it be you? "Why couldn't my son be visiting your family?"

They didn't articulate that. It was just a feeling you got. Instead they said, "Why didn't you play hockey or basketball or something else?"

We'd all had such a great time together too. It was a very happy expedition, the best of times. When Geoff and Merv and I get together, we remember what a happy time it was. It helps when we think of our quiet and shy friend. He was a geologist, by the way. Had a future.

❋ ❋ ❋

They spent that night huddled on a ledge, in a shock of quietly held weeping. Gabites and English didn't think Hillary would last the night. When Hillary whimpered for help in the night, for his sleeping bag to be drawn higher, Gabites in his grief and injury and exhaustion would think dark thoughts, and then wearily do his best to help. It was a long night. It was a long and tedious time getting down, three days. For Hillary each moment a grinding agony, as there was a limit as to how much the others could help him, given the fly walk country. Much of the time all the others could do was to scream at him to keep moving. It often got quite desperate.

As Merv English later wrote: "Peter was lying against the ice about thirty feet from the bivvy ledge. For the past half hour I've been watching him clutching and clawing to gain ten feet along the rope. Now he's against a little ridge in the ice, three or four inches high. For a long time he tries to get over it, moaning with pain and whimpering with desperation each time he tries and slips back. Eventually he collapses, hanging on the rope, a pitiful heap against the ice, and says he can't do it.

"It would be extremely difficult to help him, so I brutally abuse him and immediately feel heartless, but I also know that nothing brings the fight out in Pete more than being told he's no good. As he tries again, Geoff and I both encourage him and call praise each time he does something positive, even if it's only lifting the ice hammer a couple of inches. Each time he stops I abuse him again. Eventually he gets there."

They were all in tears when they got to the bottom, to safety.

Only Hillary persisted with high altitude climbing. Ama Dablam was just the beginning for him.

❊ ❊ ❊

I am a part of all that I have met;
Yet all experience is an arch wherethrough
Gleams that untravelled world, whose margin fades
For ever and for ever when I move.
How dull it is to pause, to make an end,
To rust unburnished, not to shine in use!
As though to breathe were life.

Alfred, Lord Tennyson, "Ulysses"

Time passed.

Day sixty-nine, January eleven, nineteen ninety-nine: With the Pole a hundred and fifty miles away, another fifteen days away, Hillary and company had seven days' worth of food remaining in their sleds. Twice they had been told a resupply of food and fuel was coming their way. But the planes had been grounded, unable to reach them in the chaos. Now the chaos had lain down. The day was clear and near windless.

> **And yes at about four p.m. a Twin Otter flew over, low, giving us all a fright. It circled, then landed among the sastrugi. Out jumped Henry and Max, the pilots. We spent a pleasant fifteen minutes chatting and repacking and then off they go with all our excess gear and turds in plastic bags. We now have twenty days' fuel and fifteen days' food. We'll get to the Pole well fed and secure.**
>
> **At seven-thirty p.m. we climb into the tent, and I called New Zealand's Prime Minister, Jenny Shipley, for a pleasant**

talk about the expedition and the need to inspire and moti-
vate people.

We then enjoyed a few treats that were sent to us from Scott
Base. Like, smoked oysters and crackers. We didn't say no this
time. It was all very welcome. (But no new stove.)

But there was something disturbing and unsettling about
the ease with which Henry and Max had dropped into our
lives. The isolation, the routine, they were suddenly broken,
interrupted. It put a hole in our heroic hell. Mockery, in part.
And a threat too, of the real world to come.

Of course our story was hotting up back home. The food,
the fuel, the days pinned down by storms. We'd become exciting.

Time passed moving up higher, following the gradual rise of the
Titan Dome, where the plateau bulges against space, a vast and
dimpled lump on the bottom of the world, drawn up and out by
its turning. Ten thousand feet, eleven thousand feet. The sleds
were lighter now but their pace heavy with weariness and illness, the cold chaos.

From the polar diary:

Day seventy-one, December thirteen, the coldest day yet. Minus forty to minus fifty, with spindrift blowing from the
Southeast, the plain to nowhere. Sometimes I wonder if it will
ever end.

After the afternoon break, Eric can't warm his hands and
feet, and they become white and wooden. We have to stop
early. Jon removes Eric's boots and stuffs him into his sleeping
bag while I put up the tent around them. Jon and I are worried
that Eric's already frostbitten toes and thumb will turn to severely frostbitten hands and feet. Eric doesn't dress warmly
and often prefers to do things without his mittens on. So far it
seems this has been a close call and hopefully he will be okay
and we can continue the last one hundred and forty miles or
so to the South Pole. We hope to be there later next week.

Day seventy-two, minus forty-five degrees, with squalls of strong southerly fronts loaded with spindrift, shrieking cloud. They went out into the swirling blank, through the choir of ghouls, white on white, no gravity. Philips out in front and floating high in the air. Muir behind Hillary, floating a long way below him. An hour into the march there was a thickening in the blind violence. Hillary stopped, waited for Muir to catch up. Muir pushed on to catch up with Philips. Philips was disappearing, thinning to nothing.

As I sped up to try and keep them in view, to bring them back, a squall of spindrift swept across the plateau and we were drowned. It was like being cocooned in cotton wool. My heart was pounding. Fear rose up like bile. I began to ski more rapidly, following the ski tracks of the others. To my horror their tracks were being brushed over. An occasional scar upon the snow showed their passing. I could barely see the tips of my skis.

A self contained solo skier has advantages in conditions such as these, as everything he needs is in the sled behind him. Our essential gear was spread among the three of us. But in my distrust of Philips I'd made sure I had enough to survive all the same. I didn't have the tent but I had the bivvy sac, I had one of the stoves, the cooking pot with its soot and congealed food. I had fuel, food, a GPS, the emergency beacon and the satellite telephone. But nothing beats the tent with three men working together to put it up in a howling storm.

I had to find them.

Fifteen minutes passed, and no sight of the others. Hillary was frantic, hauling with the energy of a drowning man in high seas. He'd heard stories of men separated from their fellows in sub zero storms. They weren't happy stories, but his mind began dredging them up. He flailed with his ski poles, holding on to his rough sense of up and down, following a line of travel that seemed right to him. He started making plans, wondering how long he would survive if the storm blew for days.

Frankly, it didn't bear thinking about.

Twenty minutes and he spotted a gray smudge.

Was it them? Or just another swarm of spindrift?

The gray image split into two. It was swaying.

> I forged ahead, hope rising. And then I saw them, hunched. I waved my ski poles in the air. I had never been so happy to see them. Without stopping for long, we put our heads down and skied on, agreeing to stay close together.
>
> Half an hour later Muir dropped out of sight, behind us. I halted, waited. Philips kept going. I moved after him a little, yelled out to him. He stopped. We waited, just standing in the maelstrom. After a few minutes Muir emerged from the storm and we stood together in the middle of nowhere, muttering our feelings. And then we moved on again, close together now.

Two hours on, they stopped for their first hot drink. As they were about to start the next session, the blind violence again thickened. They retreated into the bivvy sac to wait it out. Time passed. Then the storm found its stride. It was minus forty-five, eating them alive. They very carefully put up the tent and sat out the rest of the day.

Day seventy-three, minus forty, shrieking, blind, they stayed in the tent, no miles.

Day seventy-four, they stayed in the tent, made phone calls.

The next four days they hauled in gentler weather, little wind but still very cold.

Day seventy-nine, chaos, stopped early.

Day eighty, January twenty-two, they stayed in the tent, no miles. And still the stove blew black smoke, fumes. The stove had been damaged after being pulled apart too many times during the dirty fuel crisis.

Over the following days, the last four days, a gray smudge appeared on the horizon, the frozen exhaust of the big Hercules flying in and out of the South Pole station. For Hillary, the smudge raised visions of Kathmandu streets, of funeral pyres, of long-ago campfires, cities. And as they drew closer, a small town began taking shape under the smudge.

The long gray smudge on the horizon that was our journey's end hovered above a collection of dark specks—polar huts—at the bottom of the world. It was so strange, the idea of reaching the end of our lonely polar quest. All three of us talked about how we didn't want it to end and yet we were each desperate for it to be over. We were worn out. We all talked about feeling worn out. Ill, injured, wasted. We were all confiding in our diaries our desperation to be reunited with our loved ones. And yet this journey's end was so ill defined. And that's a mixed business.

There was no spectacular summit, no landmark indicating that this was the point about which the whole damned globe rotates. Instead, there was a ring of flags, a striped barbershop pole set at ninety degrees South, and a huddle of buildings that made me think of a far flung mining camp in Alaska or Siberia. I dunno.

Strangely, as we approached the Pole we shared a rare camaraderie, in its honor I suppose. Philips sang us a song about life on the ice (thankfully not about our life on the ice but a pleasant and imaginary one). Muir seemed smitten with the idea of reaching the South Pole; striding strongly, his powerful jaw clenched and his eyes intent, set dead ahead beneath his possum fur hat. We were still some distance from the base, and the people hadn't come out yet to line the ice road and cheer our long coming.

For me the line of tiny dark shapes expanded into buildings at such a retarded rate that it felt as if we would ski on forever. We'd been walking at such a slow beat for such a long time. And suddenly there was the sensation of wild acceleration.

We were hurtling toward the world of people again, toward the living. I could feel it.

❊   ❊   ❊

I was in India when I heard the news about my mother and sister, in seventy-five. I'd been having such a marvelous time. I flew to the gray smudge of Kathmandu. I went to our house. It was empty. My father and sister Sarah were at our friend Dudley Spaine's house at the British Embassy compound, not far from where Mum and Lindy had been cremated by the river, atop pyres of sandalwood.

I met up with Dad and Sarah in a lane near the house. They were driving to meet me. I remember Dad getting out of the car and I'd never seen him broken. Not like this. It was then that I really knew they were gone. The three of us hugged in the middle of the road, such misery. We've never hugged like that again.

Because I'd missed the funeral, and because I needed some kind of ritual as a means of accepting them gone, I went out to where they died and gathered up bits of their clothes scattered in the paddy field. I remember finding a piece of Lindy's jeans. I took them back to the house and made a pyre in the backyard. But I used too much petrol and nearly blew myself up.

Also recovered from the scene were Mum's amber beads. They'd come unstrung, were scattered in the mud of the paddy field. They're now in one of the display cases, in the coffee table I designed in my head while on the haul. It's a miniature museum, that table.

Out there on the Polar Plateau, out there in the middle of that sparkling white plain, on a day of no chaos I walked with Mum again—as I had done many times on the shelf. But it was different to those times. On that last occasion she came like a "specter of the brochen," when a shadow is projected by a beam of sunshine on to a cloud. She came like a ghost. Just as the smudges of my two companions drifted in and out of focus, so too did my mother's image with the wavering of my thoughts. As I have done before, I asked her: if she was still alive, would she come back for me? But my logical self leapt forward before she could answer.

It was out there on the plateau that I realized: it's too late. The sudden return of my beloved mother would be pure emotional chaos, carnage. I said goodbye to her, and for some time I wept bitter tears.

✳   ✳   ✳

When Shackleton, Crean, and Worsley were making their crossing of South Georgia, at the end of their tethers, they saw ghosts in the shadows, and they felt that there was someone else with them, what they came to call and cherish as the "fourth presence," who walked at their side and made itself felt to all three of them. Apparently they all believed it to be true—that there was someone walking with them, as a spirit guide of sorts they pondered.

It was only some weeks before I visited Shackleton's grave that I first heard about this side to Shackleton's story. I was a little dismayed to hear he regarded the "fourth presence" as a mystical experience. I suppose I see the whole business as some kind of collective hysteria. Or was it simply they suffered the same spooky trick of the nerves, and they chose to talk about it?

In the wonder poem "The Waste Land," that marvelously conjured pastiche of dazed grief, banality, and mystical symbolism, T. S. Eliot wrote of Shackleton's "fourth presence" experience. However, he mistakenly (or perhaps with a modernist's truer than true intuition) placed the event upon the Antarctic ice, as follows:

Who is the third who walks always beside you?
When I count, there are only you and I together

But when I look ahead up the white road
There is always another one walking beside you
I do not know whether a man or a woman
But who is that on the other side of you?

"The Waste Land" was published in nineteen twenty-two, the year Shackleton died while anchored off South Georgia, on the road again, six years after his epic journey there. Shackleton never knew that he'd been immortalized in a literary classic (but he may have expected it). He was aware, however, that the "fourth presence" story had made him a poster boy for the Spiritualist and revivalist movements that flourished after World War I. In a way, it was his last laugh on Captain Scott.

While the mythic name of the Captain was invoked during the war by English clergymen to inspire, if not shame, the nation's beautiful young men into the trenches, the name of Ernest Shackleton was invoked for some years after the carnage to comfort all those grieving mothers, to illustrate that the dead were still out there, walking around, at the elbow of those in need.

> **Oh, yes. They're still out there. I still see them come and go, making the world a movie show. And I still don't know what to do with them. Isn't that how it is for everybody?**

ACKNOWLEDGMENTS

This autobiographical tale has been a long time coming. For a couple of years the mere mention of the book would elicit a boom of laughter from my father. A "just do it" from my wife and as my children passed from one school year level to another, a nonchalance born of familiarity, "oh that one." Still they have been among my great supporters as I have been encouraged, assisted, pushed and uplifted by many, many people.

It is interesting how a few words of encouragement can keep the whole project on track and how some loyal backing gives you faith to keep on "keeping on" and how a colleague becomes a friend. Of that I am particularly grateful. It's perhaps even stranger that this business of summits and poles and hard won goals is really a people business (with all the vagaries of human relationships). It is the trust between a provisioner of funds, services or equipment and the expeditionary entrepreneur (because we manage risk for richer or poorer, in sickness and in health, for the duration of the expedition) that is the benchmark of the total adventure—it underscores it—makes the whole thing possible in the first place. We cannot do without you. You are all greatly valued. Thank you.

The essential but incomplete list:

Gillian Wratt and Chris Mace and Antarctica New Zealand, John Haley and Iridium South Pacific, Andrew Fyfe and Fairydown Adventure, Natural History NZ, Gary Carmody and AMCOR, HIH Winterthur, James Strong, Andrew Cannon, Roddy Mackenzie, Ed Hillary, John Philbrick, Kim Logan, John Elder, and finally, but most especially, to my wife, Yvonne Oomen, for her unfailing support and encouragement.

And now on to the sequel.

Peter Hillary

This book grew out of the dangerous mix of friendship and ambition. It became an often grueling and maddening process for both of us, and for everybody else close to us. Hence, a big thank you to PH that we 're still best friends (even though the stitches are yet to be removed from the long and deep incision on his psyche that he generously allowed me to make).

Perhaps ``get well soon" cards should also go to our agent and my old friend Bob Mecoy, and our editors Bill Rosen and Liz Stein. Indeed, thank you to all the people at Free Press whose names we know: Stephanie Fairyington, Andrea Au, Carol de Onís, Jeanette Olender, and Jennifer Weidman. It's a hell of a thing for me that you all believed in what we were trying to do. Likewise, my beautiful and hilarious wife Rachelle Dale; she never doubted this thing would get done, regardless of my frequent doubting hysteria.

For their expressions of faith, belief and kind encouragement (over the last 25 years of aspiring penmanship) I thank David Naylor, the late Jules Zanetti, Bruce Pascoe, Deborah Bibbie, John Huxley, Martin Sharpe, Mr. John Manners, Malcolm Maiden, Les Carlyon, Andrew Rule, Bruce Guthrie, Garry Linnell, Ken Merrigan, Steve Foley, Malcolm Schmidtke, Andrew Holden, Dominic O'Brien, Rikard Sandstrom, Phil Blatch, Roger de Lisle, Amy Sinclair, Thuy On, Fran Bryson, Milo Beatrice, M. J. Hyland, Ms. H. A. Burden, A. J. Dusting, Mrs. V. Lascaris, Ms. S. Tippins, P. L. Toohey, and my siblings Mark, Victoria, Susan and Matthew. And for dragging me out to a pool hall on occasion, I offer all sedated and grounded gratitude to the dear and wild Mark Roberts.

Thumbs up to Auden, the Australian Antarctic Division, Bowers, Cherry-Garrard, Conrad, Eliot, Hemingway, the Goons, Homer, Job, Oates, Sartre, Scott, Tennyson, and Thompson for some fine lines. A heroic hail to Huntford for the ``fourth presence" story in his Shackleton book.

For all those rudely overlooked in all this excitement, send me a postcard and you'll get your dues in the next one.

John E. Elder

REFERENCES

Fiennes, Ranulph, Sir. *Mind Over Matter: The Epic Crossing of the Antarctic Continent.* New York: Delacorte Press, 1993.

Huntford, Ronald. *Shackleton.* New York: Athenum, 1986.

March, Jennifer R. *Cassell's Dictionary of Classical Mythology.* New York: Cassell, 2001.

Mear, Roger and Robert Swan. *A Walk to the Pole: To the Heart of Antarctica in the Footsteps of Scott.* New York: Crown, 1987.

Sockley, Raymond. *The Melancholy Diary.* Published privately. Heddon Gretta, New South Wales, Australia, 1999.

Solomon, Susan. *The Coldest March: Scott's Fatal Antarctic Expedition.* New Haven, Conn.: Yale University Press, 2001.

Stroud, Mike. *Shadows on the Wasteland—Crossing Antarctica with Ranulph Fiennes.* London: Penguin Books, 1994.

Taylor, A. J. W. *The Antarctic Psychology.* Wellington, N.Z.: Science Information Pub. Centre, 1987.

Venables, Stephen. "To Breaking Point and Back Again." *Daily Telegraph* (London), 18 September 1993.

Wheeler, Sara. *Terra Incognita: Travels in Antarctica.* New York: Random House, 1999.

Wood, Gareth. *South Pole: 900 miles on foot.* Victoria, B.C.: Horsdal & Schubart, 1996

ABOUT THE AUTHORS

When **Peter Hillary** climbed Mt. Everest in 1990, thirty-seven years after his father's historic first ascent in 1953, they became the first father and son to touch the top of the world. It was just one of more than thirty major expeditions to the Himalayas, the Andes, the Katakoram, the Arctic, and the Antarctic. Peter Hillary works as a speaker, a writer, and an adventure travel operator. He is married and has four children.

John Elder is a senior writer for *The Sunday Age* newspaper in Melbourne, renowned for writing about the more desperate side of the human experience. In 1986, as a crewmember of the "In the Footsteps of Scott" Antarctic expedition, he stood on the pack ice and watched his ship *Southern Quest* sink to the bottom of the Ross Sea. He is married, and he has two daughters.